Naked
at
Lunch

Also by Mark Haskell Smith

Nonfiction
*Heart of Dankness: Underground Botanists,
Outlaw Farmers, and the Race for the Cannabis Cup*

Fiction
Moist
Delicious
Salty
Baked
Raw: A Love Story

Naked
at
Lunch

A Reluctant Nudist's Adventures
in the Clothing-Optional World

Mark Haskell Smith

Grove Press
New York

Published simultaneously in Canada
Printed in the United States of America

FIRST EDITION

ISBN 978-0-8021-2351-0
eISBN 978-0-8021-9178-6

Grove Press
an imprint of Grove/Atlantic, Inc.
154 West 14th Street
New York, NY 10011

Distributed by Publishers Group West

www.groveatlantic.com

15 16 17 18   10 9 8 7 6 5 4 3 2 1

For David L. Ulin and Tod Goldberg

You're born naked and the rest is drag.
—RuPaul

Contents

I'm on a Boat

"**W**e are safely away and you can now enjoy a . . ."

There was a pause, as if the cruise director was having trouble choosing what, exactly, he should call what was about to happen. Finally he said, ". . . a carefree environment."

The announcement was still reverberating through the ship when the scrotum airing began in earnest; shorts and shirts dropped to the ground and penises dangled in the South Florida sun. Permission had been granted. Now buttocks could swing from side to side without restriction, and breasts—finally released from the prison of blouse and brassiere—burst into the open, to be caressed by soft tropical breezes. We were on a boat. One thousand eight hundred and sixty-six nudists living the "anti-textile" dream.

Not that some of them weren't almost nude before the cruise director gave the all clear. Many were in various states of undress, itching to toss their clothes aside. A skeletal man in his eighties wandered around the ship wearing only a fluorescent thong, his loose skin draped around his bones in cascades that looked like freckled frosting, and a gigantic, barrel-chested man—he looked like he'd eaten an actual barrel—lumbered around the lido deck on an industrial-strength cane wearing only a loincloth. A few people soaked in Jacuzzis, surreptitiously slipping out of their swimsuits, while the less rebellious sat by the pool, looking somewhat forlorn, waiting for the green light. These were nudists, after all. And they had paid big bucks to frolic in the buff. When the all clear was sounded, they didn't hesitate.

I had never been on a cruise ship before—I'd never even been interested in being on a cruise ship—but this wasn't just any cruise, this was the Big Nude Boat, a special charter offered by Bare Necessities, the premier "nakation"* travel agency. Not only that, the cruise was on board the *Nieuw Amsterdam*, one of the Holland America Line's more luxurious ships, which meant this wasn't a backwoods RV-park nudist resort or Hippie Hollow down by the lake; this was the deluxe version of nonsexual social nude recreation. Meaning nudism. Or naturism. Depending on who you ask. There are several theories floating around about which word means what— historically speaking there are some actual distinctions—but the reality was that I was on a boat with almost two thousand people who weren't wearing clothes.

I am fascinated by subcultures: the Dead Heads and Juggalos who've built unique cultures out of following their favorite bands as they tour the country, the amateur mechanical engineers who build robots in their garages, the home brewers who experiment with beer in their kitchens, and the foodies who eat at illegal restaurants in people's homes. People do strange things. They collect stamps and watch trains, they

* "Nakation" is a portmanteau of "naked" and "vacation," but you probably figured that out on your own.

dress their pets to look like famous characters from movies, they dress themselves to look like anime characters, they go to conventions in woodland animal costumes and have group sex in "plushie piles." All of these activities have their own culture, a network of people who speak a specific kind of lingo that outsiders don't understand. I'm especially fascinated by subcultures that are deemed morally suspect or quasi-legal: the people who pursue their passion even if it means possible imprisonment or stigmatization by society. I can't help it. I like the true believers. The fanatics.

My first nonfiction book was about the culture of cannabis connoisseurs and the underground botanists who source heirloom varietals of marijuana from all over the world. Cannabis culture has a rich history filled with colorful characters. These are men and women who defy oppressive antidrug laws and good-naturedly don't give a fuck about societal norms. It wasn't much of a leap for me to become intrigued by the world of nudism. Or as my wife said, "First you're stoned all the time and now you're going to be naked? Why can't you write a book about cheese? You like cheese."

The loudspeaker on the ship crackled to life and the cruise director added a caveat: "I would like to remind you that you must wear a cover-up in the dining areas."

Which didn't really keep anyone from being naked in the dining areas. Or in the bars. Or anywhere for that matter. They were naked on deck and in the screening room, the library, the casino, and the buffet line. Nudists crowded around the piano bar and requested songs by Elton John and Billy Joel. The large theater where stage shows were presented was filled with naked men and women. They were in the elevators, walking down the corridors, playing Ping-Pong, lifting weights in the gym, and guzzling cocktails by the pool.

In the fitness center someone asked the ship's in-house yoga teacher if people had to wear clothes in the yoga classes. The teacher gave her a curious look and then, as the true reality of the question sunk in—what I can only imagine was the image of a roomful of naked people doing down dog flashing through her head—her face bloomed in panic and she said, "Oh yeah. In the class. Clothes. You have to wear clothes."

But other than the yoga class, everywhere you looked, testicles and breasts hung low and pendulous, swaying side to side as the boat rocked in the open ocean; billows of bulbous flesh spilling off torsos, flowing earthward like the goop inside a lava lamp. The entire human body presented in all its natural nature was unavoidably on display.

I was sitting at what was called the Ocean Bar that first evening when I overheard a man, a silver-haired smoothy, complain loudly that there were too many old people on the cruise.* "I'm guessing the median age is sixty-five," he said. He was sixty-two.

When old people complain that there are too many old people, then you really know there are too many old people.

Most of the passengers were retirees and most of them were American. Which is to say that there were a lot of overweight people strutting around in their birthday suits. That they did so unself-consciously, without any hint of the neurotic body obsession that has created generations of diet-obsessed, bulimic, anorexic, or just plain miserable people,

---

* He had an alarming obsession with photographing women's vulvas. To his credit, he always asked for permission.

was something that I found almost inspirational. They weren't ashamed of their bodies, they seemed to accept themselves and one another for who they are and what they were, and, best of all, they had fun doing it.

Not all of them were retired. I met a Harvard professor, a radiologist, a tool salesman, and a couple of people serving in the armed forces. There were pharmaceutical sales reps, retail clerks, photographers, scientists, doctors, corporate executives, teachers, lawyers, paralegals, and people who really didn't want to talk about work while they were on vacation.

And of course not everyone was fat and saggy. There was a large LGBT contingent who were on the healthy end of the body mass index, and there were some actual bona fide young people, trim and tattooed men and women in their twenties who clung together as if the naked retirees were harbingers of some sort of terrifying apocalypse. The naked twentysomethings gazed at the naked seventysomethings as if they could suddenly see the future, like a portal had opened in the time-space continuum and revealed a dystopian world where gravity and a sedentary lifestyle conspired to make everyone expand and sag. It was heartbreakingly inevitable. Perhaps this glimpse into the abyss explained some of the uninhibited alcohol consumption among the younger set.

The guests on the nude cruise were predominantly Caucasian, although there were a few South Asians, East Asians, and African Americans in the clothes-free contingent. They came from all over. Some were trying to escape the polar vortex that was bringing freezing wind and record snowfalls to cities like Chicago, Milwaukee, Cincinnati, Philadelphia, and Boston; others were from warm climates like Tampa, Phoenix, Los Angeles, and San Diego; nudists from Kansas, Iowa,

Oklahoma, and Texas represented the heartland. There were foreign nudists too: Canadians from Toronto and Quebec, and real outliers, people from far-flung countries like Finland, Australia, Germany, and the Netherlands. All these people, coming all this way, for the express purpose of standing around on the lido deck of a cruise ship and letting it all hang out.

Some clutched their daily drink specials in fluorescent plastic cocktail glasses, some relaxed in chairs, others danced to the thumping sound system, a few cavorted in the hot tub, but most of them were just talking and laughing and being extremely friendly with one another.

And no one wore clothes.

What would make seemingly ordinary people spend thousands of dollars for the opportunity to waggle their penises around other waggling penises? What were they thinking? What's the appeal? Were they getting some kind of exhibitionistic thrill? Or were they voyeurs? Did the topless women playing blackjack feel empowered? What was happening?

That's what I was here to find out. The idea of eating a slice of pizza and drinking a beer naked on the deck of a cruise ship with hundreds of other naked people seemed bizarre to me. At the very least it made me uncomfortable; and I really like pizza and beer. But if I wanted to experience the culture of nudism, if I wanted to understand what made someone risk their job or their freedom or even their reputation to do this, well, I had to get naked like everybody else.

9 Interview with a Nudist

pparently, there are rules for being a nudist. It's not enough to drop trou and waggle your genitals in the sunshine. That might be fun—or, depending where you are, get you arrested—but it's not nudism. You can take off your clothes and run across a football field, but that's not nudism, that's streaking. Jump in a lake and frolic naked with several of your friends? That's skinny-dipping. Fun, but not nudism. Even bathing in a Japanese *onsen* isn't nudism. Sure you're naked and with a bunch of other naked people in a hot spring, but after you've cleaned and soaked and refreshed in the cold plunge, you get dressed and go out for ramen. A nudist would eat noodles naked, with other naked people.

I am not a nudist. Except for a few occasions of teenage skinny-dipping, I have mostly kept my genitals covered. At least when I'm in public. I don't practice "social nudism" or "backyard naturism" or any kind of nudism, really, but that doesn't mean I don't enjoy being naked. I sleep in the nude, I take baths and showers in the nude, and I happily cavort au naturel in the privacy of my own bedroom. I'm not a prude; I just don't hang around with other people without wearing some kind of clothing. Except for with my wife, but she's used to me.

I have never felt an impulse to shed my clothes in public. In fact, I feel a strong compulsion to keep my clothes on and to be around other people who also keep their clothes on. I even try to wear a combination of clothing that approximates something I think of as *style*. You can blame it on social conditioning, but I know I'm not alone in this. The body image issues that advertising and media inoculated me with from an early age—those feelings of inadequacy, the fears of being ridiculed for being pudgy or hairy or circumcised or just, you know, uncool—are deeply embedded in my consciousness and shared by most of the people I know.

So what is a nudist? In his eccentric omnibus *The Nudist Idea*, historian Cec Cinder provides a kind of kitchen sink definition: "the nudist idea is the foundation of a distinct, entire and wholesome philosophy, one much, much larger in scope than simple collective nakedness, one that embraces sexual sanity, anti-militarism, good health, robust conditioning, inter-gender respect, political libertarianism, religious tolerance, animal rights, First Amendment political freedoms, population reduction and shrinking government and bureaucracies."[1]

I'm not sure that nudism is about animal rights or population reduction or shrinking the size of the government—those sound like an author tacking on some political talking points—but then again, I'm just getting started looking at nudism; maybe it is all those things.

Social nudism came to the United States from Germany in 1929, and since that time various nudists and nudist groups have struggled to define what constitutes nudism. For some it's a lifestyle choice that includes healthy eating habits, exercise, and an appreciation of nature. Others take a more philosophical view and look at nudism as a political stance against a repressive "textile-centric" society that promotes consumerism and rapacious capitalist growth at the expense of our environment and mental health. Some nudists like the fact that their bodies are accepted for how they really are and not what fashion and advertising say they should look like. Some folks just like the way it feels to relax in the sun without any clothes on.

But while various groups have different agendas and interpretations, they all pretty much agree that nudism is a social activity. If you're alone without any clothes on, you're just naked, but if you are in a mixed group of men and women engaged in the conscious practice of standing around in the buff, then you are a nudist practicing nudism.[2]

So why do some people like to get naked and hang out with other naked people? What's the attraction? Is it some kind of primal urge? If society didn't tell us we had to wear clothes, would we all just strip down and frolic in the fields?

My son Jules, when he was a toddler, used to race around the house wearing nothing but a small superhero cape made out of a counterfeit Hermès scarf. I would tie it around his neck and it seemed to propel him, like it gave him actual superpowers. He'd splutter rocket sounds as he ran, trying to go fast enough to make the scarf billow in his slipstream like a proper superhero's cape. Sometimes he would turn his head to admire his cape as he ran, which was not always sensible, but the occasional collisions with furniture or walls or trees only seemed to make him more determined.

Naturally the cape was the only thing he wore and he refused to wear clothes when he was home. No shoes, no diaper, no T-shirt. It was hard to argue with him. We lived in Southern California and it wasn't like he needed clothing to stay warm. So he ran and played and terrorized his older sister's playdates and watched television wearing nothing more than his faux Hermès scarf. Was he just pretending to be a superhero? Or is it deeper than that? Is there some kind of innate impulse to be naked that society has shamed out of us?* Even in the Bible it says that Adam and Eve "were both naked, yet they felt no shame." So, like, what happened? When did hanging out in the nude become illegal? When did it become something that only weirdos and hippies did?

I decided that a good place to start was to talk to a real red-blooded card-carrying American nudist, so I arranged an interview with prominent American naturist Mark Storey and bought a ticket to Seattle. Not only is Mark Storey a board member of the Naturist Action Committee and founding member of the Body Freedom Collaborative, a group that advocates for clothing-optional beaches and started World Naked Gardening Day, but he's also an editor at *N, The Magazine of Naturist Living*, and author of the book *Cinema Au Naturel: A History of Nudist Film* and editor of *Theatre au Naturel: A Collection of Naturist Plays*. In addition to that, he's written prolifically on the history of nudism, civil disobedience, and legal issues involving public nudity.

In other words: he's a nudist's nudist.

. . .

* Even though he now lives in San Francisco, Jules no longer runs naked through the streets in a superhero cape. At least, not to my knowledge.

Seattle is, on a good day, a cool and drippy climate; a place where lichen grows abundantly, the flora is lush and verdant, and the light is tinged with a soft gray quality—one of those subtle, almost institutional colors, like something you might find on the walls of the Swedish Institute for Depression Studies. I used to live in Seattle so I came prepared for a certain amount of moisture. But an unusual cold front had moved in and temperatures had dropped to near freezing. I tightened my scarf and pulled my beanie down over my ears as I stood shivering in the drizzle at a bus stop, wondering how many days a nudist in the Pacific Northwest gets to be outdoors without developing hypothermia.

Storey had agreed to meet me at Bauhaus Books and Coffee, a groovy espresso bar stuck in a kind of no-man's-land between Seattle's downtown and the hip Capitol Hill neighborhood. To be honest, I didn't know what to expect from this meeting. Would he be some kind of freaky evangelist for nudism? The Johnny Appleseed of skinny-dipping, the Che Guevara of weenie wagging? Would he be wearing clothes? Worse, would he insist I take my clothes off to interview him? It was way too cold for that.

I found the coffee shop without a problem; in fact I used to live a couple of blocks away, but that was years ago, when the word "barista" was just a twinkle in some marketing executive's eye. Bauhaus has large windows that face the street and let in enough light to keep you from feeling that you're going to get seasonal affective disorder and a wall of shelves that give the place a Goth library vibe. It also has a second floor, a loftlike space, which is where I found Mark Storey sitting at a table, surrounded by stylish young people sipping coffee and staring intently at digital devices.

Storey has a handsome, expressive face, and he shifts easily between open laughter and thoughtful introspection. He is also tall, six foot three, which makes him a large nudist. And for someone whose day job is teaching philosophy at a local college, he looks like he's pretty athletic.

"I got into the cliché nudist volleyball, and started touring western states doing the nudist volleyball tournaments. That was fun."

Apparently the bump, set, and spike used to be quite popular among nudists.

"Oh yeah. I have gotten to referee the National Nudist Women's Volleyball Tournament. That is something no one can take away from me. That was an amazing thing."

I can't tell if he's joking or serious, until I realize he's both. Although being a nude volleyball player is not without perils, as illustrated when Storey described the hiring process for his current teaching position.

"The very week that I'm going through the interview process, getting my first full-time job at a school I really wanted to teach at, the magazine I work for decided at that time to put me on the cover, full frontal, blocking the volleyball. It was the volleyball issue. I thought, 'Oh, this is going to screw me up so bad.'"

"Maybe they didn't look at your face," I suggested.

He shrugged. "Later, I'm chair of the department and I'm having to deal with an adjunct instructor. I take him out to lunch, we're chatting. He tells me his tale of woe or whatever. It was all academic stuff. And then he said, 'Well, it's nothing like your story.' I go, 'What are you talking about?' And he said, 'Well, the magazine. You with the volleyball cover.' I said, 'You know about that?' And he says, 'Everybody knew about that!'"

"Maybe that kind of thing is expected from philosophers."

He smiled. "I work with some cool people."

We paused and sipped our coffees. I had to admit that Bauhaus made a pretty good cup. Fortified with a jolt of caffeine, I cut to the chase.

"So how did you get into naturism? I'm assuming you didn't wake up one morning and decide to stop wearing clothes."

Storey laughed. "Everybody's got their own story, but for me, my dad would take my brother and me fishing in the Sierra mountains. My dad was totally cheap. If we hooked a lure on a log in the stream, we had to go get it. For the first few years, I would do it, but I'd be all wet the rest of the day." He paused and took another sip of coffee. "We were out in the boondocks, there was nobody around. And one time I decided I'm going to take my jeans and shirt off to go in. As soon as I got in the water, because I'm in sixth, seventh grade, I'm thinking, 'This is the coolest thing in the world.' I started hooking lures like crazy thereafter, just so I could go in there and go capture them. My dad could not figure out why I was snagging lures all the time. Then, of course, I got to sit out and dry off. 'While I'm sitting here drying off, might as well go explore the forest.'" He sipped his coffee. "This is as a teenager."

"You just did it because it felt good?"

He nodded. "Then I think when I was about twenty, I remember this vividly. I was laying in bed on a Saturday morning, thinking, 'I want to do something I've never done before.' Don't have a clue what it would be. Wash the dishes, anything. Then I thought, 'I'll go to a nudist camp.'"

His early lure retrieval sounds a lot like my son's cape wearing. "Do you think there's kind of an innate impulse in people to be naked?" I asked.

He paused, shifting in his seat before answering. "I do, but I haven't seen it written anywhere and I haven't written it myself yet. But I do. I have come to believe this. This just comes out of my Aristotelian totalism, if you will. I just love Aristotle, Thomas Aquinas, and Confucius. These guys would say that we're fundamentally, essentially social beings. Natural beings. I think once people start skinny-dipping, particularly with others—I'm not talking about sexual situations, but particularly with nonsexualized social nudity—I think people are opening themselves to each other in a way that is incredibly, almost lifesaving for some."

I admit I was skeptical of this. I cocked an eyebrow. "Social nudity saves lives?"

Storey nodded. "I've seen them start crying. They can just feel this big release, because they feel alienated. I actually think that social nudity can reduce alienation, and to the degree we're less alienated from one another, we're able to flourish as human beings."

I realized he was being totally serious. I tried to imagine a bunch of naked people sitting around sobbing—which just sounds like something ripped from my nightmares—while he continued. "Not that I need to be naked to flourish. That would be absurd. That's kind of like broccoli. You don't need broccoli for health, but it's a contributing factor towards health, and I think that social nudity can be a contributing factor towards de-alienation."

I'm not sure being naked with other people will make me feel less alienated, in fact I think it would make me feel even more alienated, so I ask him to clarify what he means.

"A lot of the makeup we wear, the clothes we put on, is just to hide who we are. We don't like who we are so we have to hide things from other people."

That reminded me of a convention I attended once in Philadelphia where I saw herds of men and women, all looking uniform and comfortably corporate in primary-colored polo shirts sporting identical logos. They had ceased to look like individuals and had become extensions of corporate branding strategies. Add in the penchant for khakis and cell phone holsters and suddenly a pod-people *Invasion of the Body Snatchers* scenario emerges.

Of course the flip side of logo wear is the label-spouting snobbery of fashionistas who define who they are by the cost of the clothes on their backs.

I found myself agreeing with Mark Storey about a lot of things. He is persuasive. People do hide themselves, their true selves, in the clothes they wear. Uniforms are a good example. They identify a person's role in society, not as an individual, but as a police officer or firefighter or soldier or FedEx delivery woman.

I can see why clothing can be alienating or, at the very least, depersonalizing, but does shedding your clothes really de-alienate you?

"Certainly. If you just drop trou and walk a hundred yards out in the woods, you'll feel closer to nature."

Or closer to being arrested for indecent exposure.

Storey continued. "I believe it's kind of grounded in our nature as social beings, that this openness to others, when it's in a safe, comforting kind of context, it can kind of be life affirming. Whether people recognize it or not, I actually think that's oftentimes what's happening. Everyone who's been skinny-dipping the first time says it's absolutely fabulous."

"I like to skinny-dip," I said.

Which is a bit of an exaggeration, to be honest. What I really mean is that I enjoyed skinny-dipping with my high school girlfriend at a lake near where I grew up in Kansas City, but then I was seventeen and madly in lust and probably would've walked across hot coals or handled rattlesnakes if it meant I got to be naked with her. But I don't tell this to Storey.

He leaned forward and looked at me. I could sense a philosophical inquiry coming on.

"Well, why do you like it?"

I started to answer, but he interrupted. "Yeah, there's a kind of surface physicality. It's sensuous, it's pleasant. But there are a lot of things that are sensual and pleasant that we don't put our jobs on the line for, or put friendships on the line for. Somehow this is more important to a lot of people. I've been trying for years to figure out what it is. Why do people actually do this kind of stuff and put that much on the line for it. You can go to jail. Montana can give you life imprisonment for skinny-dipping a third time."

He's not joking about Montana's laws. A first offense can get you up to six months in jail, a second offense up to a year, and by the time you've been caught with your pants off a third time, the minimum sentence is five years, with the possibility of life in prison.

I took a sip of my coffee and looked around at all the twentysomething hipsters staring at their digital screens. They didn't seem interested in connecting with other people, not in the flesh anyway. Their brows were furrowed in concentration, and it occurred to me that having two boisterous dudes talking about frolicking naked in the sunshine while they sat in the chill and gloom of a January afternoon in Seattle might have a disturbing effect on their ability to focus.

I turned back to Storey. "Humans are sensual beings, your skin is a sense organ, so isn't nudism more of a kind of hedonism?" I am not ashamed to admit that I am a hedonist, not in a self-indulgent sense, but in the classic definition of hedonism as the belief that pleasure and happiness are the highest good. That means that I find as much or more happiness in a good cup of coffee or a fresh mango or a walk in the park as some people feel when they make a lot of money or their team wins the championship. Simple pleasure is underrated. In fact I'm considering joining Hedonist International.[3]

I looked at Storey. "I mean that as a good thing."

He nodded. "There can be that. It can be good or bad. It can go either way. But if what we truly are is rational, social beings, like Aristotle would say, then anything that is allowing me to develop my rational nature and develop my social nature is going to be prima facie good. Anything that keeps me from socializing with people in a good way would be alienating me from others."

"So you're saying the impulse to be naked is more of a social impulse, not a personal one?"

"If we do have an essential nature of being social, and clothing does do something towards alienating us from each other, nudity helps break down alienation. I think that's why so many people like it. Whether they recognize that's why they like it or not."

He took a sip of coffee before he looked at me, almost apologetically.

"This isn't a developed argument, but you asked. I don't know of anybody else saying that. Usually you get the most naive, dingbat answers, like, 'I'm doing this because it's a sense of freedom.' Freedom from what? To what?" He held out his hands and shrugged. "Usually it's just a cliché people heard once."

As I've begun to look into why people would want to take off their clothes and socialize with other people who want to take off their clothes, I've heard all the clichés. The freedom that nudism theoretically provides is freedom from the paradigm of body image worship that the culture has foisted on us, the bullshit that tells people that their worth as humans depends on how young, fit, and beautiful they are. Multibillion-dollar-a-year mega-industries that constantly remind us through carpet-bombing advertisements that we need to remove unwanted hair, bleach our teeth with laser beams, suck unwanted fat deposits out of our bodies with liposuction, insert saline pouches into our breasts, and go on the Paleo diet, the South Beach diet, the Atkins diet, and whatever new diet someone will invent next. The last thing the diet-industrial complex needs is a bunch of de-alienated people with positive body images. Maybe taking off your clothes and frolicking in the forest can dislodge the cultural brainwash that makes so many people so completely miserable.

I looked at Storey. "I don't want to sound cynical but do you think that's really the reason people enjoy being naked?"

He shrugged. "The answer could be rich. It could be different for different people."

Skin in the Game

I don't know where the expression "skin in the game" comes from, but if I was going to get an understanding of nudist culture I'd have to be willing to visit nudist resorts and clothing-optional beaches in my birthday suit. Despite whatever awkwardness I might feel being naked in front of other naked people and then doing whatever it is that naked people do when they're naked together, I was also going to be exposed in another way; I'd be putting some skin in the game. Specifically, my pasty-pink, easily sunburned skin.

There's a reason why I slather on sunscreen before driving to the grocery store and why I prefer to go to the beach and watch a sunset rather than go in the middle of the day. The old Coppertone ad that said, "Tan . . . don't burn," doesn't seem to apply to me. All I do is burn.

I wondered if I had any kind of genetic disposition, any built-in protection, against chronic sunburn, so I drooled into a tube provided by the recreational genetic testing company 23andMe and sent the saliva to a lab. Despite a promising start—I was 0.7 percent Native American and in a subgroup of E1b1b1a, which meant I had a distant connection to North Africa and the Iberian Peninsula—it turned out that my ancestors were predominantly British, Irish, and "non-specific Northern European." Which meant I needed some professional advice before I dropped trou in broad daylight.

I live in northeast Los Angeles, not far from downtown and the hipster enclave of Highland Park. My dermatologist used to have her office in Pasadena, just a quick ten-minute drive from my house, but she's since moved, so I made an appointment to see her and schlepped across town, toward the ocean and her office in Pacific Palisades.

I'm not a huge fan of doctors, I have to say—I typically go to a Chinese doctor, an acupuncturist, for any medical issues—but I really like my dermatologist. Dr. Dana Jo Grenier has a wry sense of humor, she's funny and fun to talk to, but she also has the kind of detail-obsessed personality that you often find with people who run long distances as fast as they can for fun. Which she used to do. She still looks like a long-distance runner, she's lean and wiry, and when she puts on her magnifying glasses to examine your skin, she looks a bit like a praying mantis.

As I took off my clothes for the exam—I didn't know at the time that this would mark the beginning of a year of undressing in front of people—I explained what I was planning to do. She laughed and shook her head.

"When I was first starting out we had a patient who was a nudist and he liked to do headstands in his backyard."

She began examining me, putting her face a few inches from my body, slowly scrutinizing my dermis like a Belgian diamond appraiser examining a stone.

"How long can someone stand on their head in the sun?"

She lifted my arm and stared at it.

"Long enough to develop squamous cell carcinoma on the underside of his scrotum."

She said this matter-of-factly, as if it's information she's just passing along and not some kind of freaky cautionary tale. I wondered how someone could get a sunburn on the underside of his scrotum and then go out the next day and do it again and again. Isn't once enough? Isn't a toasted nutsack a warning sign?

I tried to remain calm. "I'm not planning on doing any inversions in the sun. I'm not even planning on laying out in the sun."

She lifted her magnifying goggles and gave me a twisted smile that was a mix of bemusement and genuine concern. "That's good because genital skin is extremely sensitive."

Which is sort of the point of genital skin, am I right? But I didn't say that. Instead I said, "I've got that spray-on sunscreen. I can cover all sensitive areas."

She nodded. "Remember the spray comes out as particles. You've got to rub it on. And you need at least SPF 30."

She made a note in my file, which I'm guessing recommended I seek psychiatric help, and then looked at me. "And reapply every two hours."

. . .

In my personal hierarchy of the arbitrary importance of organs, I usually think of the brain or heart or genitals as my most important organ depending on what I'm doing at the time. But if I really think about it, skin is the most interesting organ. It's the biggest and, no offense to the spleen, most aesthetically pleasing. Skin function is complex: it's relatively durable and protects us from germs and infection, it holds our guts inside our skeleton, it stretches to accommodate us through our daily grind of bends and twists and exertions, and it's a profoundly acute sense organ.

While the collective attributes of skin are important—most people would say that keeping our organs inside our body was enough—it's our sense of touch that gives meaning and value to the world. We are sensual animals. We like textures. We place a premium on things that feel good. Cashmere, silk, and Egyptian cotton are valuable commodities not because they smell nice or taste good, but because of how soft they feel against our skin. Pressing your skin against someone else's skin generally feels good and our brain takes this sensation and gives it emotion. Touch creates intimacy. It's how babies bond with their parents.

Which makes it kind of weird that we spend so much of our lives keeping our skin covered. We are born naked and before we even take our first breath we are swaddled, bound up in cloth as if our skin might somehow peel off if it makes contact with air. It's our first barrier to intimacy and connection, and it sets in motion a progression of textiles, through diapers and jumpers to dresses and jeans, until we attain adulthood and proudly hang the symbols of modern civilization, Coco Chanel's Little Black Dress or a classic Navy Blazer, in our closet. Then comes a series of jeans and khakis and skirts and capris and pajamas and bathrobes until we finally get around to kicking the bucket and are laid to rest in our Sunday best or wrapped in a shroud and immolated.

No wonder babies are born screaming.

No wonder we are obsessed with skin.

Western society equates skin with sex. When we're consciously trying to be sexy, we wear clothes that "hug our bodies" and "show some skin." Plunging necklines, backless dresses, miniskirts, and fishnet stockings all reveal ample amounts of skin and are considered evocative of sexuality. Our celebrity culture feeds on flesh; hemlines and cleavage and nipple slips are analyzed and dissected by pundits on television and in magazines. People are judged by how much skin they show and how they show it. And in Los Angeles, people are judged by their tattoos and how they show them. It's skin as mobile art gallery.

The dark side of this is when a woman who is "showing some skin" is sexually assaulted and then accused of "asking for it" because of the way she was dressed. On January 24, 2011, a law enforcement officer in Toronto, Canada, famously advised victims of sexual assault to "avoid dressing like sluts." Which is a stupid thing to say, obviously, and launched a wave of protests called "slut walks," where women march against victim blaming and "slut shaming" by dressing however the hell they want. If you listen to what the fashion industry says, what the media tells us, what the obsession with self-portraits plastered on social media reveals, then you could be brainwashed into believing that looking sexy is the ultimate achievement of a human being alive in the twenty-first century. But if something bad happens to you, it's your fault because of the way you were dressed. That is a fucked-up kind of thinking.

Strip away the marketing campaigns designed to sell you stuff for your skin, ignore the television ads and reality programs where showing skin is a sign of sexuality, and look at skin as the simple sense organ it is, and you quickly realize that skin is the gateway to hedonism. Of course it is. Skin looks good, it feels good; you want to touch it, you want to be touched. Which explains why some societies find it threatening; too much skin is too much connection, too much intimacy, too much sex. I think of the burka and niqab as examples of extreme anti-skin apparel, though to be fair, every culture has dress codes.

This compulsion to keep our skin covered is a relatively recent development in human evolution. According to archaeologists, we didn't start wearing jeans or haute couture or velour tracksuits or any kind of clothing until about forty thousand years ago. For the hundred or so thousand years that preceded that moment, humans lived in tropical climates and wore very little except the skin they were born with. There are still indigenous peoples living this way in the world: the Zo'é people of the northern Amazon rain forest, the Mursi and Himba tribes of Ethiopia, and the Kombai of Papua New Guinea are just a few of roughly a dozen societies that live textile free. Which is not to say they don't accessorize their bodies with various piercings, tattoos, lip extensions, body paints, and penis gourds—even an isolated tribe likes to have style.

Humans are relatively hairless compared with other hominids—chimpanzees and gorillas, for example—because, evolutionarily speaking, we were meant to live in a tropical climate. This whole cold-weather, reindeer-sweatered, fondue thing is an aberration. Unlike other animals, we developed the ability to process the heat and humidity of equatorial regions. In other words: we sweat. As anthropologist Nina G. Jablonski states in her book *Skin: A Natural History*, "For an active primate living in a hot environment, having a functionally naked and actively sweating skin is the best way to maintain a steady body temperature and—literally—to keep a cool head."[4]

Most animals have very few sweat glands and are wrapped in fur that insulates them. For example a dog can only cool itself by panting, which is why they tend to overheat in hot weather. Our ability to sweat gave us the evolutionary edge, keeping our bodies cool and allowing early humans to go about the hard work of foraging for food, often covering large distances. This cooling function gave us the physical stamina for what's called persistence hunting—basically chasing antelope or other furry animals on a sweltering day and annoying them until they dropped dead of heat stroke. Some evolutionary anthropologists have theorized that persistence hunting led to an increase of protein-rich foods in human diets, which led to brain development, which led to technological innovations like bronze and iron, which led to Coco Chanel and her Little Black Dress or, if you're so inclined, the velour tracksuit. For those who take a more faith-based approach to human development, you could say that God put Adam and Eve into the Garden of Eden—implying that the Garden of Eden must've been somewhere in the tropics—but they were still naked, hairless, and sweaty.

However, none of these evolutionary theories means that I'm going to run naked through the streets of Los Angeles persistence hunting my favorite taco truck. That would be crazy. I could get sunburned on my genitals.

Aside from being a sophisticated cooling system, our skin allows our bodies to absorb vitamin D, which is essential for calcium assimilation and healthy bone development. Without adequate exposure to sunlight, a person can develop rickets, a disease that creates a softening and deformity of the bones and can lead to bowleggedness and other abnormalities. When the industrial revolution began cranking up its smokestacks and people crowded into coal-smogged cities to work in factories, rickets became rampant.

In 1875 a Scottish missionary and physician named Theobald Palm moved to the city of Niigata, in Japan, where he engaged in the traditional missionary work of healing the sick and converting the locals to Christianity. Trained at the Edinburgh University School of Medicine, Palm had seen firsthand the toll taken by rickets, which, at the time, affected an estimated 60 to 80 percent of children in the United Kingdom. But in Japan, rickets was virtually nonexistent. Palm was intrigued by this and began writing to doctors and missionaries in countries around the world, compiling a study of rickets based on geography.

Medical science in the nineteenth century had a lot of theories, but doctors didn't really know what caused the disease. They speculated that rickets was an infection, or maybe a congenital condition, or something caused by urban crowding and air pollution, or perhaps it could have something to do with a lack of vitamins, like scurvy.

Theobald Palm made it his mission to figure it out.

Not that he didn't have other things to do too. He also had to convert heathens to Christianity, which, in a predominantly Buddhist country, didn't go as smoothly as he'd hoped. In the summer of 1879, a crowd attacked Palm and destroyed his "preaching-place" because they felt that a cholera epidemic was caused by Christians.[5]

In 1885 he returned to northwest England and was again struck by the prevalence of children with rickets in the cities. But Palm had lived for a time in Tokyo, which, while a crowded urban environment, didn't have incidents of the disease, so he knew that the cause wasn't as simple as overcrowding, it was simpler. Studying maps and the anecdotal accounts he'd gathered from missionaries around the world, Palm posited that the main difference between areas that had rickets and areas that did not was sunlight.

In 1890 he published a paper called "The Geographic Distribution and Etiology of Rickets" in a medical journal called *Practitioner*. Of course in 1890 no one understood how sunlight caused the synthesis of vitamin D, and the medical establishment largely ignored Palm's observations.[6]

But other researchers were looking into the benefits of sunlight, and in 1903 the Danish scientist Niels Ryberg Finsen won the Nobel Prize for his work on light therapy and its ability to inhibit bacteria growth—in other words, sunlight as an antibiotic—and by the time 1920 rolled around a doctor named Auguste Rollier had opened "sunshine schools" in Switzerland. Early photos of these schools show shirtless children sitting outdoors, their desks arranged in neat rows as they studied and tanned at the same time. Heliotherapy— after Helios, Greek god of the sun—soon became the rage. Daniel Freund, in his excellent book on the subject, *American Sunshine: Diseases of Darkness and the Quest for Natural Light*, quotes a typically gushing article that appeared in the *Los Angeles Times* in 1927 describing "the curative effects of sunlight therapy on dry and scaly skin, asthma, tuberculosis, bladder conditions, runny ears, polio, and of course, rickets."[7]

Nowadays we don't worry too much about rickets, although a 2012 report from the Royal College of Paediatrics and Child Health in England suggests we should, warning that cases of rickets have risen fourfold since the mid-1990s.[8] This new outbreak is blamed on a number of factors, such as children spending the majority of their time watching television and playing on their computers, and in a 2013 BBC News report, a six-year-old boy in Leicestershire developed rickets because his mother constantly slathered him in SPF 50 sunblock.[9] Of course not getting enough sunshine is only one of the problems related to the disease; poverty and malnutrition play major roles as well.

Then there's seasonal affective disorder (SAD), which is a kind of moody depression and ennui that affects people who live in northern climates with extremely long dark winters. It's more common in extreme places like Finland and northern Alaska, but has been known to affect people in New England and the Pacific Northwest. One effective treatment for SAD is to spend a few hours a day getting bombarded by bright lights and UV radiation. Obviously humans need a certain amount of sunlight to thrive both physically and mentally but, just like really tasty cocktails or an unlimited amount of free gelato, too much of a good thing can be a bad thing.

It used to be that lying out in the sun was supposed to be good for you—sunshine gave you a healthy glow. People would slather cocoa butter or baby oil on their bodies with the intention of broiling themselves a rich mahogany color. But as these glowing, healthy tans began to age, signs of solar wear and tear became evident. The deeply bronzed sex appeal of George Hamilton and the sun-kissed vigor of girls in bikinis gave way to precancerous growths, crinkled skin, and leathery hides. The Saint-Tropez tan has gone the way of the cigarette and the three-martini lunch. Things once considered glamorous are now suspect habits and health risks.* You'd be nuts to tan like that in this day and age. Now a sunburn is more

* A two-margarita lunch is, however, perfectly acceptable.

than just a painful and unpleasant condition; overexposure to ultraviolet radiation from sunlight can damage cellular DNA and lead to all kinds of skin problems. As Jablonski says, "UVA has been implicated as a major culprit in the premature aging of skin caused by sun exposure (known as photoaging), and it has been associated in epidemiological studies with the most dangerous form of skin cancer, malignant melanoma."[10]

Back in the examination room, Dr. Grenier lifted my arm and peered at some freckles. She took off her magnifying glasses and looked at me. "You know, this is a dangerous assignment. Any damage you do, you'll live with for the rest of your life."

Which sounded dramatic. It's not like I'm headed into a war zone on a mission behind enemy lines. But then I'm not sure I want to be the old geezer who points out misshapen warts and precancerous moles while telling stories about that nudist resort I went to.

I tried to reassure her. "I won't be laying out in the sun. I'll put on lots of sunscreen. And I'll wear a hat."

She didn't seem convinced. She handed me a list of recommended sunscreens and shook her head.

"They should give you combat pay."

Gymnophobia

"**G**ymnophobia" is the technical word for "a severe and abnormal fear of nakedness." It's easy to mock sufferers of this phobia, as David Cross did so brilliantly as the character Tobias Fünke in the television series *Arrested Development*. In the show Tobias has "never-nude syndrome" and wears a pair of cut-off denim shorts at all times, with a tube sock underneath so that no one, including himself, ever sees his genitalia. In the show it's taken to an extreme for comic effect, but for people who really are gymnophobic, just the thought of getting naked can cause shortness of breath, irregular heartbeat, and nausea; the sight of people without clothes can induce a panic attack; and a stroll au natural through a nudist resort could result in a full-blown psychotic episode.

It's hard to estimate how many people suffer from this phobia because nobody really wants to admit he or she has it. Being gymnophobic can expose you to ridicule and mockery, even if it does come from body image anxieties, shame, and possible sexual trauma. Some psychologists speculate that it is related to obsessive-compulsive disorder.

I think that most of us can relate to the anxiety that arises from being naked in front of other people. Just think back to high school gym class and walking into the showers. Or the locker room at your health club. And how many people prefer to have sex with the lights off? When you start to think about it, it seems like there is a low level of gymnophobia running through almost everyone. Being naked, or seeing someone who's naked, can be an uncomfortable experience. Unusual, to say the least.

One of the treatments for this phobia is cognitive behavior modification through what's called "exposure therapy." It's pretty much what you think it is.

I can't say I suffer from gymnophobia. I don't have a fear of seeing other people naked and I'm not necessarily fearful of being naked myself. Which is not to say I'm immodest. I'm not the guy who struts around the locker room swinging his wang for everyone to look at; I'm adept at wrapping a towel around my waist. But then I had never been to a nudist resort. I had never experienced being naked in front of other naked people in a place where every single person is naked. You can't not be naked—being nude is the entrance fee, the prerequisite to entering this realm. The gymnophobic need not apply. Or as the sign clearly states: SWIM ATTIRE IS NOT ALLOWED IN THE POOL AREA.

Finding a nudist resort for my first experience of non-sexual social nudism wasn't as difficult as I thought it might be. Nudism is a predominantly warm-weather activity and in Southern California, where I live, there is a surprising number of places that cater to anyone seeking a little exposure therapy.

Palm Springs is only a two-hour drive from Los Angeles, and with its average temperature of 73 degrees and annual precipitation of less than six inches, it is an ideal spot for nude recreation. The area was originally settled by the Cahuilla Indians who lived near a large lake fed by the Colorado River. The lake dried up a long time ago but that hasn't stopped people from turning Palm Springs into a swinging resort town. Nowadays it's an upscale desert oasis dotted with spas and golf courses and tennis courts. People come from all over the world to lie out in the sun and look at palm trees.

I wasn't particularly surprised to discover that the former playground of Frank Sinatra and his cocktail-quaffing cohorts is also a nude tanning mecca, but I was surprised at how many there were. There are at least a half dozen "clothing-optional" resorts in Palm Springs, but only two that I found that don't cater exclusively to gay men. I briefly considered going to one of the gay resorts but, I'll be honest, I am not a gay man, I am shockingly heteronormative.

On its website the Terra Cotta Inn proudly acclaims itself as Palm Springs' "most popular topless and nude sunbathing resort" and cites a *Huffington Post* article proclaiming that the inn is ranked number one of the "Top 11 Nudist Resorts around the World to Visit." It also boasts that it is a great place for your first nudist experience. As the brochure says, "Not a nudist or naturist? Never vacationed at nude beaches before? No problem!"

But when I called to make a reservation there was a problem. I was informed that it was a "couples only" resort. Or as the woman who answered the phone said, "We have a lot of first-timers and we like to reassure the ladies that the men here are all married and with their wives."

As if married men weren't just as capable of gawking and leering at naked women as single men.

"I'm married," I assured her.

"You're more than welcome to come with your wife. We'd be happy to have you." She sounded unnaturally chirpy when she said this.

"But my wife doesn't want to come."

Which was true. She had zero interest in being naked around other naked people. When I told her the Terra Cotta Inn wasn't going to make a reservation unless she came along, she shook her head and said, "No fucking way."

It's not because she doesn't look good naked—I'm biased, but I think she looks fantastic—or that she suffers from any anxiety or hidden fears. She definitely doesn't have gymnophobia. She just doesn't want to try nonsexual social nudism. At least not at a resort in Palm Springs. In fact, she finds it fairly laughable that I'm going to run around naked with other naked people. At least *she* laughs about it.

A lot.

I reminded her that this was all part of the process. You can't study a culture from a distance, you've got to immerse yourself to gain any true understanding.* Like Dian Fossey might've said, if I'm going to study gorillas, I've got to go out into the mist.

I tried again with the reservationist at the Terra Cotta Inn. "It'll be my first time and you guys are famous for first-timers."

I heard a sigh on the other end of the phone.

"Like I said, we're a couples resort." She said this with that resigned there's-nothing-I-can-do-about-it voice and then said good-bye. I found her attitude especially annoying because on the resort's website it says, "The Terra Cotta

---

* Nothing annoys me more than someone who writes a book about cannabis and then claims to have "never smoked it." Really?

Inn is the best not because we are exclusive and snobby (we jokingly recommend those people to go elsewhere). Quite the contrary, we're the best because we have such a friendly atmosphere and the guests have so much fun. If you naturally have a smile, you will love our nudist resort."

I naturally have a smile, I'm smiling right now, but I guess I'll never grin and bare it at the Terra Cotta Inn.

While the Terra Cotta Inn might be biased against single men seeking a clothing-free experience, the nearby Desert Sun Resort is not in the discrimination business. It welcomes single men and women, but with the excellent caveat: "Behavior requiring an apology is not tolerated."

I packed up a variety of sunscreening and sunblocking products—creams and sprays and gels and sticks of anti-ultraviolet technology—and threw them in my trusty Subaru Forester along with a hat and some towels. Normally I'm someone who travels with a swimsuit; even if I'm going to Moscow in February I'll pack it because you just never know, you might get invited to jump into a natural hot spring or swim in a hotel pool, so it felt slightly unnerving, like I was courting disaster, to leave my swim trunks at home.

I kissed my wife good-bye and hit the road.

I know what you're thinking and I have to admit that it did feel strange to be going to a nudist resort to lie around naked with other naked people without her. But I had questions that needed answers. Questions like: What did it feel like to be naked in a social setting? What was the appeal?

I would like to say that the drive from Los Angeles to Palm Springs was, as Joan Didion famously said, "haunted by the Mojave just beyond the mountains, devastated by the hot dry Santa Ana wind,"[11] but really the freeway is a traffic-clogged strip of concrete bordered by an endless barrage of logo litter—corporate signage for Applebee's and Del Taco and Petco and everyone else who's got some business selling something out there with a sign to prove it—punctuated by the occasional billboard for a "gentlemen's club" and cell phone towers disguised as non-native trees.

It's only after you enter the pass that cuts between the San Jacinto and San Bernadino Mountains that the landscape begins to change. The sprawl of suburban housing developments and shitty fast-food restaurants gives way to scrubby desert, railroad tracks, and a high-end outlet mall where busloads of tourists gorge on discounted luxury goods and designer clothes. The freeway passes the mall and then you're greeted by an architectural aberration, the skyscraperish Morongo Casino, run by the Morongo Band of Mission Indians, which juts out of the surrounding desert like an unwanted boner.

Past the casino, mountains rise up on both sides of the freeway and the road drops down into the Coachella Valley, a vast expanse of brown dotted by more than three thousand windmills, their white blades rotating in the wind. Normally I love seeing the windmills, but this time I got a queasy feeling. Were they a metaphor for my own quixotic quest? Or was this the first hint of heretofore unknown gymnophobia?

There's a buzzer at the entrance to the Desert Sun Resort. There are no windows, no flashing neon, just a discreet sign and a large wooden door. A security camera eyeballed me from overhead. I pushed the button, announced myself, and a friendly voice told me to "come on in."

The resort is on one of the main streets just north of downtown Palm Springs, but you wouldn't know it was a clothing-free facility if you walked by. It looks like most of the other Mojave-blasted stucco complexes in the area, only this one has high walls and lush foliage creating a barricade against the outside world.

An affable man in a bright yellow polo shirt checked me in and walked me through a surprisingly extensive list of rules. Many of the rules were typical of any resort—admonitions to shower before entering the pool, to use the hot tub at your own risk, and not to bring pets into the guest rooms. Then there were some that I had never seen before:

- Overt sexual behavior, or the appearance of overt sexual behavior, is strictly prohibited.
- Proper naturist etiquette requires use of a towel while seated when nude.
- Do not use cell phones/laptops/cameras/stereos anywhere on the resort except for inside hotel rooms. iPads, Kindles, or tablets are permitted on the grounds *if* a Desert Sun Resort business card is taped over the camera lens.
- Do not gawk at guests.
- Do not wear swimming suits/undergarments at any time for any reason. No clothing is necessary at any time, anywhere within the facility.

Which didn't mean that nudity was required everywhere at all times. You can slip on a pair of shorts or a shirt if you really want to. Just not around the pool.

The resort is large and attractive, with villas and courtyard suites set around landscaped ponds and man-made streams. There are tennis courts, a restaurant, a spa, and three separate pool areas. My room was in what they called the Chaparral Hotel, which turned out to be a classic motel that had been given a cosmetic upgrade and was right next to the activity pool. The room was completely generic—it looked like every motel room in North America and reminded me of the time I got caught in an ice storm and my wife and I were forced to spend Christmas in a Motel 6 in Abilene, Texas—although there were odd touches of Palm Springs glamour like a marble shower and lemongrass shampoo. I opened the cupboard and found a half-eaten bag of Cool Ranch Doritos and six cans of Sprite. Did the previous guest leave them for me? Was the resort a cool ranch kind of place?

Actually, the room was fine, and it's not like people come to nudist resorts to sit in their rooms. I was mostly concerned by the fact that there wasn't a chain or bolt lock on the door and no in-room safe, just the doorknob with a key lock, which anyone who has ever watched an episode of network television knows you open by sliding your credit card between the door and the doorframe. How could I walk outside without a stitch of clothes on and leave my wallet, cell phone, and laptop in a room a twelve-year-old could break into? Or was I using my security fears to keep from leaving the room? I had never been in a nudist resort. I'd never strolled around naked with other naked people, and now that I was in a place where that was not only encouraged but required, I was obsessing about the lack of a deadbolt. Was I just making excuses?

I stood naked in front of a mirror and checked my body. What was I looking for? Gravy stains? Some physical deformation that was so humiliating that I should just call this whole thing off for humanitarian reasons?

I took a canister of spray-on waterproof sunblock and covered my skin with a thick SPF 45 coating. I remembered Dr. Grenier's warning and made sure I sprayed sunblock everywhere; I was not going to get squamous cell carcinoma on *my* scrotum, or anywhere else for that matter.

Satisfied that I had blasted every inch of my body with several layers of sunblock—and really, what was I doing? Putting on sunblock like it was a pair of jeans?—I took a deep breath, opened the door, and walked out of the room. I strolled toward the pool trying to look as normal as I could. Without any clothes on. In public.

I carried a towel and, being an intrepid immersive-style journalist, a mechanical pencil and a Moleskine notebook.

I heard a song start thumping out of the poolside speakers right on cue, as if they knew I was coming, like I had my own theme song. It was "Super Freak" by Rick James, the sound track for my entrance into the world of social nudity.

There was a small brass plaque on the wall that read, ABANDON CLOTHES ALL YE WHO ENTER HERE, and that's pretty much what was going on. There were about twenty naked men and women sitting in chaise lounges around the pool. And it is not paranoia, I am not making this up, as I walked out by the pool they all turned their heads to look at me.

My first thought wasn't *Wow, we're all naked here!*

No.

My first thought was *Wow, these people are really old!*

They sat blinking at me from behind sunglasses, peering over magazines and books. One man in his early seventies cleared his throat and went back to reading the newspaper. A woman who looked a lot like the actress Maggie Smith* took a sip of seltzer water. I caught a whiff of what smelled like something cooking and turned to see a man in his midsixties stretched out in the sun, his skin tanned the color of teak, glistening with cocoa butter.

It could've been a scene from any retirement home in America, except that they were all stark naked. An elderly woman walked past me and smiled. I smiled back. Have you ever seen a seventy-year-old woman with her pubic hair shaved into what's called a "landing strip"? I have.

If you ask the American Association for Nude Recreation (AANR)—the self-proclaimed "credible voice of reason for nude recreation"—they'll tell you that a nakation offers "Relaxation, stress relief, freedom, fun, great people, positive body image and increasing self esteem."

The fact that everyone is naked is supposed to help you connect with others—the de-alienation I heard about earlier—and let go of your body obsessions, your fears, and your shame. Ideally, the nudist experience creates a level playing field where everyone is equal. And it's true that once you're in a place where everyone is naked, there is a sense of it being a level playing field, only this playing field wasn't level, it sagged. I would guess the average age around the pool was sixty-five, maybe older. And the inexorable pull of gravity had exerted its force on their bodies. It occurred to me that if people lived long enough, we would all eventually melt into lumpy puddles of flesh, like squashed basset hounds.

---

* It was not the actress Maggie Smith.

As I was standing naked in front of these people, I have to say that I didn't feel a sudden sense of liberation. But I didn't feel afraid or ashamed either. My self-esteem didn't increase or decrease. Mostly I felt a little awkward. I've never talked to a naked stranger while being naked before and I was unsure what to say. Like, how was I supposed to greet people? Would my saying hello be interpreted as overt sexual behavior?

And what were they thinking about me? Did I appear unhealthily pale? An obvious first-timer? Nudists refer to people with untanned buttocks as "cottontails." I'll be the first to admit that my ass doesn't see a lot of sunlight. Were they all scoffing and muttering "cottontail" under their breath?

I noticed that a couple of the women were violating the "don't gawk" rule. They were staring at me, their eyes wide.

I quickly realized why.

It was not my physique or lack of tan that was making them goggle; it was the fact that my penis had become incredibly shiny in the sunlight. It looked as if it had been coated in a glossy lacquer like some kind of Shang dynasty artifact. The spray-on sunblock that I had so scrupulously and thickly applied had turned my dick into something resembling a solar flare. I could've sent a distress signal to a search and rescue team.

Fortunately, I did not get an erection.

If the number of times this question is brought up on nudist resort websites is any indication, one of the biggest fears men have is getting an erection in public. At the Desert Sun Resort they offer these reassuring words: "On the rare occasion that this does occur, just simply cover up with a towel, turn over or take a quick dip in the pool."

I honestly don't think that's what most men are afraid of when they go to a nudist resort. The fear isn't that you'll get an erection; the fear is that your testicles will ascend, your penis will retract, and you'll stand there looking like a Ken doll.

The throb of Rick James was followed by the up-tempo innuendo of George Michael as I sauntered away from the "activity pool" toward what was called the "quiet pool." I walked past a few people soaking in the Jacuzzi. I nodded at a semicircle of naked people playing guitars and singing a wretched version of "Layla" in the shade of some trees.

The quiet pool was quiet. No music blared, and the conversation among the few couples that lounged around it was a barely audible murmur. I did not gawk. I spread my towel on a chaise and settled in.

Occasionally someone would get up and swim in the pool for a few minutes, but mostly people kept to themselves. They might nod and smile at each other, but there was not a lot of conversation.

I thought maybe I could start a conversation but then I began to obsess about the rules. What if I said something that could be taken as a sexual provocation? Was it like making a joke while going through airport security?

As a single man, I felt like I was eyed with suspicion. As if some kind of primitive alarm bell was going off in the other men's reptile brains. Was I some kind of swinger? Would I swoop in and steal their mate? But perhaps it was just a flash of sunlight reflecting off my penis that caused people to squint and look away.

I swam a little. I read a book. I watched a youngish woman with a flower tattooed on her butt walk to the bar and fetch a couple of drinks. I was enjoying nonsexual social nudism at a bona fide nudist resort. The AANR calls membership in its organization a "passport to fun," which seems a bit of a stretch. It's not that it wasn't fun, but it really wasn't that different from any other Palm Springs resort I'd been to. The main difference was that the prohibition against "the appearance of overt sexual behavior" seemed to give a strained Kabuki stateliness to people's demeanor. In other words, they were trying so hard to be nonsexual that there was a formality, a stiff decorum, to the way people carried themselves. Even at the active pool there wasn't much activity. It seemed weird to me. Typically you get a bunch of people around a pool in swimsuits and they'll flirt and gawk and do cannonballs off the diving board, but there was a playfulness to typical poolside behavior that was missing here. Maybe it was because it was an older crowd, or maybe it was the tension created by trying to be nonsexual when everyone is naked. Typically humans get naked for sex, but in a setting where everyone is naked and even the appearance of sexual interest is strictly forbidden, it's easy to see why people start to act strangely prim.

Historian Paul Fussell, in an essay titled "Taking It All Off in the Balkans," writes, "Naturists agree that, given the cascades of sexual stimuli poured over us by contemporary civilization, at stated times and places a little contrived, conscious sexlessness is good for you."[12]

"Conscious sexlessness" sounds about as much fun as a juice cleanse.

After a couple of hours of lounging and scrupulous non-gawking, I got hungry and wandered into the restaurant for lunch.

The restaurant was crowded, every table full except for one by the bar. I sat down on my towel and surveyed the room. There were dozens of naked people sitting at tables eating lunch. Following proper nudist etiquette, they kept towels between the furniture and their bodies. Compared with the morgue-like tranquillity of the swimming pool, everyone in the restaurant was positively chatty. Conversations would spill from one table to the next and people would jump up to greet friends or stand at another person's table chatting away. I would've been somewhat uncomfortable to have someone's penis that close to my french fries, but it didn't seem to bother anyone else. In fact the restaurant scene was livelier than your typical Palm Springs lunch joint. Maybe this social nudism thing *is* a passport to fun.

The waiter, who like all the other employees at the resort was fully clothed, handed me a menu. I watched him walk off and deliver a couple of cheeseburgers to a table. Is being a waiter at a nudist resort the weirdest job in the career of a food service professional? Or is it just another day at the office? Did they train you not to stare at the guests' genitals? And how could you not? I had a lot of questions.

I ordered a veggie burger and an iced tea, and just as I was about to ask him what it was like to work around all these naked people, his boss appeared. I could tell right away that she was the owner of the resort. She carried herself like someone who was in charge, only instead of a briefcase and business suit she was topless, a sarong jauntily tied around her waist. Her sunglasses were jammed on top of her head holding her blond hair off her face and she looked younger than most of the guests I'd seen. She seemed smart and friendly, a hands-on kind of boss—in a distinctly nonsexual way—one of those proactive managers who was making sure everything was running smoothly and all the guests were happy.

I felt for the waiter. How weird would it be to stand there and listen to your employer give you instructions while you desperately tried not to look at her large, and admittedly attractive, naked breasts.

Imagine that sexual harassment training film.

And so I sat there and ate my lunch. Naked.

After lunch I went to check out the library and game room, which was really just a shelf of books and board games off to the side of a very modest fitness center that housed a few creaky elliptical trainers and some dumbbells. I entered the room to find a naked woman looking through the books. She was probably seventy years old and tilted her head back so that her reading glasses would focus on the titles. Although I tried not to gawk or stare, I have to say that for someone her age, she looked to be in pretty good shape. She gave me a quick once-over. And I have to admit that I was taken aback. Weren't we supposed to not look? Isn't that what the sign says? Or is a quick once-over different from a gawk or stare? But that's something I noticed about nudists: for all their talk about nonsexual this and don't gawk that, they always take a peek. It's a normal human response to seeing a naked person. I look too. You can't help it.

The library comprised a few shelves of paperbacks that looked to have been abandoned by previous guests. Among the usual suspects, the thrillers and romance novels and best-selling business books, were some literary fiction titles. Zadie Smith at a nudist resort? Maybe not in the flesh, but a copy of *White Teeth* was here.

The naked lady pulled a dog-eared paperback off the shelf and turned toward me. "Have you read this?"

I made a concerted effort to look her in the eye and said, "I'm not really a Clive Cussler reader."

She put the book back and continued looking. Only now we were looking together, side by side, a naked man and a naked woman, strangers trying to find something to read to pass the time. I picked up one of Lee Child's novels. "Have you ever read him?"

She nodded. "He's good. Can't say I cared for the movie."

We chatted about authors and books for a few minutes, and just as I was wondering how the conversation might turn if I picked up the copy of *Fifty Shades of Grey* sitting on the top shelf, she chose a Harlan Coben thriller and said good-bye.

Would this have been an encounter worth writing about if I hadn't noticed the gray hairs on her pubic region? Doubtful. But there it was. My first nude conversation with a stranger. Awkward, but not unfriendly.

I went back to my chair by the pool. Was this a more enjoyable experience than sitting by a pool and reading with a swimsuit on? If I'm honest, I have to admit that it was. It felt good to let the sun and the warm desert breeze dry my skin after a dip in the water without the feeling of clammy fabric sticking to my body. Admittedly it was strange to look around and see naked people, but they were doing a pretty standard version of what people on vacation do, reading or snoozing or drinking cocktails and laughing—all in a nonsexual way, naturally. Nobody gawked, nobody said anything offensive or racy, it was all very proper. I suppose, for me, it was a bit too proper. But after a while I got used to it. I didn't feel weird or embarrassed or uncomfortable being naked around these people, and the few who would dare talk to a lone naked man were totally friendly.

There was nothing else to do but kick back and relax, so I laid out on the chaise lounge, my penis reflecting the desert sun like a chunk of fool's gold.

A Very Brief History of Early Nonsexual Social Nudism

Nudity isn't new. People have been expressing their natural nature from the beginning of civilization. Ancient Greek Olympians competed in the nude; sculptures of early athletes reveal rippling muscles, curly pubic hair, and genitalia in exacting detail. In decorative drawings on ancient wine ewers, the wrestlers, discus slingers, and javelin heavers are all depicted sporting in the buff.* Not only were they naked, but their bodies were slathered with olive oil to enhance the viewing pleasure of fans and the gods, who apparently liked the look of shiny, well-articulated male musculature as much as anybody.

But nudity in ancient Greece wasn't limited to just sports, the Greek word *gymnos* means "naked," and early gymnasiums were not musty places to practice free throws and hold homecoming dances. They were institutions where young

---

* Modern beach volleyball, with its skimpy bikinis and sunscreen-shiny skin, pays unwitting tribute to the ancient games.

men discussed philosophy, science, and literature—Plato and Aristotle both taught at gymnasiums—and practiced physical exercises called gymnastics. The ancient Greeks were way ahead of us in understanding the value of going to the gym. That the young men in the gymnasiums were nude and slick with oil as they studied and exercised is, depending on your point of view, awkward or kinda hot.

The Romans came along and decided that lounging around in the nude discussing philosophy wasn't a good fit for a civilization in the business of world conquest. Much like the corporations of today, they didn't need philosophers and aesthetes, they needed soldiers and workers who could take orders, so they declared the gymnasiums immoral and closed them. Rome's conversion to Christianity only reinforced this attitude, and the once brazenly naked and heroic Greek statue was deemed shameful and required to wear a plaster fig leaf. Western culture seems to be stuck in this quasi-military patriarchal mode, and any form of intellectualism or philosophical discourse is relegated to bohemian enclaves, college campuses, and the Internet.

I often think of organized religion as being the nexus of all the prudery and sexual oppression that inhibits free expression in our culture. It starts when Adam and Eve eat from the tree of knowledge of good and evil and then suddenly find their genitalia embarrassing. Connecting original sin and the fall of man with covering your junk[13] is disingenuous at best and, don't take this the wrong way, could be where everything went off the rails. I can't imagine we'd be a society with the same body issues and eating disorders, and all the guilt and shame that comes with having sexual desire, if we had attended school wearing nothing but extra virgin olive oil. Then again I imagine that sitting in Mr. Speight's sociology class in the nude might've ended up being a perfect storm of raging teenage hormones, spontaneous erections, and teen pregnancy.

But while I think of organized religion as a colossal funwrecker when it comes to nudity, religious groups have practiced nudism throughout history. Dozens of them, in fact. Members of the Digambara sect of Jainism believe that clothing can cause attachment to material things, and so monks live completely nude and have been doing it since the fifth century B.C. The Adamites, a Christian sect that flourished in parts of North Africa from the second to the eighteenth century, believed in returning to an Edenic innocence by taking their fig leaves off and practicing "holy nudism."

In the fourth through sixth centuries, a Spanish sect known as Priscillianists believed that Satan, like an all-powerful and evil Karl Lagerfeld, invented clothing to prevent the healing power of God's sunlight from reaching our human skin, and so refused to wear clothing; and in the thirteenth and fourteenth centuries, a French Christian sect called the Turlupins believed that clothes were designed to keep people from sinning and that, logically, the faithful didn't need clothes because they wouldn't be tempted to sin. Because they were faithful. So they walked around nude. And in the sixteenth century a group of proto-hippies called the Dutch Anabaptists practiced communal living, nudity, and free love. History is littered with crackpot religious sects that practiced nudism, and that's not counting the Druids, Wiccans, and assorted pagans who performed ceremonies and initiations "skyclad."

I'll admit that nudist religious sects have a certain zany appeal, but I'm less interested in people who took off their clothes for religious reasons—people do lots of unusual things for religious reasons. I want to look at the people who have taken their clothes off in a social setting for the simple reason that it felt good. To do that, we fast-forward to 1891 and the Fellowship of the Naked Trust.

...

By all outward appearances Charles Crawford was a model of humdrum administrative industry. His father was a priest in the Church of England, he was educated at Marlborough College, and as soon as he turned twenty-one he joined the Indian Civil Service—then a part of the British Raj—and was sent to Bombay.

In the late nineteenth century Bombay was, as historian Daniel Brook writes, "a kind of bizarro London, where the punctiliously planned efforts of the British were refracted in the fun-house mirror of the teeming, multicultural subcontinent."[14] The city boasted a world-class university built in the Gothic style of Oxford and Cambridge, a library based on the Doge's Palace in Venice, and a train station that wouldn't have looked out of place in any major European city. Yet despite having technological advances like gas streetlights, sewage was still put out in front of homes in buckets to be picked up every evening by "night soil" collectors, and while the British and European residents enjoyed a lavish lifestyle, the majority of the population lived in cramped slums amid squalor that would produce frequent epidemics of virulent fever and bubonic plague. In other words, Bombay of 1891 was not that different from Mumbai of 2015.

It was the British East India Company, as rapacious a corporation as any in history, that initially ruled over the

Indian subcontinent, shipping Indian opium and cotton around the world, all the time running a profit-skimming operation that would make a Las Vegas mobster proud. In 1858 the company gifted the administration of India to the Crown, and the British government took over the job of squeezing whatever it could out of the Indian people.

It was in this chaotic and cosmopolitan milieu that Charles Crawford unspectacularly worked his way up the bureaucratic ladder, starting as a magistrate and eventually becoming, according to the 1894 edition of the India Office List, a "3rd class Sessions Judge in Ratnagiri." When he turned thirty he married a nice Scottish girl and they had a son, whom he named Osbert.

No one knows if it was a consequence of the boiling heat and humidity of Bombay, the repressive hierarchy of the Raj, the untimely death of his wife from complications stemming from the birth of their son, or some long-buried secret desire, but under the three-piece wool suit and high-collared shirt was a man who was desperate to get naked.

This was an unusual passion in Victorian England, where the stout and gimlet-eyed young queen—a monarch who oversaw a society that exploited child labor in the mines and sent homosexuals to the gallows—was busy making sure that tablecloths were of a sufficient length to cover the legs of tables. This is not a euphemism. Back then a well-turned table leg held an erotic charge that's hard to find in a contemporary IKEA. "Bathing costumes" were mandatory and nude swimming, which had been common in England in the early part of the century, was banned.

Despite the institutionalized prudery of the times, Crawford had a dream. Leaving his son in the care of relatives after his wife's death, he returned to Bombay and made the acquaintance of two young American brothers named Kellogg and Andrew Calderwood. The Calderwoods, sons of a missionary, shared his vision of a clothing-free frolic and the Fellowship of the Naked Trust was born.

No one really knows how it all got started. In fact what little is known about the fellowship is due to Crawford's letters to the English writer and philosopher Edward Carpenter, a leading proponent of socialism, vegetarianism, and a kind of pagan sandal wearing, who lived with his lover in a gay community in the English countryside near Sheffield. Carpenter was a prolific writer, justifiably famous for his 1889 book *Civilisation, Its Cause and Cure*—which posited that civilization was an affliction that passed through mankind every so often like a bad case of salmonella—and *The Intermediate Sex*, published in 1908, which became a seminal text for the early gay rights movement. Carpenter was a member of the socialist think tank the Fabian Society[15] and close friends with a diverse group of artists, philosophers, and writers like Walt Whitman, Mohandas Gandhi, Isadora Duncan, D. H. Lawrence, and E. M. Forster. Despite the sophisticated circles he swam in, Carpenter was off the grid before there was a grid to get off. He was an advocate for a simple, natural lifestyle and lived in the countryside with his partner, George Merrill. Remember that this was around 1895, the same year that Oscar Wilde was tried and imprisoned on charges of sodomy and gross indecency, so for Carpenter and Merrill to live in an open homosexual relationship either points to how isolated they were or how badass and influential Carpenter was. Photos of Carpenter show a stylishly dressed and strikingly handsome man with a well-groomed beard and an eccentric penchant for the socks-and-sandals look, who wouldn't be out of place fronting an alternative folk rock band in Brooklyn or mixing bespoke cocktails at a bar in Los Angeles.

Carpenter was a prominent advocate of what we would now call an alternative lifestyle, so it makes a certain sense that Charles Crawford chose to write him about his nudist dream. Although they had never met—Crawford apparently found Carpenter's address in a magazine advertisement—Crawford saw a kindred spirit in Carpenter and wrote him on August 18, 1891, detailing his plans for the fellowship. He did, however, take the precaution of requesting that their correspondence be kept confidential: "for personal reasons it would be inconvenient for it to be associated with these views—so easily misrepresented—by those who oppose them."[16]

Enclosed in that first letter were "The Rules of the Fellowship of the Naked Trust," which were fairly straightforward: "i. Every member (1) to go stark naked wherever suitable (2) to encourage others to do the same (3) to be plainspoken when desirable on sexual and other subjects usually tabooed, and to discourage unnecessary reticence about them in others (4) to comply with the following rules."

The rules go on to declare an official motto, *Vincat Natura* ("nature prevails"), describe a secret handshake, and list eyeglasses and false teeth as exceptions to the stark-naked rule.

In a second letter, dated October 25, 1891, Crawford admitted to a lifelong passion for nakedness and his delight that he had found kindred spirits in the Calderwood brothers. He added that they were hoping to get more members, including women, and then outlined a "Statement of Motives" for the fellowship. Crawford broke these down into three groups: physical, "because no costume that has ever been invented is equal in comfort to perfect nakedness"; moral, "because the false shame of our own bodies and morbid curiosity as to those of the opposite sex which result from always wearing clothes, are the chief sources of impurity"; and aesthetic, "because the human body is God's noblest work, and it is good for everyone to gaze on such beauty freely."

In the same letter Crawford described a meeting of the fellowship: "In June, Andrew Calderwood and I had a grand day. We went away to a bungalow in the Tulsi Lake without servants and spent from dinner time Saturday till 5 pm Sunday in nature's garb."

I don't know about you, but when I go to a lake house with a friend and spend the day naked, I call that a "dirty weekend." Or as Vishwas Kulkarni wrote in a recent story about the fellowship in the *Mumbai Mirror*, "It is however the club's philosophical connect to the sepia-tinted beginnings of the queer movement in Victorian England that makes it more exotic . . ."[17]

Was the fellowship some kind of homosexual liaison filtered through Crawford's starched bureaucratic brain? Is that why he codified it with rules and official motives? It makes a certain sense; homosexuality was illegal at the time and the bureaucratic foundations of a "society" could've acted as a kind of cover story. But the only real connection is that Crawford reached out to Carpenter, who was known as an early advocate for homosexual rights. It's also difficult to say how much influence the fellowship had on future nudists. Crawford's activities were discreet and only briefly mentioned by Carpenter ("the existence of a little society in India—of English folk—who encourage nudity") in his 1892 travelogue *From Adam's Peak to Elephanta: Sketches in Ceylon and India.*

Sadly, Crawford didn't get the opportunity to expand his group or continue frolicking "in nature's garb"; he died at the age of forty-four in 1893 in Bombay from what was officially listed as an intestinal obstruction. The Fellowship of the Naked Trust, the first organized social nudist group in history, had three members and lasted only two years.

...

There's a synchronicity to the world, whether it's punk rock or probiotics; ideas tend to pop up independently in multiple places, so it should come as no surprise that in 1907 a young health food freak in Stuttgart, Germany, named Richard Ungewitter, would publish one of the first and most influential books of nudist philosophy. The book was called *Die Nacktheit in Entwicklungsgeschichtlicher, Gesundheitlicher, Moralischer und Künstlerischer Beleuchtung*, or *Nakedness in an Historical, Hygienic, Moral and Artistic Light*. The book struck a nerve with the German public and became a bestseller. Not bad for a man who had previously tried his hand at selling whole-grain health bread.

Any book urging men and women to take off their clothes is going to get attention, and Ungewitter's book not only titillated the masses but also annoyed the church and state. Especially when he was preaching a hippie-dippie back-to-nature message during what was a boom time for German industry. Companies like Krupp were manufacturing steel; Bayer and BASF were making dyes, pharmaceuticals, and agricultural chemicals; and the country was connected by an efficient railway system. Germans flocked to the cities looking for higher pay and a taste of the good life.

It was the fin de siècle, the old century was gone and a new one was beginning. In the cities of Europe a vital and energized bohemian counterculture had sprung up, and new ideas about art, life, sex, and politics were suddenly in the zeitgeist. German expressionist painters like Ernst Kirchner and Max Pechstein had formed a group called Die Brücke and written a manifesto that was redefining art. Cabarets and theaters flourished, with avant-garde plays like Oskar Kokoschka's *Murderer, The Hope of Women* being produced, and literary journals sprang up filled with prose and poetry that challenged the status quo and attempted to subvert the dominant patriarchy and militarist culture of the previous decade. And while the barons of industry sat comfortably in their factories raking in huge profits, the working classes were being exposed to revolutionary socialism. At the same time Germans were putting *Die Nacktheit* on the bestseller list, the International Socialist Congress was gathering in Stuttgart to coordinate the policies and efforts of all the socialist parties around the world.

Local authorities were caught between keeping enlightened workers from turning Germany into a worker's paradise and trying to get freethinkers like Ungewitter to keep his pants on. They attempted to ban *Die Nacktheit* and, when that failed, took to regularly harassing its author, stopping him on the street and dropping by his house to try to catch him in the throes of some indecent high jinks so they could discredit him and lock him up. But as much as his message annoyed the authorities, there was something profound in his writings that resonated with the deep German desire—or perhaps deep *human* desire—for a romantic connection to nature and a spirituality unrelated to organized religion.

But while an artist like Ernst Kirchner was experimenting with "impulsive love-making and naked cavorting" in his Dresden studio,[18] Ungewitter was after something more pure. He was considered something of a killjoy by his critics, a vegetarian who eschewed alcohol, coffee, tea, milk, and sugar. He thought public dancing was immoral and railed against the publication of trashy literature.* To Ungewitter, nakedness was a panacea, a cure for almost every physical ailment, spiritual turmoil, and societal problem that afflicted humanity at the turn of the century. Even masturbation could be cured by nudism as "nakedness is calming on the sensual drive." Which, in my limited experience, I don't believe for a second. Everyone knows masturbation is cured by orgasm.

Revolutionary ideas are a response, a revolutionary needs something to revolt against—Thomas Jefferson had King George III, Karl Marx had capitalism, Charles Crawford had Victorian repression, and, nearly a century later, the Sex Pistols would have disco. For Ungewitter, it was the increasing industrialization and urbanization of Germany. Heavy industry and mass production were in full swing, and Germans had moved from a life spent frolicking in bucolic pastoralia to one toiling in toxic factories and overcrowded cities. A robust agrarian lifestyle was replaced by decadent urbanity, and the populace had become obsessed by materialism, debauchery, and fashion. Ungewitter saw this as a problem. In a later work, *Kultur und Nacktheit: Eine Forderung* (*Culture and Nudity: A Demand*), Ungewitter described his fellow countrymen with an acid dollop of health freak snark: "men walk about with reddened,

* No booze, coffee, dancing, or pulp fiction? I don't think we would've been friends.

fixed, glassy eyes, bald heads, breathing only in gasps, with a sagging gut and spongy, flabby muscles, behind whom women, first as corseted marionettes, later in the greatest corpulence, waddle."[19] Ungewitter was reacting to a society that, in his eyes, had become morally rotten and physically weak.[20] American historian Chad Ross, in his excellent book *Naked Germany: Health, Race and the Nation*, distills Ungewitter's rage succinctly: "Germany, bluntly put, had become too intellectual."[21]

After World War I something strange happened in Germany: nudism became hugely popular. As Ross puts it, "during the Weimar Republic nudism became a mass cultural phenomenon in which millions of Germans participated, whether as members of nudist leagues or more simply (and far more likely) as weekend beachgoers."[22]

Defeated in war, their economy wrecked and burdened with reparations, Germans needed some relief. Nudism let the German people have fun again. They hiked through the forests and swam in the lakes and rivers, embracing the healing rays of the sun, all the while naked. There are even photographs from that period of German men and women skiing naked in the snow. Amazingly, they are smiling.

And it wasn't just an outdoorsy phenomenon. Ungewitter was joined by authors like Hans Surén, whose 1924 book *Der Mensch und die Sonne* (*People and the Sun*) was reprinted seventy-three times in its first year, and Heinrich Pudor* on the bestseller list, and magazines devoted to *Nacktkultur* began

---

* Pudor went from being the author of naturist books like *Naked Men* and *Rejoice in the Future* to self-publishing anti-Semitic books with titles like *Germany for Germans* and *Preliminary Work on Laws against the Jewish Settlement in Germany*. By the early 1930s he was the editor of a magazine called *Swastika*, which, if you can believe it, criticized the Nazi Party for being too tolerant of Jews.

springing up across the country. These were lifestyle magazines that used nudism as a platform to promote a wide range of topics from Eastern religions to poetry and dance, sex reform and politics.

The 1920s saw dozens of new organized nudist clubs with cultish names like German Friends of the Light and Leipzig League of Friends of the Sun, as well as Orplid in Danzig and Ungewitter's own club, the Lodge of Rising Life, a group with a stringent anti-Semitic admission policy that, according to Ross, "would remain an important presence in the nudist world for years."[23]

All that chatter about the German ideal of physical fitness and finding optimum health in the fresh air and sunshine had a dark underbelly. As Ungewitter wrote in *Kultur und Nacktheit*, he saw nudism as key to "bettering of the German race by promoting marriages between blonde-haired, blue-eyed types."

Failed watercolorist Adolf Hitler was torn on the issue of nudism. Many of the nudist clubs that had sprung up, notably around Berlin, were popular with Marxists and artists and political agitators, while others were hotbeds of German nationalism and anti-Semitism. In case you're just tuning in: Hitler preferred the latter. As Ross writes, "Given the constant, unavoidable viewing of participants at the nudist park and the racial anti-Semitism that permeated *Nacktkultur*, one is tempted to conclude that nudism was also a means of identifying otherwise well-assimilated Jews."[24] You get the subtext, right? There is no better place to spot dudes with circumcised penises than a nudist camp.

Hitler's advisers were equally ambivalent. Some believed that organized nudism would lead to moral decay. Hermann Göring declared that nudism "destroys women's natural feeling of shame, and causes men to lose respect for women, thereby destroying the basis for any real culture." Is he saying that real culture comes from women living in shame? What does that even mean? Others were less prudish, but feared that nudist camps were havens of communism and homosexual activity.

But what self-respecting Nazi wouldn't be attracted to nudism as espoused by racist ideologues like Ungewitter? The more Hitler and his cronies looked at ideas like eugenics, clean living, and the romantic notion of pure-bred German *volk* frolicking in the Schwarzvald, the more appealing nudism became. Besides, it was popular. People enjoyed naked outings in the Black Forest and skinny-dipping in the Rhine. Hitler, being a political animal, decided to split the difference. In March 1933 he ordered all nudist clubs closed—especially ones with ties to Marxist and communist organizations—and in January 1934, he reopened Nazi-approved nudist clubs under the sponsorship of the National Socialist Party and the newly created Kampfring für Völkische Körperkultur, which was later renamed the Bund für Leibeszucht, which Google Translate regurgitates as "Confederation for Physical Breeding."

...

But Germany wasn't the only place where people were thinking of ways to congregate in the nude. In England, a man named Harold Clare Booth began promoting the nudist ideal, beginning pseudonymously with an article titled "The Nude Culture Movement" published in the health journal *Physical Culture* in 1913. Fads and fashion travel, so it's no surprise that the idea of enjoying sunshine and fresh air unencumbered by clothing had drifted across the English Channel. Nudism was suddenly being discussed in magazines including the *New Statesman* and *Health & Efficiency*, a publication promoting healthy living, diet, and exercise. Booth continued to publish articles on the subject, and in 1923, perhaps influenced by the writings of Swiss physician Auguste Rollier on heliotherapy, he and a group of like-minded people founded the English Gymnosophist Society (EGS). Other groups began to spring up shortly after that, notably the Sunshine League and New Health Society organized by London physician and heliotherapy advocate Dr. Caleb Saleeby.

At the time in England, it was against the law to "conspire to outrage public decency," so nudist groups tried to keep their activities as quiet as possible. But as the EGS began to grow, and fear of infiltration by Scotland Yard became a real concern, Booth spun off a splinter faction of core members that called itself the Moonella Group. It was an exclusive club—there were only about a dozen members—but they were committed to nonsexual social nudism and began to hold weekly meetings at the Essex estate of one of their female members.

Early nudists loved to write manifestos, create rules and regulations, and otherwise codify their intentions in written documents, and the Moonella Group was no different. Fueled by what I can only call paranoia, the members drafted the "Resolution of the Moonella Group for the Due Ordering of Its Affairs," which swore participants to secrecy. Not only were they not allowed to tell anyone about the existence of the group, but they weren't allowed to divulge who the other members were, going so far as to give themselves "gymnic names" when they joined. I guess the first rule of a nudist club is no one talks about the nudist club.

Naturally they had a secret handshake.

It's easy to mock the paranoid behavior of early nudist groups, but it helps to keep in mind that in 1925 there were public decency laws on the books and a nudist could easily have been sentenced to prison for cavorting in the buff outdoors, especially if men and women were naked together. Not only was the idea of naked men and women enjoying sunshine together illegal and scandalous, but there were fears that nudists were either communists or, as revealed in Nesta H. Webster's ludicrous shit-stirrer *The Socialist Network*, part of the German-Russian-Jewish-led international conspiracy against Christianity.

Eventually Booth and the others looked to set up a more permanent camp for their philosophizing and purchased some land near Bricket Wood outside of London. The "camp," as it was known, was established in 1927 and formally named the Fouracres Club. Over time it evolved into the Fiveacres Club.* It was the first nudist camp established in England and is still, eighty-seven years later, a functioning nudist retreat center. I wonder what Booth and the other early gymnosophists would've said when Pink Floyd played there on Guy Fawkes Night in 1966.

...

The French have long loved fashion, and they weren't about to be left out of this new clothing-optional fad. So in 1927, a couple of brothers, the naturopaths and physicians Gaston and André Durville, founded the Société Naturiste, and shortly

* I'm guessing they bought another acre.

thereafter published *Fais Ton Corps* (*Make Your Body*), a book that looked at the curative effects of sunshine, fresh air, and a healthy vegetarian diet. Like Ungewitter and other naturists at the time, they believed urban living was the cause of many of the diseases that were afflicting people and, like Ungewitter's, the brothers' books were bestsellers. As their popularity increased, they began publishing a biweekly magazine called *Naturisme*, and leased an island in the Seine at Villennes-sur-Seine that they called Physiopolis.

Although the brothers would've preferred a fully nude retreat, there was pressure from the local police and the French minister of public health to keep breasts and genitals covered. Men wore shorts and women wore bras and panties. Jan Gay, author of *On Going Naked*, visited Villennes in 1931 and said, "Without being too harsh, one can call this island a pseudo-naked French Coney Island."[25] Which is actually kind of harsh.

Another group sprung up about the same time as a counterpoint to the Durville brothers. The Amis de Vivre (Friends of Living) didn't go in for vegetarianism or abstaining from alcohol; they ate pâté, drank wine, and smoked cigarettes—in other words, they were French—but they did it in the nude. A collection of doctors, writers, and professors, they weren't especially dogmatic about their pursuits; they just thought being naked was the most important part of nudism.

As you would guess from the name, the Amis de Vivre was an easygoing bunch. Nudity wasn't required unless members were in the "nudarium" area. Louis-Charles Royer, a writer and member of the Amis, wrote a serialized fiction about the group called *Au Pays des Hommes Nus* (In the Land of Nude Men), which became a bestseller and led to other branches of the club springing up in Lyon, Perpignan, Marseilles, and other French cities.

Meanwhile the Durville brothers had become frustrated with the restrictions imposed on them at Villennes and set out to find a place where they could build a true naturist paradise. In 1931 they settled on the small island of Levant off the French coast in the Mediterranean where they built a rustic retreat they called Heliopolis. It was undeveloped, close to nature, and bursting with fresh air and abundant sunlight. Better still, it was a private island where everyone could be totally naked all the time. A nudist utopia, if you will.

...

There have always been pockets of nakedness scattered around the United States—wacky religious sects, anarchist personality cults, utopian communities, and dudes that just liked to be naked on the farm—but none of these was organized in the manner of the German nudist clubs. However, it didn't take long for the siren song of clothes-free frolic to spread from Germany to New York City, where, in 1929, an enterprising young German named Kurt Barthel placed an ad in a local newspaper looking for kindred spirits interested in bringing *Nacktkultur* to the United States. Barthel had organized a few nude sojourns out in the Hudson Highlands, mostly with German expats and a few curious Americans, but now he wanted to do something a little more serious. A small group met at the Michelob Café on Twenty-Eighth Street in Manhattan on December 5, 1929, and formed the American League for Physical Culture (ALPC). It was a strange time to be planning a nudist club. Wall Street had crashed just two months earlier,

Prohibition was in full swing, and according to the National Weather Service records, it was 32 degrees Fahrenheit outside. But then again, now that I think of it, if I were broke, sober, and freezing, I might look for something fun to do. The ALPC started out simply enough. The group rented a gym with a swimming pool and held weekly meetings. A *Miami Daily News* article from 1933 describes one of these meetings, reporting that the basement gymnasium was "more than faintly redolent of perspiration and disinfectants." A typical session would go like this: members would perform calisthenics to warm up, maybe play a little volleyball or generally exercise, and then relax with a swim in the pool. Surprisingly—and unlike many of the clubs in Europe—the league had almost equal numbers of men and women from the beginning. The American nudists took a more pragmatic approach to being in the buff. They ignored the bans on coffee and tobacco and didn't require strict vegetarianism, and they weren't writing books and pamphlets about a return to a romantic idealized kind of naturism. They just liked to take off their clothes and hang out.

Membership in the ALPC grew rapidly, that is until someone dropped a dime on them and the police raided one of the gatherings, arresting seventeen men and seven women for public indecency. Fortunately they found a sympathetic judge and the charges were dropped. But Barthel knew he needed to find a location where he and his friends could practice nonsexual social nudism without threat from overzealous law enforcement or religious prudes. Besides, with more and more people coming, they were quickly outgrowing the gymnasium. The ALPC eventually leased some land in Ironia, New Jersey, and dubbed it Sky Farm.

Like many of the other nudist or naturist retreats founded in the early days of the movement, Sky Farm continues to operate in the same location as a "members only" nudist club. Sky Farm set the template for American nudist clubs and, as more and more people tried nonsexual social nudism, clubs and resorts gradually began springing up around the country. It was a start, but as we'll see in later chapters, the real boom in organized American nudism was yet to come.

I Left My Cock Ring in San Francisco

I didn't realize that public nudity was legal in San Francisco until it wasn't.

I mean, I'd seen naked people in the city before; there was the naked Christlike dude who walked down Polk Street carrying a red telephone and telling people "It's for you," and I'd witnessed the gay men sitting around and catching some sun in the Castro, one of the oldest and largest gay neighborhoods in the country. And then there is the Pride Parade, a clothing-optional celebration of gay culture, which, after the Rose Parade, is the largest parade in California; the seven-and-a-half-mile Bay to Breakers race where contestants dress in goofy costumes or nothing at all; and the largest fetish festival in the world, the Folsom Street Fair. All of these events featured ample public displays of male and female genitalia and nobody seemed to notice or care. Getting naked was just part of San Francisco's freewheeling culture. It was the kind of thing that made the city special.

Not just because of the parades and fetish fairs, but because San Francisco has a history of tolerance for nudism.

According to the *San Francisco Bay Guardian*'s "Nude Beaches 2012" report, there were three quasi-official nude beaches—Golden Gate Bridge Beach, North Baker Beach, and Land's End Beach—within the city limits. And then there were the hippies who danced naked in Golden Gate Park.

And then, on February 1, 2013, it was banned.

This came as a surprise to a lot of people, but it's not like there were never no limits on public nudity. You might have been able to walk down the street naked, ride the bus or the subway, and sit down in a restaurant and have dinner, but you couldn't sunbathe in the city parks. That ban was put in place by the San Francisco Recreation and Parks Commission to discourage the aforementioned hippies from taking off their clothes, waving their arms in the air, and twirling around to a psychedelic jam session. Although, if you ask me, it's a totally weird law because isn't a park the place where you'd prefer nudists to go? Maybe they should've just banned hippie dancing.

Public nudity was also banned for sexual purposes, which I guess is more of an erection ban. In fact, according to California Penal Code Section 647(a) nudity is legal in California except when a person "solicits anyone to engage in or . . . engages in lewd or dissolute conduct in any public place or in any place open to the public or exposed to public view."

So it's not like San Francisco was a totally freewheeling pleasure dome of nakedness, but then again, compared with every other city in the country, it kind of was. Until it wasn't.

I was surprised to see that the ban had been led by Scott Wiener, the San Francisco supervisor from District Eight, which includes the Castro, Noe Valley, Diamond Heights, and other neighborhoods. Not only is Supervisor Wiener a gay man, but he lives in the Castro, and you'd think that he would be sympathetic to the gay men who sunbathe in public there and you'd be right. It turns out that he is sympathetic to the nudists in the city, but the Harvard Law graduate is a politician, and he found himself caught in a political struggle that is a lot more complex than it looks on the surface.

I sent Supervisor Wiener an e-mail asking for an interview and he responded with a tentative yes, although he was honest enough to say he hoped I wasn't writing a "hit piece" on him. I hopped on a plane and, on a stunningly beautiful February morning, found myself going through security at the magnificent expression of Beaux-Arts architecture that is the San Francisco City Hall.

I walked down a long corridor, past a group of women speaking Chinese and wearing yellow plastic hard hats, and found Supervisor Wiener's office. When I was finally ushered in for our interview, I was taken aback. Scott Wiener is a tall man—six foot seven according to *SF Weekly*—trim and fit with a close-cropped beard. He was wearing a checked shirt that coordinated in an off-kilter way with a zigzag pattern tie, which indicated he had style and a sense of humor.

I knew I was a weird appointment in his busy schedule, but he was gracious and friendly as we sat at a table in his office and he popped open a Diet Coke.

"I'm curious how this became your issue."

He smiled and said, "Can you remind me again—I didn't go back over your e-mail—you're writing a book?"

Now that I have a pretty good sense of what nudism is, I'm trying to understand why there are so many laws against it. My personal experience has shown me that nudists are, for the most part, not kinky freaks or weirdos; they're not exhibitionists or voyeurs or anything other than people who just like the way sunshine feels on their naked bodies. And here in the United States, more often than not, they're grandmas and grandpas. Hardly a revolutionary demographic.

I explained what I was doing to Supervisor Wiener in general terms and it seemed to put him at ease. He nodded, took a swig of soda, and began.

"We have a long history of nudity in San Francisco. At the beaches, at all the fairs, and as long as I've lived in the Castro, which is going on sixteen years, there's always been the occasional naked guy who walks through the neighborhood. There are always two or three of them that maybe every week or two you would see. I don't remember anyone complaining about it. It wasn't a big deal. It was sort of part of the spice of the neighborhood and the city, but it was fine." He took another sip of soda. "It coincided right about the time that I took office at the beginning of 2011." He paused and gave me a rueful smile. "Lucky me. I actually did go back and talk to my two opponents in the race and I said, 'Do you remember this ever coming up as an issue during the campaign?,' and none of us could remember it ever coming up."

Supervisors typically campaign on broad platforms like public safety and quality of life issues like fixing potholes, planting trees, constructing bike lanes, dealing with problems like homelessness, and improving public transit. They rarely get involved in civil liberties debates.

"What changed?"

"There was a group of guys that would be primarily at Castro market, but elsewhere in the neighborhood, hanging out naked pretty much seven days a week. Then it expanded with guys coming in from around the Bay Area to get naked in the Castro, because they couldn't do it in their hometown.

It went from this occasional quirky fun thing to something else. I think at the very beginning when it happened, people sort of raised an eyebrow and maybe it got a little annoying but thought, 'Okay, this is just . . . this is interesting.' After a few months of that, people started to get more and more unhappy about it."

"What kind of unhappy?"

He sighed. "Primarily this is painted by some as straight people imposing values in the Castro, but it was mostly gay men who were upset about this in the neighborhood. It wasn't just at Jane Warner Plaza. I got quite a few reports of—again showing just incredibly poor judgment—some of these guys walking right by elementary schools, even when class was getting out. I heard from McKinley, from Sanchez Elementary, and again just showing very, very poor judgment."

Naked men walking in front of elementary schools doesn't strike me as a protest for body freedom or liberation; it's an intentionally provocative gesture.

Wiener continued. "For the first, almost two years, there were just huge amounts of e-mails and calls and people stopping me on the street demanding that I ban it. I really resisted those calls. It's not what I wanted to be legislating. It's not the issue I wanted to be known for . . ." He paused and gave me a kind of helpless look. I realized that a guy with a last name that's a euphemism for penis wouldn't want to be known as anti-nudity. Obviously.

I laughed, I couldn't help it. Supervisor Wiener has a good sense of humor.

". . . And frankly, I didn't want to ban it." He paused, collecting his thoughts. "After a while it just became completely untenable and there's a pressure that was building in the neighborhood, and elsewhere because Castro market is such a prominent physical place, the pressure that was building was just . . . it was becoming explosive. There was a lot of anger being directed towards me for not taking action. So I started just asking people, 'What do you think? Should I do this?,' and by and large a lot of them were like, 'You know a year ago I would have told you no, but I think you need to do it.' Ranging from Cleve Jones to other people, mostly gay men, and I sort of came to the conclusion that although I had always thought that this will run its course . . ."

Cleve Jones is a gay rights activist and cofounder of the San Francisco AIDS Foundation, and was a colleague of assassinated gay rights leader and San Francisco city supervisor Harvey Milk.

Wiener sat back in his chair, his extremely long legs splaying out. "It was just getting more extreme. There were days when you would go out there and there would be ten, twelve, fourteen of them congregating in the plaza, walking around the neighborhood. The whole issue with the cock rings started—"

"Cock rings?" I interrupted.

He nodded. "Despite what some people say, this legislation wasn't about cock rings, but that was just an example of them getting more extreme."

Naked men love wearing cock rings.* It makes their penises look bigger and, well, men like it when their penises look big. There was a bit of controversy over cock rings and some of the Castro nudists claimed that a San Francisco police

---

* Not to be confused with an Arab strap, which, though similar, is a different thing entirely.

"cock ring patrol" was targeting them. For the police, wearing a cock ring constitutes lewd behavior, but for nudists like Lloyd Fishback, it wasn't about being sexual: "You shrivel up in the cold. It kinda helps you stand out a little more, make you look a little bigger."[26]

"The Castro Theater was just apoplectic because that theater is . . . we're lucky that it's still open. One of the areas where they are able to make money so they stay open is they do the sing-alongs. Sing-alongs to *The Sound of Music*, sing-along to *The Little Mermaid*, and those are extremely popular, with lines of families and kids around the theater. Some of the naked guys would just walk up and down those lines and then people would say they're not coming back. It was just a combination of things that were just bringing it to a boiling point. That's what led me to introduce the legislation."

The idea of a cock ring parade in front of little kids waiting in line to go see a Disney movie baffled me. Even if you buy into the idea that nudity is okay in any context, they must've known they were pushing the envelope with this behavior. Why be so provocative?

Wiener nodded. "Right? The sense I got . . . it was marking territory. There was an attitude of 'this is our neighborhood,' whatever that means, and keep in mind there have always been a lot of straight people in the Castro. There have always been children in the Castro. There's elementary schools, three of them, within a few blocks of Castro market that predated all of us. But it was sort of 'This is our neighborhood and we can be as edgy as we want and do whatever we want and we don't want you here.'"

Wiener leaned forward and fixed his eyes on me. "A woman contacted me. She had brought a troop of Girl Scouts to sell Girl Scout cookies at Eighteenth and Castro on a Saturday afternoon, and there was a naked guy who walked by. Fine, he walks by, and she said in a fifteen-minute period he walked back and forth past the girls five times. It was very obvious to her what he was doing. It sort of went above and beyond."

According to an editorial in the *Bay Area Reporter Online*, an LGBT newspaper, the Castro nudists would "shake their dicks at oncoming traffic." I don't know why, but I find the image of a dozen or more naked men shaking their penises at traffic kind of funny. But I can also see where the joke might wear thin after a while.

Normally, city supervisors deal with more mundane issues. Look at some of the legislation that Wiener has passed recently and you'll find he's been behind the move to license professional dog walkers, revise restaurant codes to help small businesses, regulate food trucks, help janitors earn a living wage, and all the typical street resurfacing and park beautification you'd expect from a locally elected official.

But feeling pressured to do something, Wiener proposed a stiff ban—and now I think you see why he didn't really want to be associated with this. In addition to the local coverage of his proposed legislation, the ban was noted in articles in the *Wall Street Journal, USA Today, Guardian, Daily Mail*, and other national and international media outlets such as CNN and BBC.

"I knew when I introduced the ban that it would get a lot of press. I still underestimated the sheer volume. The fact that the whole process around the legislation straddled Thanksgiving, and the number of people who went to various parts of the country home for Thanksgiving and then came back and told me that's the only thing that anyone wanted to talk about at the Thanksgiving dinner table."

Wiener's legislation wasn't exactly popular with his fellow city officials. Supervisor Christina Olague was opposed and was quoted as saying, "When it comes to priorities, this seems absurd to me." Supervisor David Campos, who represents the Mission District, thought the ban was a misuse of police and city resources, and Supervisor John Avalos said, "I will not put on this fig leaf. I just can't do it."[27]

But other members of the board of supervisors, notably from tourist-heavy districts like Fisherman's Wharf, supported the ban and it ended up squeaking by 6 to 5.

When the vote was announced, a number of spectators in the gallery immediately took off their clothes and began haranguing the board. Deputies showed foresight, and an understanding of San Francisco politics, and appeared with blankets to cover the naked protestors seconds after they disrobed. One of the nude protestors was a man named Stardust who was quoted in the *San Francisco Chronicle* saying, "It's telling people they should be ashamed to be naked, and that's totally wrong."[28]

The response from nudist groups in the city was predictably virulent. England's *Daily Mail* ran a headline that said "Naked Fury: Protestors Strip Off and Storm San Francisco City Hall as Officials Approve Legal Crackdown on Nudity." Wiener was called, among other things, a "fascist," a "Republican clone," a "whore," and "the only wiener that doesn't belong in San Francisco." Whenever Wiener made a public appearance, nudists would show up shouting and taking their clothes off.

Wiener was surprisingly philosophical about the reaction.

"Locally I actually think it was a really fascinating, and frankly an important debate that happened. Particularly within the gay community, but I think more broadly. I do truly believe that the legislation had strong majority support generally and within the gay community. But there was definitely a very passionate minority, which I always respected. There are a lot of people, particularly LGBT people, who came to San Francisco—and I include myself in this category—we all came here because you can be who you are in San Francisco. People won't judge you. A lot of people growing up were perceived to be 'freaks' or not normal, and they come to San Francisco and they are accepted for who they are. For a lot of people they would say, 'Listen, I don't get naked in public. I don't really like it, but that's who they are and I don't want to tell them what to do.' We see that in San Francisco in particular. There's this strain of hesitancy to tell other people what to do. If you want to take your clothes off, if you want to lay down in your vomit on the sidewalk, if you want to camp out anywhere you want. Someone might say I'm conservative if I tell you you can't do that. It was a very fascinating debate."

A group of nude activists continued the debate and challenged the ban in federal court. They believed that the ban violated their First Amendment rights. But in his opinion U.S. District Court judge Edward Chen refused to block the ban and wrote, "In spite of what plaintiffs argue, nudity in and of itself is not inherently expressive."[29]

For the time being, Wiener has won.

But doesn't this ban have consequences beyond San Francisco? Isn't there some kind of core human impulse that should be honored?

Wiener smiled at me. "Well, we can have a broadsided philosophical debate about whether it should be okay for people to be naked in public and if society accepts that, that's fine. Here we're trying to address a particular situation that arose in a particular neighborhood that most people weren't okay with. We try to strike that balance about where you . . . there are places where people can be naked. Whether you have . . . I mean, I don't know, is there an impulse to be naked? Maybe on some level, but the fact that most people really would never even think about being naked makes me question that."

I reminded him that, from the nudists' point of view, he'd taken away their constitutional rights.

He nodded. "Their arguments are not illegitimate. Again, this is a difference of opinion for when it's appropriate to let your stuff hang out. I actually—I was at an event right after I introduced the legislation and I started talking to these three guys. They were from Oakland and one of them said to me, 'Oh, we're nudists,' and I thought, 'Uh-oh, here it comes, they're going to yell at me . . .'"

"Or take off their clothes."

". . . Or just be mad at me and tell me how awful I am. He said, 'We're nudists and we support your legislation because that's not nudism. We go to gatherings in people's backyards or we'll rent out a campsite, or whatever. We all gather together and we're naked together and everyone there consents to that and that's what we want and that's what we do.' He said, 'Nudism is not about walking on the sidewalk naked by people who have no desire whatsoever to see me.' It was interesting . . .

"The other interesting thing, and this is just a quirk of San Francisco, in the early eighties the city banned nudity in parks. Before I passed this legislation it was illegal to be naked in a park, but legal everywhere else, and that always struck me as backwards. If you are going to allow people to be naked anywhere, it probably should be in parks. You see that in Europe and they kept making the European comparison. This is very European where in Europe they don't walk down the street naked. If you get . . . like in Germany and I think elsewhere, there's parks where they will sunbathe."

I wondered about the "slippery slope" argument that nudist activist Mitch Hightower posited in the *Wall Street Journal*. He said, "Today it is naked people, and next week it will be drag queens, and then the week after that it will be people who wear leather."[30]

Wiener took a sip of his soda.

"The legislation is actually much more narrow than the city's other nudity bans in parks and on court property. It basically only applies to genitals. It doesn't cover women's breasts and it doesn't cover buttocks. I actually removed buttocks in the legislation after meeting with the folks from Folsom and they said, 'We're not thrilled about the legislation but we understand why you're doing it. We just would like you to remove buttocks because of the people who want to wear assless chaps.'"

Only in San Francisco would you find this kind of sensitivity to people who wear assless chaps.

"They kept saying that this is no different than banning gay people from kissing in public, banning drag queens, requiring women to wear burkas. If you ban anything you may as well ban everything, so therefore ban nothing. I don't buy that argument. We make distinctions all the time in society."

And with that he looked at his watch and gave me a friendly nod. I realized that our time was up. I thanked him;

he had been more forthcoming than I expected, and he seemed genuine and sincere about trying to balance San Francisco's radical instincts with what I'd call a more gentrified point of view.

I walked out of the building and stepped into the sunshine. I was meeting my son for lunch at Zuni Café, so I strolled down Market Street and wondered how we, and by "we" I mean us as a society, got to the point where our own bodies and the bodies of our fellow human beings cause so much commotion. I mean, seriously, we all have bodies and for the most part they are all the same. Why does seeing someone naked cause offense? And why do some people insist on showing their genitals to other people? Is a nude painting offensive? Probably not if it's hanging in an art museum. Is a grown man waving his dick at a car offensive? Maybe. Maybe not. In some states that would be called "flashing" and bring criminal penalties. But flashing by definition is not nudity; it is done to shock, for sexual gratification. Flashing is lewd. But even if flashing is lewd, do we really want to spend our tax dollars keeping wienie waggers incarcerated? Is that the kind of world we want to live in?

The Rise of Nudist Clubs
in America

Nudism has become a big business. It seems that there are more people than you'd think who'll plunk down their hard-earned dollars and pay for the privilege of being naked around other naked people. There are so many of them that the nakation business is, according to the American Association for Nude Recreation (AANR), "conservatively estimated a $440 million industry." That's a big chunk of change and one that could, with the wave of a wand of oppressive legislation, disappear in the blink of an eye. Which is where the AANR comes in. Like the local tourist board or chamber of commerce, the AANR's job is to protect and promote the business of nonsexual social nudism, particularly as it pertains to its member clubs.

The AANR is a nonprofit organization that calls itself "the credible voice of reason on issues relevant to nude recreation and Nakationing in appropriate settings." Which seems like it's claiming ownership of the topic while backing away as quickly as it can. The "in appropriate settings" is a hedge against naked people running amok, say, in the mall or on the golf course, and keeps the AANR positioned as a respectable entity and not some organization promoting anarchy. The AANR PR material boasts that it is "a gold and silver award-winning member of the American Society of Association Executives" and has won "four Golden Bell communications awards from the Hospitality Marketing and Sales Association International (HMSAI), two Silver Mercury Awards and an SATW Cushman Award in recent years."

I don't know what any of that means, but it certainly sounds impressive.

And the AANR is impressive. Depending on which promotional brochure or press release you read, the organization has 34,000 members, or "now serves over 213,000 individuals," or is "serving more than 52 million individuals who enjoy skinny-dipping and clothing-optional recreation." It claims to have more than 250 affiliated clubs, resorts, campgrounds, and related businesses scattered across the United States. Some of these clubs, like the Desert Sun Resort in Palm Springs, are designated "landed clubs" because they have their own property and facilities, while others are called "travel clubs" because they have to move around and find temporary or public places where their members can enjoy nude recreation.

The "passport to fun" that membership in the AANR provides costs about fifty-eight dollars a year or, as it says in the press release, "less than the price of a bathing suit." In the AANR's drive to remove any stigma from nudism and recruit new members, it presents a wholesome, reassuring tone; it's a voice that wants to help people "recapture the freedom and innocence" of their first skinny-dipping experience. All of its marketing is focused on getting its members to visit official AANR clubs.

To further promote the interests of its member clubs, the AANR sponsors the Trade Association for Nude Recreation (TANR), which provides advertising and outreach for member businesses. The TANR also hosts an annual conference that, according to its website, "is especially aimed at improving the viability and marketability of all naturist enterprises in which risk-takers have invested capital, careers and family futures."

I should note that my attempts to arrange an interview with someone from the AANR were never acknowledged; my e-mails were never replied to; and when I spoke to someone on the phone at its Kissimmee, Florida, headquarters I was advised to "download the press kit."

Looking at the press materials, it is clear that the AANR isn't much concerned with the legal issues, civil liberties, or moral imperatives at play in the wider world of nudism. That may be because the resorts and campgrounds it represents are private, for-profit, clothing-optional areas and it doesn't cost a dime to go to a nude beach or a clothing-optional hiking trail, so why promote something that would be competition for its member businesses.

Although this may be changing. Recent postings on the AANR home page have revealed a schism in the organization, and some members are pushing for a more politically engaged and activist vision.

Today's AANR began in that meeting at the Michelob Café in 1929, where Kurt Barthel and his friends started the American League for Physical Culture and then did naked jumping jacks in a smelly gym. A few years later, in 1931, a man named Isley Boone—who liked to be called "Uncle Danny" because of some strange fixation with Kentucky frontiersman Daniel Boone—took over the organization from

Barthel and jazzed up its image by first calling it the International Nudist League and then the American Sunbathing Association (ASA).

The early ASA grew at a relatively modest pace, gaining converts and earning money through the sale of its lifestyle magazine, *Sunshine & Health* (formerly the *Nudist*). Which is not to say it was always smooth sailing. Boone battled local authorities and religious leaders who tried to close nudist camps; fought with the U.S. Postal Service, which would routinely refuse to deliver his magazine on moral grounds; and basically steamrolled anyone who tried to thwart the growth of his burgeoning nudist empire. Nudist historian Cec Cinder sums up the pre–World War II state of American nudism: "By now Boone had developed a sort of nudist conglomerate which consisted of nine rather mysterious interlocking corporations or companies, with himself the controlling (and perhaps only) officer of most and certainly in control of them all."[31]

Boone's control freak mentality created conflicts, mutinies, and splinter groups. All of which went on hold when World War II broke out. Boone couldn't have foreseen it, but the war proved to be a turning point for American nudism.

There's not a lot of privacy in a war zone and soldiers by necessity spent much of their time being naked together. They changed clothes and showered and sometimes skinny-dipped together. I don't know why the Pentagon thought that it would be a problem. For a long time it was given a pass, maybe something to do with boys being boys, or perhaps ever since George Washington asked German military officer and alleged homosexual Friedrich Wilhelm von Steuben to join him at Valley Forge, there's been homosexuality in the armed forces that the general public isn't aware of, but whatever the reason, the military brass became concerned that men left in the company of other men for extended periods might turn to homosexuality to relieve the stress of combat. There has always been homosexual activity in the armed forces, but between 1938 and 1941 there had only been thirty-four soldiers convicted of sodomy and related offenses,[32] a significantly small number when you consider that more than 16 million men and women served during World War II. And while the statistics may not have given cause for alarm, there was anecdotal evidence of soldiers hooking up, or, as Quentin Crisp famously said of cruising American GIs during the London blackouts, "Never in the history of sex was so much offered to so many by so few."

The Pentagon thought all this man-on-man action would somehow have a negative effect on troop morale. And while it wasn't willing to sanction supplying actual pornography to the troops, it decided that a nudist magazine like *Sunshine & Health* might be a reasonable compromise. There were ample photographs of naked women to help soldiers do the five-knuckle shuffle, and at the same time, it promoted a vision of a wholesome American lifestyle. Historian and author Brian Hoffman writes, "*Sunshine & Health* contributed to a widespread effort by the military to boost troop morale through a policy that attempted to address the sexual needs of soldiers without resorting to prostitution."[33]

In other words, it's better to let soldiers jack off than have them unfit to fight thanks to STDs.

As the popularity of the magazine grew among soldiers, the editors of *Sunshine & Health* responded by amping up the raciness of the photos. As Hoffman says, the magazine "attempted to use the soldiers' erotic longings to draw new members into the movement."

To a surprising degree, they succeeded.

But while the military might have seen nudism as a healthier alternative to prostitution and sodomy, the home front didn't see it that way. The idea that people might be cavorting naked on private property was met with outrage from the religious leaders and morality police of the time.

In 1935 New York State passed the McCall-Dooling Bill. The bill, written under pressure from the New York Archdiocese, amended the penal code to state that "A person who in any place willfully exposes his person, or the private parts thereof, in the presence of two or more persons of the opposite sex whose persons, or private parts thereof, are similarly exposed, or who aids or abets any such act . . ."—it goes on at some length, but you get the point. The law made it a misdemeanor to be a nudist and, perhaps unintentionally, made participating in a ménage à trois a criminal act. A watchdog group called the Legion of Decency* was quickly formed to monitor nudist activities and, perhaps, report any suspicious three-ways.

Four years later, on the other side of the country, the Los Angeles County Board of Supervisors passed an ordinance banning nudism. The city of Los Angeles enacted similar legislation and, in 1940, raided a ranch used by a nudist group called Fraternity Elysia. This headline from the May 27, 1940, *Freeport Journal-Standard* gives a good indication of the law enforcement attitude at the time: "Burrs Are Punishment Enough

---

* Not to be confused with DC Comics' *Legion of Super-Heroes* or *Legion of Doom*.

for Hollywood Nudists." The police are quoted describing the women being "on the fattish side of 40" and openly chuckled at the nudists' attempt to flee into the surrounding hills: "When they get through picking out the burrs after running through Sagebrush hills, that'll be penalty enough." The nudists apparently took off with nothing "but badminton racquets."

The owner of the ranch and one of the guiding forces of Fraternity Elysia was Lura Glassey, an attractive young woman who sported a pixie haircut and a sly smile. She had previously run a nudist club with her husband, Hobart—photos of Hobart depict an intense young man with a hipster mustache—called Elysian Fields.* After a falling-out with their business partner, she and her husband moved their nudist camp to the ranch at La Tuna Canyon, not far from Los Angeles. Hobart died in 1938 in a freak accident when he slipped from the top of a kiln and broke his neck. By all accounts, Lura was intelligent and feisty and not afraid of authority figures; faced with a ban on mixed-sex nudity, she contrived to get around it by having men and women take turns being naked—a whistle would signal the change—but as clever as she was at circumventing the rules, she was ultimately arrested. She appealed this, and several other convictions, taking her case all the way to the Supreme Court, where, in 1947, she argued that "nudism is a social belief, and not legally limited unless there is a danger to society."[34] The court didn't see it that way and Lura Glassey became one of the few American citizens to ever serve prison time for nudity.

* Fun Fact: Seismologist Charles Frances Richter and his wife were frequent guests.

The history of nonsexual social nudism is littered with similar stories, and as the postwar era turned into a boom time for American nudism, with established clubs getting new members and new clubs and colonies popping up across the country, more and more complaints about immorality and obscenity began making their way to local authorities.

Things began to change when, in 1956, police raided the Sunshine Gardens Nudist Resort in Battle Creek, Michigan, and arrested several nudists. Even though they were on private property, the nudists were convicted of indecent exposure. Which, if you think about it, is bizarre. If you're naked with a group of other naked people and you are gathering for the express purpose of pursuing group nudity on private property, what's public and indecent about it?

To their credit, the Michigan nudists fought the charges and, in a verdict that had ramifications across the country, had their convictions overturned by the Michigan Supreme Court. Of his decision, the justice and avid fly fisherman John D. Voelker* said he was not going "to burn down the house of constitutional safeguards in order to roast a few nudists."[35]

The Sunshine Gardens verdict came the same year that "Danny" Boone and the American Sunbathing Association won a landmark case in the U.S. Supreme Court, overturning provisions of the Comstock Act.

The Comstock Act was enacted in 1873 during the presidency of noted Old Crow aficionado Ulysses S. Grant. I'm not saying that it was hypocritical for a notorious boozehound to pass a law banning the transportation of obscene material and

---

* Judge Voelker was also an accomplished novelist and author of the bestseller *Anatomy of a Murder.*

contraceptive devices through the mail, but I will suggest that he might've been drunk at the time he signed it.

The law was named after Anthony Comstock, a postal inspector and founder of the New York Society for the Suppression of Vice, the self-appointed morality police who mostly targeted girlie magazines and publications they deemed to be pornographic or that promoted homosexuality. In their zeal to keep New York safe from salaciousness, these vigilantes managed to ban *Ulysses*, *Lady Chatterley's Lover*, and the work of Oscar Wilde, along with scores of other books and magazines. In 1927 they even managed to close a Broadway play called *Sex* starring Mae West.

The Comstock Act empowered the U.S. Postal Inspector to snoop in letters and packages, approving or disapproving the content of various publications. This overreach led to a ten-year legal battle between the postal service and *Sunshine & Health*. The inspector general would, if it suited his whim, declare certain issues of *Sunshine & Health* obscene and undeliverable. The magazine would then go to court and get an injunction forcing the postal service to deliver the publication. The next issue would come under similar scrutiny, be banned, and the process would start again.

As *Sunshine & Health* grew in popularity during the war, the postal service bans became more frequent and the magazine was forced to go to court to stay in business, seeking protection under the First Amendment. The court battle would drag on for years, but on January 13, 1958, Uncle Danny and *Sunshine & Health* prevailed. Now the magazine could be delivered to anyone in the United States with a passing curiosity or interest in the nudist lifestyle. Other nudist magazines quickly sprung up in the wake of this ruling, and the 1950s and 1960s saw publications like *Modern Sunbathing, Sundial, Nude Living, Nudism Today, Jaybird Happening*, and others, including one that wasn't necessarily about nudism, called *Playboy*.

Early nudist magazines are almost comical in the way they had to pose the models, twisting their bodies so that the women's breasts were prominent but the pubic area was turned away, or airbrushing genitalia out altogether so that nudists playing catch on the beach looked more like Mattel toys with a pixilated smudge for a crotch.

...

American nudism was never a wildly popular fad like it had been in Germany before the war, but it was gaining converts. According to naturist historian Lee Gregory, "In 1949 there were 30 naturist clubs and 3,000 members nationwide in the American Sunbathing Association."[36] By 1964 there were approximately 140 nudist camps across the country, 100 of them members of the ASA.*

As more and more people began trying nonsexual social nudism, cultural references became more common; nudists and nudist colonies were often used as material by comedians.

---

* Of course there were other nudist organizations in the early days. The American Gymnosophical Association (AGA), for example, was one of the groups that split off from the ALPC in 1930. It was run by a sociology professor named Maurice Parmelee and had its own resort at the Rock Lodge Club in the New Jersey countryside. But the AGA was small and, like other upstart organizations, never grew to possess the clout that "Uncle Danny" Boone's ASA had or the AANR still has. Nonetheless, the Rock Lodge Club is still an active nudist club and an affiliate of AANR.

Here's a classic: "Q. How can you spot the blind guy at the nudist colony? A. It's not hard."

Badda boom!

Nudist-themed films, which had struggled after the Motion Picture Production Code* was enacted in 1930, slowly began to find audiences. Titillating titles like *Garden of Eden* (1954), *For Members Only* (1960),** *Gentlemen Prefer Nature Girls* (1963), *Take Off Your Clothes and Live* (1963), and *Girls Come Too!* (1968) portrayed the nudist lifestyle as natural, healthy, and—just like the AANR does today—decidedly nonsexual.

Mark Storey writes in *Cinema Au Naturel*, "To the degree that nudists were involved in the making of a nudist film, they would have been intent on mitigating the preconceived notions in the public's mind that the camps and clubs were havens for sexual libertines and host to daily orgies."[37]

The films had the additional challenge of not showing pubic hair, avoiding full-frontal nudity, and dodging any depiction of sexual behavior. That they had to be entertaining, on some level, goes without saying. Storey describes the standard plot of nudist-themed films as "girl is introduced to nudism, girl discovers innocent delight there, girl finds the man of her dreams."

Nudist films were not box office hits and it took a popular film to give the general public an idea of what a nudist camp might be like. *A Shot in the Dark* (1964) is the second in the successful series of Pink Panther films, with British actor

---

* Better known as the Hays Code, a set of moral guidelines defining what was acceptable in motion pictures.
** Also known as *The Nudist Story* and *Pussycat Paradise*.

Peter Sellers portraying the bumbling Inspector Clouseau of the French police. This installment features the inspector's hilariously awkward visit to a nudist camp called Camp Sunshine. It is arguably the best example of how nudism and nudist clubs were portrayed in mainstream culture in the early 1960s and it's a fantastic bit of comedy; taking off his clothes to go undercover, Clouseau covers his genitals with an acoustic guitar as he tries to find a suspect lounging in the "recreation area."

But it's the depiction of Camp Sunshine that is perhaps more revealing of the public's fantasy of what a nudist camp might be like. Clouseau walks past a naked jazz band playing a riff on Henry Mancini's Pink Panther theme, while naked men and women—their backs to the camera—groove to the music under a stand of pine trees. The inspector makes his way to a small lake where groups of nudists sit in chairs and a man and a woman standing a few feet apart from each other toss a beach ball back and forth. This scene, perhaps more than any other, gave the general public the idea that nudist colonies were jazzy centers of male-female beach-ball-tossing fun times.

In 1995, in a switcheroo of acronyms, the ASA was renamed the AANR and the mission became, as Gloria Waryas, the current president of AANR-East, said in a recent interview, "predominantly a vendor-driven organization."[38] That is, it sold memberships and promoted the pleasures of nude recreation in official nudist clubs.

Presently there are AANR-affiliated nudist clubs in almost all fifty states—Arkansas, North and South Dakota, Mississippi, and Alaska being notable exceptions.

Show Me Acres—"For those who enjoy the beauty of bareness!"—is fairly typical of a well-appointed landed club.

The resort has more than three hundred acres of woodlands in the Missouri Ozarks, as well as a large swimming pool and clubhouse. Typical of clubs in less temperate climates, Show Me Acres is open from May to September and only on weekends. It hosts a "Hawaiian Luau Potluck Weekend" and a "Christmas in July" party in addition to barbecue and chili cook-off competitions. One of the things I like about Show Me Acres, in addition to having a state-specific name that also acts as a clever double entendre, is that unlike many nudist clubs, it allows singles.

Another example of a landed club would be Serendipity Park, about a ninety-minute drive from Atlanta, Georgia. They are "6-time national award winners for outstanding friendliness" and, judging from some of the activities they mention on their Facebook page, like "hot tub beer pong" and a "pirate costume party," it does sound like a friendly place. Like other landed clubs it has a pool, wooded areas, cabins for rent, and campgrounds.

There are dozens more landed clubs: Prairie Haven in Scranton, Kansas; Bare Backers Nudist Club in Boise, Idaho; Shangri La Ranch in New River, Arizona; White Tail Resort in Ivor, Virginia; the Willamettans Family Nudist Resort in Springfield, Oregon; Solair Recreation League in Woodstock, Connecticut; Gymno-Vita Park in Vandiver, Alabama; and Cypress Cove Nudist Resort and Spa in Kissimmee, Florida, to name just a few.

Non-landed—a.k.a. travel clubs—are different. They don't have acres of land or pools or clubhouses. They have to find their nude adventures where and when they can. A good example of a non-landed AANR-affiliated club is the Hill Country Nudists of Austin, Texas, which hosts one or two skinny-dipping events a year and does monthly outreach meetings preaching the gospel of nonsexual social nudism to Texans. Like a typical landed club, the Hill Country Nudists holds wine tastings and themed potluck dinners, movie nights, and parties with live music. Unlike landed clubs, it sometimes has to deal with the public and public spaces, like Hippie Hollow, a designated nude beach on nearby Lake Travis, or when it hosted a moonlight bike ride through downtown Austin.

The North Carolina Naturists is another non-landed club, but unlike the Austin nudists who have Hippie Hollow, the North Carolinians tend to meet in their backyards and homes for nude potluck dinners and pool parties, like the Valentine's Day luncheon hosted by members Karen and Jim or a pool party at Frank and Rhonda's. How strange would it feel to be a new member sitting in Karen's kitchen, eating red velvet cake with a bunch of nudists? Maybe not that strange at all.

I'd had a taste of American club nudism at the Desert Sun Resort, and while it gave me one view of what nude recreation could be, I felt like if I was ever going to understand what would make a person want to go to a nude potluck dinner, it was time to get serious. I had to jump into the deep end of the culture. So I booked my tickets, packed the bare minimum of clothing into a small carry-on suitcase, and headed for the motherland of nonsexual social nudism. Europe.

Vera Playa

The experienced sunbathers rise with the morning light and claim the best chairs around the pool. This is about real estate—location, location, location—and these are the positions that promise optimal conditions. The old pros can read the movements of the sun like an astronomer, calculating what time a shadow might fall across their position; they know how far they are from a cool dip in the water, the relative distance to the bar and bathrooms. Their skin is smooth—body hair only gets in the way of the sunlight—and uniformly deep brown and leathered. If you can imagine Dutch actor Rutger Hauer turned into a purse, you've got the picture.

By nine the best seats have been claimed. Amateurs will have to settle for the fringes, chairs that are far from the pool and under palm trees that offer only dappled exposure to the sun.

On the beach a naked man jogs past, his penis whipping wildly in circles like a rubber chicken. He passes a group of topless women doing some kind of stretching exercise. They reach their hands up to the sky and then swing their torsos from side to side. It's not yoga. I don't know what it is. I'm still drinking my coffee.

It wasn't easy to get to Vera Playa. I flew from Los Angeles to Dallas to Madrid to the dusty coastal town of Almería in southwestern Spain. From there I rented a Fiat 500 and drove another hour through the beautiful and desolate Spanish desert until I finally circumnavigated my way through the maze of roundabouts and gated *urbanizaciónes*—what we would call apartment complexes or condominiums—and found myself in front of the Hotel Vera Playa Club.

As I checked in I was greeted by the sight of what appeared to be a tribe of naked people surrounding a large swimming pool and, for a brief moment, I had a flash of what Captain Cook must've felt when he landed on the shores of Kealakekua Bay. Except here I wasn't set upon by warriors and beaten to death; I was met with benign indifference.

The Hotel Vera Playa Club has the unique honor of being the only naturist hotel in Spain and the centerpiece for what is arguably the largest naturist development in the world. And yes, it seems to me that the words in its name are in the wrong order too. But the hotel is lovely, with a soaring atrium painted a shocking blue and lined with decorative tile.

I walked past a massive birdcage next to the entrance and a large tropical parrot twisted his neck sideways at me and squawked. Could the parrot, who must've been accustomed to naked humans by now, see that I was a pretender? An interloper in the land of naturists? I realized that if a single avian squawk could send my brain spinning into paranoid fantasies, then I was feeling somewhat unnerved being in a clothing-optional city.

Past the lobby is the pool area, the main stage for nude activities, a large biomorphic structure with shallows for small children and water slides built to look like a pile of boulders. While the pool gives off a *Flintstones* vibe, the massive terra-cotta-tiled area surrounding it is more like a giant tandoori oven built for the slow roasting of human flesh. Hundreds of chaise lounges are scattered under a grove of palm trees. If you're like me and hear your dermatologist's voice echoing in your head, you can position your chair in the shade, and if you're a member of the smooth-skinned sun-worshipping elite, you can catch all the Spanish rays you desire.

It was only my second visit to a nudist resort and I was feeling vaguely debutante-ish as I strode out toward the pool wearing nothing but a half a can of sunscreen and a pink towel slung over my shoulder. It wasn't that I was nervous exactly. I'm not worried about what someone might think of my body and I had learned from my first experience to be prudent in applying the sunscreen so as not to make my penis look like it had been freshly Turtle Waxed. It's more like being invited to join a club but, aside from the hygienic stricture to always sit on a towel, no one had really explained the club's rules to me. Maybe there weren't any.

Where there had been a formality to people's behavior in Palm Springs, here that formality was replaced by a refreshing normality—in Vera Playa people were just getting on with their vacation. There were the typical elderly couples roasting their hunched and saggy carcasses in the sun, but also middle-aged men and women, young professionals, a smattering of hipsters from Barcelona, and lots of families with children.

The kids surprised me. I hadn't been expecting it and, honestly, I don't know why. Although I guess it's because if you were naked around kids in the United States you'd probably be arrested as a sex offender or something. But really, why wouldn't you take your kids to a beach resort? It's normal in Europe for families to go on naturist holidays together, and the hotel went out of its way to accommodate them with babysitting services and a range of activities for kids of all ages. The little ones do art projects, make excursions to the beach, or have specialty parties like "Cowboys and Indians" and something called a "princess party," while the older kids can "catwalk around the pool" and "be a model for a day," sing karaoke, and enjoy a "mini-disco." The little kids and preteens seemed evenly split between wearing swimsuits and going nude, but the teenagers—hyper self-conscious—piled on as many clothes as they could.

I heard some shouting and turned to see the youth activity director waving a bunch of kids over to where she was standing. I'm guessing it was some kind of morning roll call before they went off to play. But why she decided to gather all of them a few feet from the chair where I was splayed out is something I do not know. In a matter of seconds my chaise was suddenly adjacent to a school yard, thirty or forty kids of all ages lining up to hear instructions from their teacher. I looked up from my book to see a huddle of teenage girls acting like they weren't looking at me. I returned the favor, acting like I wasn't looking at them acting like they weren't looking at me. That way no one had to feel uncomfortable. For a second I considered covering my crotch with a book, but I was reading Jess Walter's excellent novel *Beautiful Ruins* and, well, I may be getting older but it's too soon to apply *that* label to my genitals. Besides, doing anything would've been an acknowledgment that I was feeling uncomfortable and my being uncomfortable might've made them uncomfortable, or at least think that they should be uncomfortable when, really, nobody has to be uneasy about any of it as long as we all act like we're not looking.

After what to me seemed like an hour of lying naked on a playground, the kids got their orders and ran off to do various fun things, but before I could turn back to my reading I heard some strange sounds and looked over to see a group of men and women standing in a circle doing what I can only call organized rhythmic clapping. There wasn't any music playing that I could hear, just a group of naked people in a circle clapping out a beat. Some kind of traditional sun worship warm-up? I had no idea what they were doing, but it reminded me of the horror film *The Wicker Man* and I was sufficiently unnerved that I required a beer from the bar.

Except for these occasional outbursts it was quiet. Birds in the trees chirped, the waterfall in the pool made a continuous aquatic rumble. Occasionally someone would dive in. This tranquillity would be broken from time to time by announcements over a loudspeaker. PA feedback would squeal, heralding another incomprehensible broadcast as the hotel tried to shove a good time down our throats. Or maybe it *was* fun. I know one of the announcements trumpeted the start of "flower power mojito hour" and an exuberant young man in a kind of hippie clown outfit came bounding out of the bar to round people up for a free shot of mint-tinged booze. As much as I enjoy a good mojito—and believe me when I say with all sincerity that the mojito is one of mankind's greatest achievements—I couldn't be bothered to get out of my lounge chair. Besides, the clown outfit scared me. Would we all take a shot of flower power mojito and then stand naked in a circle rhythmic clapping?

People lined up for the free mojito shots but then went back to their chairs for more sunbathing. A few of the wilder ones jumped into the pool. Which is to say that the pool area returned to normality, a totally normal resort normality. Couples played *pétanque* on small sand pits. People read books and applied sunscreen. A couple of younger women sat in their lounge chairs obsessively sending text messages. Kiddies splashed in the shallow end. No one used the water slide. A mother played Ping-Pong with her ten-year-old son—which in America would spell years of therapy for both parent and child, not because of the Ping-Pong but because of the naked-ness of the Ping-Pong players; but here it seemed innocent, cute even. In other words, it could've been any resort hotel anywhere in the world, except at the Hotel Vera Playa Club everyone was naked.

Playa means "beach" and *Vera Playa* is simply "beach in Vera." But the beach has some history. It's where Hannibal allegedly landed his elephants in his bid to defeat the Roman Empire in the Second Punic War, and more recently, in what was called the Palomares Incident of 1966, it's just a few kilo-meters from where an American B-52 bomber carrying four H-bombs crashed after a midair collision with a refueling tanker. Although none of the bombs exploded, the soil was contaminated by plutonium dust, and the U.S. government spent billions of dollars digging up the Spanish dirt, shipping it home, and burying it in South Carolina.

The hotel was constructed on the ruins of an aban-doned desalination plant, and roads originally built to truck freshwater out are now used to import the area's newest economic driver: naked tourists.

I asked the Centro de Gestión y Promoción Turística del Ayuntamiento de Vera, the official tourism bureau of the city, for some statistics on tourism. Here's a rough translation of its official report: "With respect to data recorded at that point we can state that during the year 2012 there were a total of 7,687 visits, of which 73.02 percent were made by domestic tourists, and the remaining 26.98 percent, by foreign tourists."

For the number one industry in the area that doesn't seem like a lot of people. But then the data is pulled from tourists visiting the information desk at the convent in downtown Vera, which was hosting an art show by local students when I stopped by. According to the tourist bureau's data, only six Americans visited Vera in 2012. Which really surprised me. Even if you're not into naturism, this is a strikingly beautiful part of Spain. But maybe Americans really are more prudish than Europeans.

I can't imagine any of the naturists I'd seen at the beach bothering to go to the city center to look at an old convent. Not while the sun is shining and they can keep their clothes off. However, I do find the ratio of Spanish tourists to foreign tourists informative. Most of the guests at the Hotel Vera Playa Club were Spanish, with tourists from the United Kingdom outnumbering the second-largest group, Germans, 5 to 1. The rest were French or Italian with some glamorous Russians thrown in. I'm not kidding about the Russians. The men were handsome, the women were gorgeous, and they showed up for breakfast drinking Cava and wearing exquisite clothes. They were movie stars compared with the rest of us in our T-shirts and shorts. And, yes, you are required to wear clothes in the dining room at the hotel. But seeing the beautiful Russians was the first time in a nonsexual social nude setting when I thought that I couldn't wait to see what they looked like naked. It was a juvenile impulse, I admit it, but the Russians did not disappoint.

I'm not surprised that the foreign tourists are from countries with miserable weather. Why wouldn't they want to leave the cold and wet of northern Europe for the dry heat and blistering sun of southern Spain? It is semiarid desert and looks a bit like the iconic American Southwest, which explains why this part of Spain has been the backdrop for *Lawrence of Arabia*; *The Good, the Bad, and the Ugly*; *A Fistful of Dollars*; and parts of *Indiana Jones and the Last Crusade*, among others.

The beach at Vera Playa, which was designated naturist by the local government in 1979, is more than two kilometers of flat, pebbly sand. Of course now that I think about it, the Spanish authorities probably decided that an area with a history of radioactive contamination might as well be designated naturist.

In the 1980s the *urbanizaciónes* began being developed along the naturist beach. The first was called the Natsun—which I'm guessing is a portmanteau of "naturist" and "sunshine"—followed by others with names like Vera Natura, Natura World, Armony Natura, and Vera Luz. These are not super-swanky developments. They look like the condos you might find in small beach communities like Carpinteria and Encinitas on the California coast. Which is not to say they're not nice. They look perfectly fine.

The best part about living in an *urbanización* is you can walk from your condo, along pedestrian pathways, to the beach and back without wearing any clothes. That you can stop at a grocery store or a bar or a restaurant without getting dressed just adds to the appeal. No shirt, no shoes, no pants, no nothing.

Where you keep your wallet is a bit of a conundrum, and I hadn't seen anyone wearing a fanny pack.

Unlike other nudist and naturist resorts, Vera Playa isn't hidden behind walls or locked behind gates. The beach and the pathways are open to anyone who wants to drop trou and air his or her genitals. It's an audacious concept. Creating a clothing-optional neighborhood? A place that's open to the public? Why?

I should note that my use of the phrase "clothing optional" annoys naturists. For them, it's either naturist or textile, with no in-between. Which is fine in theory, but in practice people seem to wear whatever makes them comfortable. On the beach and in the *urbanizaciónes* I saw as many people wearing swimsuits or shorts as people who were totally nude.

I contacted Bob Tarr, an ardent naturist, a civic-boosting resident of one of the *urbanizaciónes*, and the webmaster of the informative site veraplaya.info, and asked him who lived in these complexes. Tarr replied, "Most of the homes here (80% or so) are Spanish owned and with relatively few exceptions they are used for the July/August summer holidays and occasionally during the rest of the year mainly at bank holiday periods." Bob's numbers seem to correspond with the data from the tourist bureau, so maybe using the convent information booth as a metric wasn't such a strange idea after all. Bob wasn't going to be in Vera Playa when I was; he said it was "a bit too hot and a lot too busy" that time of year. Which surprised me because it was early July, the weather was pleasant, and it wasn't particularly crowded.

With almost 80 percent of the owners not around all year, who rents the apartments in the *urbanizaciónes*? Bob told me that occasionally non-naturists will take advantage of the relatively low rents on these vacation homes, and that has become, as he said, "a bit of a thorny issue."

I wanted to get an idea of how the locals felt about this mix of "textile" and "naturist," so I arranged an interview with José Carmelo Jorge Blanco, the mayor of Vera. If anyone would know about thorny issues or how the locals felt about their beaches being overrun by naked people, he would.

The center of Vera is eight kilometers from Vera Playa. I left the hotel and drove around, basically getting lost, until a friendly bicyclist pointed me in the right direction and I found myself in Vera. After I wound my way through tiny one-way streets near the city center—my rented Fiat proving to be excellent at maneuvering through the narrow alleys—I turned up in the Plaza Mayor at the tourism office, where a woman named Pilar Guerra was waiting for me. Pilar is tall and attractive and reminded me of a slightly frazzled character from one of Pedro Almodóvar's early films. That she made herself even taller by wearing three-inch platform sandals only added to her charm. She was relieved I spoke Spanish, she said, because her English was "not good," and I was alarmed that she thought I spoke Spanish. Because I don't really speak Spanish, I speak a kind of Los Angeles pidgin Spanglish. But it didn't seem to bother Pilar, who just shrugged and said, "We don't get a lot of opportunities to speak English anymore here."

We decided we would muddle through together. The mayor spoke fluent German, which is admirable, but wasn't much help.

José Carmelo Jorge Blanco is an extremely affable, some might say *simpático*, individual, quick to smile and outwardly intelligent. When Pilar and I entered his office, the sixty-two-year-old grinned like a bemused optometrist. Which it turns out is what he is when he's not overseeing the municipality. He doesn't take a salary for serving the citizens of Vera, he just likes doing it.

We sat down at a large conference table made of highly polished black wood. The chairs matched the table and were upholstered in red velvet. It all looked impressive and old, like it was left over from a TV show about the Spanish Inquisition.

The mayor began by saying, "*Vera Playa es diferente. Muy singular en el mundo.*"

I nodded. Vera Playa is a unique place. No doubt.

"How did this unique place come about?"

Pilar translated my question to the mayor. He thought about it and said, "The government has defined this type of nudity, we respect it and defend it. All the different political parties and groups in this city, all of them, defend *turismo naturista.*"

While it is technically true that there are no laws against nudity in Spain, you just don't see people strolling Las Ramblas in Barcelona in the buff, walking naked through the Alhambra in Granada, or sitting at cafés nude in Madrid. So while it's legal throughout the country, it's not really encouraged. Except in Vera.

"Why turn Vera into a nudist city?"

He burst out laughing. "Why not?"

He had me there.

The mayor continued. "It's about personal liberty. We respect the rights of each person."

This I could follow in my limited Spanish, but then he went off saying something that I couldn't catch. I turned to Pilar, who bit her lip and said, "The typical tourist is compatible . . .

eh, with a naturist tourist, and each tourist can . . . eh . . . live together." Pilar looked up, apologetic. "Maybe."

The mayor seemed to enjoy the language malfunction that was occurring. He looked at Pilar and laughed. "Your English is no good."

It was a good-natured ribbing and Pilar smiled. "Next year I'm going to study in at . . . *escuela idioma* . . . I would like to . . . eh . . . *recuperar* . . ."

"Recover your English?" I ask.

She nodded. "Yes."

I'd like to recover my Spanish but I'm not sure much of it existed in the first place. I turned back to the mayor. "What is the economic influence of the naturist developments for the city?"

"Most of the jobs here are directly or indirectly related to tourism," he said.

Pilar looked at me and said, "About five years ago there was a building boom here, a lot of people were building houses and complexes, but with the crash everything stopped and now we are living in another time."

Just like in the United States, Spanish real estate prices rose almost 200 percent between 1997 and 2007,[39] and, just like in the United States when the real estate bubble popped, the banks fell into crisis and the government—with help from the European Union—was forced to step in and bail them out. This set off a chain reaction of plummeting home values, austerity measures, inflation, and unemployment as high as 25 percent.[40] Construction stopped and, as Pilar so eloquently expressed it, the Spanish "are living in another time."

The economic crash explains the empty lots, half-built *urbanizaciónes*, defunct nightclubs, and abandoned construction sites that are scattered throughout the area around the beach.

"The worst part is most of the resorts and *urbanizaciónes* are now in the hands of the banks. You can buy a house for very cheap." Pilar looked like she was about to set me up with a realtor. Not that I need a recommendation—there were For Sale signs up everywhere. According to one, you could snag a two-bedroom, two-bath condo a few blocks from the Mediterranean for about 70,000 euros.

I was thinking about Bob Tarr and the "thorny issue" he claimed existed between naturist *urbanizaciónes* and textile ones. So I asked the mayor about it.

The mayor considered my question and then said, "We don't know about any problem. *No pasa nada.* The whole sector of the beach is for naturists. Vera is a city that is very open about this."

Which made me wonder if it was more of a one-sided concern; in other words, the naturists want to keep the beach for themselves.

"What do the people of Vera think about all these naked people running around?"

He shrugged. "We have never had a problem. *Nunca problema.*"

Pilar added, "The people that don't like . . . eh, that like to stay with the clothes don't go to the place with the people without the clothes."

The mayor smiled. "I am not a naturist, but I am not afraid to encounter one."

Which I found to be a very enlightened attitude. Why couldn't it be like that on beaches in the United States? Why have laws restricting people from doing what they want? Does anyone really believe that seeing a naked person causes anyone any harm?

The mayor continued. "In the United States you just now have gay marriage. In Spain we have had this for a long time and we don't have a problem. It is the same with naturists. There is no problem. People have rights to do what they wish and you can't bother people anymore."

According to the mayor—who's a member of the center-right political party—all the political parties in Spain are tolerant of people's desires and respect individual liberty.

After the meeting I wandered around the city, enjoying the small-town bustle of the streets. I got hungry and ended up at a restaurant that Pilar had recommended. The Terraza Carmona didn't serve lunch until two, and it was only twelve thirty. I must've looked sad or hungry or some combination of sad and hungry, because they said that although the restaurant was closed, I could eat tapas and have some wine in the bar. They then carted out a few small plates. I sipped an icy Verdejo from a producer called Campustauru and ate *albóndigas de pescado*, *pimientos rellenos*, and some fresh cheese doused with the best olive oil I've ever tasted. All that and Brook Benton's "Rainy Night in Georgia" was playing on the restaurant's sound system. Everything was delicious and made me wonder why the food surrounding the naturist area was so mediocre. If the impulse to swim and lie in the sun naked is hedonistic, shouldn't that extend to gastronomy?

The street that leads to the entrance to the hotel is called "Hotel Street" by the locals. It's lined with bars, restaurants, a tiny *supermercado*, and A'Divina, a gay bar that features drag shows called *Espectáculos de Transformismo* every Sunday. There

is a sad-looking discotheque and a swingers' club. The bars
and restaurants seem to fall into two distinct camps: ones
frequented by local Spaniards and ones for tourists and expats.
There are a couple of traditional pubs dishing up fish and
chips and pints of beer for the British, an Indian restaurant,
and a Dutch pub for visiting northern Europeans.

Sitting right in the middle of Hotel Street is the Ponte
Sexy, which seems to be some bizarre hybrid of a club, a cocktail lounge, and a retail lingerie and sex-toy store. Customers
sip cocktails on rattan chairs in an open-air bar while racks
of trashy lingerie hang near the wall. A mannequin displays
some kind of clothing that looks like it's been pulled from
a Colonial Williamsburg fetish shop. The finishing touch—
and what really ties the place together, if you ask me—is the
multicolored disco ball light effect swirling over the whole
place. This may be exactly what advertising pundits mean
when they talk about "selling a lifestyle."

The restaurants and bars on the strip have an easygoing
feel. People, for the most part, wear clothes when they're on
Hotel Street, but that didn't stop a naked man from walking into a bar to get his wineskin refilled or a nude couple
in their twenties from picking up a six-pack of beer at the
little grocery store. Nobody got offended or unnerved or even
seemed to notice.

I was having a drink in a pub called Frankie's, which is
run by a British expat named Alan. The place was crowded
and a group of middle-aged men and women, their noses
crisply red from a day at the beach, were drinking pints and
getting rowdy. One man in the group came back to the table
but then realized he'd forgotten to get something at the bar.

As he turned to leave one of his friends joking called him a "dickhead." The man stopped, then turned around, dropped his pants, and waggled his penis at his friends while doing his best De Niro impression. "You talking to me? You talking to me?"

Where in most places this kind of behavior might be met with shock or arrest and prosecution—maybe even being labeled a sex offender for the rest of your life—here the response was peals of uncontrollable laughter.

While I don't necessarily want my friends waving their cocks at me when I'm out at a bar, I also don't want them to be arrested if they do. Which is why I find the ideology of mutual respect, the live-and-let-live attitude of Vera Playa, inspiring. After spending four days here, reading by the pool, walking on the beach, even working out in the gym—yes, I used an elliptical trainer wearing only my tennis shoes—I found myself getting more relaxed with the whole nonsexual social nude thing and the American attitude about the naked body became more and more laughable. Not because it's funny, but because it's so extreme. Why are we infusing our nakedness with guilt and shame? Why is skinny-dipping seen as some form of perversion?

Here the nudity is so commonplace it's almost boring. I never would've thought seeing a hundred naked people around the swimming pool would be dullsville, but it is. Sure, the occasional surprise jumps out at you, the incredibly beautiful woman who really is incredibly beautiful, or the tall man who looks like he's had an elephant trunk grafted on to where his penis should be, but these are the exceptions. Everyone else—young, old, fat, thin, tall, short, smooth, hairy, whatever—just looked naked. Which is not to suggest there are no weirdos or eccentrics in the place. For example, the guy with the elephant trunk schlong was continuously walking back and forth in front of all the sunbathers as if he'd just forgotten something and had to go and get it. I'm guessing he forgot to show us how gargantuan his penis was.

The Man in the Fishnet Diaper

The cabdriver spun the wheel and hit the gas like she was in some bad French version of *The Fast and the Furious: Tourist Season*. Already going faster than I thought was normal for a cab ride, the taxi suddenly lurched to the right and bombed around a corner, juddering and slewing, before cutting back sharply to the left and accelerating through a roundabout at top speed. With each jerk and careen, I could hear my suitcase in the trunk of the cab skitter across the floor and slam against the side, only to bounce off the roof of the trunk and cartwheel back across as we hurtled through a series of winding turns. The cabdriver looked at me and said, "See, your suitcase is so happy to be in Cap d'Agde she is dancing!"

I wasn't dancing. I'd been traveling for almost thirty-six hours. I left Vera Playa and drove my sweet rented Fiat 500 to Granada, where I caught an overnight train to Barcelona called a TrenHotel. I had an excellent meal on the train—roasted salmon and a bottle of Albariño—but sleeping in the small cabin was like trying to sleep on the back of an angry and flatulent whale. In Barcelona, after a near nervous breakdown from sleep deprivation, I caught the coastal train to Perpignan, France, where I ate a waffle from a vending machine. Fortified by a blast of sugar, I took a small regional train that slow-danced its way through the Languedoc-Roussillon, stopping to say hi to every vineyard and gas station in the area, until finally, my brain scrambled by pure Belgian sugar, I was sitting in the back of a cab listening to my suitcase being abused, on my way to what is arguably the most famous nudist resort in the world.

By the time we got to Cap d'Agde it was almost ten o'clock at night and I was dizzy with adrenaline. I climbed out of the taxi—and if I was a religious person I might've kissed the ground—to see the cabdriver dancing and shaking her ass to some samba beat only she heard in her head. I gave her a generous tip, in the hopes that I would never see her again, and walked into the security office at some kind of checkpoint.

I showed my passport, paid an entry fee, and was given my keys and a card that would buzz me through the security gates. They also handed me an indecipherable map of what looked like plans for a lunar settlement or maybe the inside of a vacuum cleaner. When I asked the security guard how to get to my apartment, she waved off into the night and said, "Go to the right."

I began walking through the darkened streets toward a series of buildings, figuring my keys might open a door in one of them. But as I pulled my suitcase along the sidewalk, I noticed something strange. For the largest naturist resort on the Mediterranean, no one was naked. In fact, people were very clothed.

A young, muscular, and deeply tanned German man walked toward me. He wasn't wearing a shirt, but that's not alarming. What caught my attention was the ankle-length leather skirt he had on. It was cut into long panels, making him look like one of King Tut's retinue drawn by Tom of Finland.* He rocked motorcycle boots, heavy black eye shadow, and several studded straps around his waist. The woman holding his hand was wearing a miniskirt made out of thin black straps that I can only describe as a Goth macramé project that exploded. They were headed toward the swingers' club. They looked ready for action.

Also ready for action was the hunched and diminutive man walking with his equally hunched and diminutive wife behind them. They looked to be in their midseventies and were also wearing some kind of motorcycle-inspired fetish gear. The geezer had the leather hat and leather vest, but somewhere he'd gone rogue; he wasn't wearing pants or chaps or even an ankle-length skirt, but a fishnet Speedo, black mesh briefs that were too big for him and hung so baggy at the back that they looked more like a fishnet diaper. And these weren't the only people on the street. Everywhere I looked it was as if I had been dropped into some nighttime fetish parade. They were pouring out of the apartment buildings, dozens of men in skirts and leather gear, women in latex catsuits or see-through minidresses, clomping in thick-soled boots or perched atop vicious stiletto heels. I knew I looked lost, completely alien, wearing jeans and pulling a small suitcase, unable to speak the language. As I watched the man in the fishnet diaper disappear into the crowd of costumed fetish freaks out for a night of

---

* Tom of Finland is the pseudonym for Touko Laaksonen, a Finnish artist known for his fetish drawings of homosexual men.

swinging, it occurred to me that there was not enough ecstasy in the world to make this seem normal.

Welcome to Cap d'Agde.

...

German and Dutch nudists had been coming to this isolated beach in the South of France for years. Unlike glamorous beach towns like Nice and Cannes on the French Riviera, the southern coast of France was mostly rural and undeveloped, and the sleepy town of Agde, not far from Montpellier, was the perfect place to practice naturism without anyone noticing. Naturists would pay a small fee to a local farmer, pitch their tents in the olive groves by the beach, and frolic au natural in what was a very rustic environment. In the 1970s, the French government began looking for a way to promote the scenic coastline of the relatively unglamorous Languedoc-Roussillon region, while local officials had been looking for an opportunity to relieve northern Europeans of their cash and improve the local economy. And so Cap d'Agde—which is about six miles from the town of Agde—was officially designated as a naturist beach in 1973. A plan was hatched to build a family-friendly village that would appeal to French as well as German, British, and Dutch naturists. That meant keeping exhibitionists and voyeurs to a minimum, so they designed a series of large apartment complexes, along with the amenities of a small resort town, and surrounded them with serious security. The naturist village, which includes a large campground, is surrounded by a ten-foot-tall wire fence and you have to buy a pass at a central security office to go in and out of the various checkpoints. There are guards stationed at entry points, as well as "park rangers" patrolling the grounds for unauthorized guests with telephoto lenses.

It's the opposite, philosophically, from Vera Playa. The Cap, as it's called, is not open to anyone wandering in, it's enclosed. But it's not as if you'd ever need to leave the enclosure. In many ways it's more like a real city than Vera Playa.

The area is massive. It holds close to forty thousand visitors a day during the high season. Imagine Wrigley Field filled with naked people. Or maybe don't. But you get the idea. The place is bustling with activity. There are almost two hundred different businesses in Cap d'Agde, and because it's in France, most of them seem to involve delicious food. There's a fishmonger, a couple of charcuteries for pâté and sausages, and a few cheese shops. I counted three supermarkets and maybe a half dozen bakeries and wine stores. There are "caterers" where you can pick up prepared food and beaucoup bistros, bars, pizzerias, and other restaurants. You can get your hair styled, ink a new tattoo, get your nipple pierced, do your laundry, buy sunscreen, and perhaps purchase that fetish wear you've been craving, all within the gates of the compound. Most of the rules are simple and similar to any other nudist resort: nudity is encouraged, photography is not allowed, sit on a towel. After that, pretty much anything goes.

The centerpiece of the development is a massive apartment complex called Heliopolis, named after the nudist island paradise built by French naturists Gaston and André Durville. The architecture is allegedly influenced by the French architect Le Corbusier; it is open and airy, giving optimal sunlight and sea view to each of the eight hundred apartments, and even cooler, it's shaped like a gigantic letter C. The structure is five stories high and all the apartments are stacked at an angle, meaning each apartment terrace is exposed to direct sunlight all day long. It's curved and sloped and futuristic-looking in the best possible way. It reminded me of an alien space station in one of the *Star Wars* movies. There's a groovy dormitory vibe to the place, like what you might find in Isla Vista, the beach area adjacent to the University of California at Santa Barbara. In fact the apartment I rented for the week looked a lot like some of the utilitarian flats I'd helped my daughter move into when she went to UCSB. Which means it was not luxurious, but perfectly workable.

When Heliopolis was first built, the C surrounded a large pool and tennis courts, but in a move to maximize profit, the recreational area was scrapped and another complex, a tacky hotel called Le Jardin d'Eden, was built. You'll recall from your Bible studies that the Garden of Eden was where Adam and Eve used to live, although I don't think God would've put them in a swingers' motel and expected them not to taste the forbidden fruit.

Cap d'Agde claims to be as family friendly as Vera Playa—and perhaps it is during the school holidays—but I found that a little hard to believe as I sat outside on a warm Monday night, eating Thai food, drinking beer, and watching the parade of middle-aged men and women strolling by. There is a uniform look to the people here. During the day most everyone is naked, or wearing a sarong or beach cover-up or wrap of some kind, but at night people get dressed up. The men wear typical resort wear—shorts or white slacks and polo shirt—and the women wear the skimpiest, most revealing clothes they can find and teeter around on ridiculous stiletto heels. This was different from the swingers in their fetish gear;

this was the going-out-to-dinner clothes. I imagine that you dress for dinner and then, if the mood strikes, you put on your swinger outfit and hit the clubs.

As a karaoke performer belted out American pop songs,* I looked around the patio in front of the 1664 Café, and was struck by the sensation that I was attending an academic conference. If you can imagine your high school math teacher dressed as an extra on *Miami Vice* and your English teacher dressed like a hooker, then you're getting close to what I was experiencing. Forgive me, Ms. Thompson, for imagining your 1974 self in a silk dress with a neckline that plunges down to your pubic bone, but I'm working on a metaphor here, which is something you taught me how to do in English class. Everywhere I looked there were badonkadonks stuffed into skintight miniskirts, rascally nipples sticking out from the gaps in fishnet dresses, the always elegant bra-and-feather-boa look, and bony torsos beneath diaphanous blouses.

Which is not to say that everyone was of a certain age. Cap d'Agde is mixed. There was a representative cross-section of modern Europe here. Black, white, old, young, fat, thin, you name it. The beautiful people were here too. I watched a couple so strikingly good-looking walk by the *pétanque* area that the players stopped playing and stared with their mouths open, cigarettes dangling off their lower lips. During the day it was common to see naturist families with children and packs of topless teenage girls on the beach; it's a very freewheeling nudist scene.

---

* Seriously, Europe, if I have to hear another crappy rendition of "Proud Mary" I might not come back.

But at night the kids are out of sight, the adults come out, and Cap d'Agde becomes a kind of sex-fantasy fantasy camp. The women are dressed to embody the male fantasy of what a sexy woman looks like when she's on the prowl for sex. And, hell, for all I know the women feel sexy dressed like that, attracting the male gaze, being in control. It could be a turn-on, for sure.

Ultimately, it all seemed pretty harmless. A little sun-burned sex anarchy in the South of France. Exactly the kind of anarchy Émile Armand had in mind when he wrote his manifesto on revolutionary nudism in 1934.

...

Émile Armand was born Ernest-Lucien Juin Armand in Paris, France, in 1872. He was an anarchist, a passionate hedonist, a writer who promoted nudism, antimilitarism, and free love, which he called *la camaraderie amoureuse.* In other words, he was an all-around counterculture superstar. It shows in photos of him. He's got a wicked gleam in his eye and a mischievous smirk; with his slicked-back hair and cool mustache, he looks like the kind of troublemaking libertine who could seduce anyone he wanted. Apparently he did.

A child of the Belle Epoque, he was raised in a time of optimism and relative prosperity. The arts were flourishing: painters like Henri Matisse and Pierre Bonnard were working in a postimpressionist style, authors like Marcel Proust and Colette were changing popular literature, and the fashion world was introducing the idea that the ideal woman should be waiflike and have a boyish figure. Bohemian cabarets were popular in Montmartre and women were dancing the cancan at the Folies Bergère. Bistros, bars, and café society thrived.

As they often are, these urban delights were built on the back of an impoverished underclass. Workers were organizing, socialism and women's rights were the talk of the town, and as a son of a participant in the doomed revolutionary Paris Commune of 1871, Armand was bound to have radical ideas. In his late twenties he began actively writing and editing several anarchist journals: *Le Cri de Révolte* and *La Misère*. He was outspoken and unabashedly fervent in his beliefs and basically caused a ruckus whenever and wherever he could. Armand was thinking about many of the same things that Edward Carpenter was, at roughly the same time, and it was Armand who echoed Carpenter on the uselessness of society when he wrote *Life and Society*: "Society, no doubt, is the crowd that screams 'Hurrah!' at the parade of the crippled from the last general slaughter."

While Armand wrote about many subjects, his point of view tended to be refracted through a lens of what he called hedonistic individualism; in other words, Armand was focused on things that made him feel good. Like sex. Lots and lots of sex. He was years ahead of the hippies and their maxim "If it feels good, do it."

But what makes Armand unique among philosophers of the time is his focus on using sexual liberty as a way to individual freedom. And he wasn't just shouting about freedom for straight people. He supported gay, bisexual, and transgender sexuality rights. Armand wrote about rehabilitating "nonconformist caresses," which, you know, sounds like a fine idea. If it feels good everybody should do it with everyone they want to in the way that they want. Of course he had to deal with some blowback from monogamists, and to that end, in 1926 he published *Le Combat contre la Jalousie et le Sexualisme Révolutionnaire*. You can probably translate that without my help. That he was writing about these issues in the 1920s seems in itself pretty remarkable.

In 1934 he published a manifesto called *Le Nudisme Révolutionnaire* (*Revolutionary Nudism*). How could an avowed hedonist *not* want to be naked? And, being a nudist, how could he *not* write a manifesto? But *Revolutionary Nudism* is a great read. It could be one of my all-time favorite manifestos.[41]

In the introduction, Armand glibly dismisses groups who use nudity for health reasons, and discounts the people who want to restore humanity to an Edenic state of innocence as crackpots. "It seems to us to be something else entirely than a hygienic fitness exercise or a 'naturist' renewal. For us, nudism is a revolutionary demand."

For Armand nudism is, individually and collectively, among the most potent means of emancipation. The manifesto is broken into three main points. The first is an affirmation. Just a reminder to his readers that they, and not the church or the state, control their individual bodies. The second part is a protest "against any intervention (of a legal or other nature) that obligates us to wear clothes because it pleases another—whereas it has never occurred to us to object that they do not get undressed, if that is what they prefer." And then he wraps it up by calling for liberation "from one of the main notions on which the ideas of 'permitted' and forbidden, of 'good' and 'evil' are based. Liberation from coquetry, from the conformism to an artificial standard of appearance that maintains the differentiation of classes." Armand wanted to liberate us from any constraints and called for the "release from the prejudice of modesty, which is nothing but 'shame of one's body.'"

It's hard to argue with a well-written manifesto, which I think is kind of the point of a well-written manifesto. But I really like Émile Armand. His ideas are profound and his call for hedonism and sex as a means to individual and societal liberation is something I think we still need to hear in our modern society.

...

I'm not sure Armand ever went grocery shopping in the nude, and I am positive that I never had before I visited Cap d'Agde. But I needed to eat and everyone else at the market was naked so, you know, when in Rome. So I went. Me, my shopping bag, and my flip-flops. I felt like an early man, a hunter-gatherer headed out to forage for sustenance. Of course I was foraging in French markets where they treated the produce and cheese with the same care Tiffany handles its jewelry, but I was naked. It seemed like a risky adventure to me.

First I went to the greengrocer and bought lettuce, olives, yellow plums, fresh figs, some cherry tomatoes, and a cucumber. Has a grocery run ever sounded so exciting? Were the other people in the store naked? Yes, everyone but the employees was pretty much as naked as I was. Were there "hot" women and "well-hung" dudes? Why yes, I seem to recall that there were plenty of both. Did it infuse squeezing the tomatoes with an illicit frisson? Did looking at the vinegar selection become compellingly erotic? Not really. Although I will admit I was incredibly self-conscious squeezing past people in the crowded aisles.

My wife demanded photographic evidence of this excursion, but when I asked the cashier if she would take a photo of me she blew air through her lips in that curious French way and said, "*Cochon.*" Which means "pig." I didn't ask for a photo at the bakery, it was too crowded, but I did get a nice little quiche with Roquefort and a fresh baguette.

I hit the wine store, where I had gotten into a lively conversation with the owner the day before. He had recommended a particularly good local wine—a Picpoul de Pinet from Beauvignac—so I asked him to recommend a rosé from the area. Perhaps it was because we had established a rapport, or maybe because he just recognized a good customer when he saw one, but he and his wife did not call me a pig; they laughed and snapped a photo. And no, you can't see it. You probably don't want to.

There's a refreshing honesty to shopping naked. In the textile world, people always check each other out, imagining what the other person might look like naked—don't be coy, you know you do—but when you can clearly see the breasts of the woman next to you or the penis of the man standing behind you—in fact, when all around you are bare breasts and dangling penises and buttocks and bodies—well, a lot of the puerile fantasy that is commonplace in our society just disappears.

Maybe it was the quality of the produce available in the market, maybe it was the excellent recommendations of the wine merchant or the smell wafting from the shop that was making a gargantuan paella, maybe it was just being in a crowd of naked people going about their everyday business, but I have to admit that shopping in the nude was kind of fun. People were friendlier than they usually are in grocery stores. Nobody got upset when the line was slow. For the most part everyone was smiling. I didn't feel nearly as awkward as I'd feared. Even when I spilled olives all over the counter. Ultimately, attempting to speak French was more embarrassing than being naked.

That night I stood on my balcony and looked out over Heliopolis. I was drinking the excellent local rosé—Château Haut Fabrègues—and taking in the sweep of the architecture as a cool breeze blew in from the Mediterranean. People were out on their terraces drinking wine, smoking cigarettes, and generally doing what I was doing, hanging out and enjoying the night air. I noticed a naked man having drinks with a couple of nude women on a balcony below mine. None of this is unusual at Cap d'Agde. Naked people have dinner parties all the time here. But I was surprised when the man stood up and stuck his penis in the mouth of a blond woman who had been sitting to his right. Although I couldn't see exactly what was happening, her head movements made what I would call a "bobbing" motion. This went on for a few moments and then the man turned and offered his penis to the woman who'd been sitting on his left. She graciously accepted and sucked on him while the blonde spanked him. I decided it would be creepy if I stood there and watched for too long, although there were several other people out on their balconies and they seemed to have noticed it too, so I went inside and refilled my wineglass.

Apparently these kinds of swingers' dinner parties are a common occurrence at Cap d'Agde. At least according to Ross Velton, author of the *The Naked Truth about Cap d'Agde*, who writes, "Nowhere on Earth will you feel so at home expressing your perversions and acting out your fantasies."[42] Which helps explain the fetish wear that I saw at night and the penis jewelry that some men wore on the beach during the day. Yes, you read that right. A significant percentage of the men here wear rings or what looked like little gold bracelets clamped around their penises. *Shaftlets?* There seems to be no sexual preference designation attached to the wearing of penile decoration, it's just something the cool nudists are into. Of course genital jewelry is forbidden by the official rules. But that doesn't stop people from wearing it and, seriously, can you imagine the security guard asking someone to remove his penis ring? Or worse, take out a piercing? But this flaunting of the anti-genital-jewelry rule upsets naturists—as you'll recall the Fellowship of the Naked Trust only made exceptions for eyeglasses and dentures—who are trying to force the swingers out of Cap d'Agde.

Without being overly dramatic, what's happening in Cap d'Agde is a clash between two distinct camps of nakedness. You have the naturists, the philosophical descendants of the Durville brothers, who believe in health, fresh air, exercise, and vegetarianism, versus the horny hedonists who fall more in the Émile Armand camp.

It didn't start out this way; the swinging happened incrementally. Originally, Cap d'Agde was a place where naturists and their families could have a nude beach experience without fear of arrest from authorities or exploitation by perverts. But anytime you have a place where everyone is walking around naked, well, you know voyeurs and swingers are not going to be far behind. The swingers took over a section of the beach and the dunes that ran behind it, and by the mid-1980s, it was common to see couples masturbating on the beach as well as more exotic threesomes, blow jobs, group sex, and even the occasional consensual gang bang.

In his book, Velton goes into great detail about the etiquette of swingers and libertines in Cap d'Agde, describing spouse-swapping dinner parties and giving advice on finding a couple who want to swing with a single man: "when a husband, knowing you are in hot pursuit, pulls up his wife's skirts and slaps her buttocks, you know your presence is not unwelcome."

Naturists were alarmed at seeing their resort overrun by libertines and a crackdown of sorts began in the 2000s. Now signs are posted on the beach warning that it is illegal to engage in lewd behavior, and park rangers patrol the area giving citations—I refuse to say "stiff fine"—to any man who is caught sporting an erection. This renewed commitment to keeping the beach family friendly didn't stop people from swinging, it just forced them indoors, and now there are more swingers' clubs and even a hotel dedicated to "the lifestyle." And of course what happens in your apartment is your business, even if everybody can see you from their balconies.

Pressure from the naturists intensified when, in April 2008, two swingers' clubs—Glamour, a *boîte échangiste* or wife-swapping club, and the Palme Ré, an orgy club—were firebombed by naturist "hardliners." And later in September of that year another *boîte échangiste*, the Tantra club, was destroyed by a suspicious fire. Police suspected it was the work of naturist "fundamentalists" with a grudge against the libertines.[43]

The resort seems equally split between libertines and naturists, and from what I can see, it seems like they manage to coexist. During the day, the naturists have the run of the place—except for the sunbathing swingers and their genital jewelry—and in the evening, especially around midnight, the swingers and fetishists come out and head to the clubs.

I didn't see any lewd behavior or pick up on any butt-slapping cues when I was at the beach. For me it was just a crowded slab of sand with thousands of naked bodies getting their melanoma on in the broiling sun. Did I mention I don't sunbathe?

For those who'd had enough UV radiation, there were beach clubs behind high fences that required cover charges. I had seen footage of the antics at these clubs on a website dedicated to the swinger side of Cap d'Agde. The pictures showed a *mousse* party, which involves couples and three-somes and foursomes getting freaky while a bubble machine spews soap foam all over their bodies. That they were pumping French rap at bowel-quaking volume made it somehow less irresistible.

It is a strange experience being in places like Vera Playa and Cap d'Agde. Not because of the nudity or swinging, but because as a man traveling alone I am looked at with suspicion. Most of the people who come to nudist resorts are couples. Although I was mostly greeted with a smile if I smiled at them or made small talk while we waited in line at the bakery, occasionally I was greeted with a look that seemed to indicate they thought I was a dangerous deviant. The language barrier didn't help either. To the people who gave me that look, I want to assure you that I have no interest in having sex with you or your wife or you *and* your wife. *Please.* That is the last thing I want to do. I'm here to learn what I can about the culture of nudism and naturism. I don't want to get spanked on my balcony, even though there's nothing wrong with it if you do. But the conversation never gets that far. As Velton writes, "The nice guy who has come to the Cap to sample its famed open-mindedness and tolerance may feel rejected by many simply because he is alone."

Which sounds way sadder than it actually is.

One night I walked over to the area with most of the swingers' clubs and watched the fetish fashion show. Why wouldn't you squeeze your sunburned body into a pair of leather short shorts and a studded leather bra before you strapped on your seven-inch stiletto heels and went clonking across the parking lot to the club? Or that latex dress? Who am I to judge? The most popular look for women seemed to be the dress with the neckline that plunged to their crotch. At that point can it even be called a neckline? Perhaps "plunging pubic line" doesn't have the necessary cachet. I recognize that these are people on vacation in a sexy swinging nudist resort and they're just having fun. And, really, why shouldn't they? The only truly disturbing news I have to report is that the ankle-length man skirt is a bona fide fad. I saw it on a half dozen men. Some were leather, others a kind of heavy canvas. It seems the ankle-length man skirt must be worn with heavy motorcycle boots, although I could see it working with Roman sandals. The female companions of these men in skirts were always dressed as characters: Catholic schoolgirl, French maid, anime femme fatale.

Describing the scene at Cap d'Agde to my wife via Skype was an unusual experience, mostly because being in Cap d'Agde was, for me anyway, an unusual experience. As the sun was setting on the French Mediterranean, she was just waking up in Los Angeles, and the full-frontal sexcapades were just beginning to be expressed by the libertines. Yes, dear, I *can* see naked people having cocktails on their balcony and, well, maybe one of them has an erection, but you can't really blame him because a naked woman in a mask is rubbing what looks like a silk scarf around his testicles. I believe her response was "Are you fucking kidding me?" These are not easy conversations to have with your wife. How do you explain what goes on at Cap d'Agde to someone who's not there to see it? It sounds either unbelievably great or unbelievably horrific or completely believably cheesetastic. And it is kind of all those things rolled up into one anti-textile hootenanny. Fortunately for me, she is a generous person with a great sense of humor, so she just shook her head and chuckled.

I began my last day in the Cap with a classic European scene. I was sitting outside a French café, drinking *café crème* and eating a croissant. The sun warmed my sunblock-slathered skin, while a gentle breeze off the ocean kept me from getting too hot, too sunbathery. At the restaurant next door, waiters were blasting AC/DC's "Highway to Hell" while they set the tables for lunch. It could have been any seaside resort in France—the coffee was good, the croissant delicious—only at Cap d'Agde I had my *petit déjeuner* au naturel. Not only that, I was surrounded by nudists from all over Europe. One woman looked like a fashion model, emaciated and gorgeous; a brawny nudist strolled past, the words LED ZEPPELIN tattooed down his spine so that it looked like a vertical marquee; a naked old man in a wheelchair was pushed past by his naked wife, who held a tiny dog on a leash; a few men smoked cigarettes and admired one another's genital jewelry; couples tapped at their laptop keyboards using the café's expensive Wi-Fi; and sitting right next to me was a professional sunbather, his body smooth and deeply chocolate brown, his shoulders mottled by places where the sun had annihilated his skin and it had fallen away, peeling off in ragged patches.

I have to admit that I wasn't expecting to like Cap d'Agde, but I found myself having a certain affection for a place that is this weird. The variety of people and lifestyles and bodies and desires that are on display creates an anarchic vibe that makes a direct philosophical connection to Émile Armand's hedonistic individualism. This kind of anarchy wouldn't work without tolerance and mutual, if grudging, respect between the naturists and the swingers. People let their freak flags fly, and once they're up the pole they are surprisingly freaky. Which makes it fun. They wear their weirdness well here in the Cap, even if it's a fishnet diaper.

I'd been to two of the most famous nudist resorts in the world, but I knew there was more to nudism and naturism than sunbathing on *la playa* or shopping for wine *sans vête-ments*. What about the German tradition of communing with the forest? What was it like to go "free hiking" in the Alps? To find out, I headed to Austria and the Naked European Walking Tour.

The Naked European
Walking Tour

I t was too cold to hike naked. At least that's how I felt. The sky was overcast and an icy breeze was coming off the mountain. The alpine blast mixed with the damp air in the valley and hung above the ground in a frosty mist. Even the cows munching on wildflowers in the field looked like they'd rather be in a nice warm barn. But the lack of sunshine and the chill in the air didn't stop several of the hikers from stripping down to their boots and hats and hitting the trail, marching up the mountain in the scrotum-shrinking cold.

If you look at photos of early German naturists, the acolytes of Richard Ungewitter and his full-throttle *Nacktkultur*, they aren't stretched out on chaise lounges by the pool; they're standing on top of mountain peaks, hiking along forest trails, and swimming in lakes and rivers. They are transforming their bodies by being active while simultaneously connecting to the soulful, spiritual side of the natural world. *Nacktkultur* is about finding virtue and health and joy and Germanness, whatever that is, by being naked and active outside.

To get a taste of what's now called *Freikörperkultur* (Free Body Culture), I traveled more than two thousand kilometers from the South of France—spending more than twenty-four hours on various trains through Paris to Stuttgart to Salzburg—to make my way to a tiny mountain village in the heart of the Austrian Alps where the Naked European Walking Tour (NEWT), an annual weeklong naturist hike-a-thon, was taking place.

We were hiking up a valley called Vögeialm on a trail with the unpronounceable German name Tauernhöhenweg toward a mountain summit that overlooked a ski resort.

Roberto, a lawyer from Rome, walked next to me. Even in his hiking shorts and Patagonia-style pullover he cut a stylish figure. With his dandyish mustache and goatee, he would probably look better in a tuxedo than most people, but here we were, about to embark on a naked ascent of an Austrian Alp.

We watched the naked hikers start up the trail and exchanged a look.

"It's too cold for me," he said.

I nodded. "Me too."

Although Roberto was an experienced hiker—he'd walked the Silk Road in Asia—this was his first time hiking, as he called it, "in the buff." I had never hiked in the buff either and the last thing I wanted was to get frostbite on any sensitive areas. We kept our clothes on.

We hiked through a pasture, alongside a stream that looked cold and fresh like a beer commercial, past Austrian cows that chewed on the wildflowers, big brass bells around their necks clanking as they walked. The sun refused to come out. We shivered. Why had I thought hiking in the Alps in July wouldn't be cold?

The Naked European Walking Tour 2013 edition was a diverse group. There were twenty of us and, except for me, all European. There were NEWT veterans: Paul, a British expat who lived in Switzerland; Vittorio, a librarian and poet from a small town in northern Italy; Harry, a sound recording engineer from Belgium; Pascal, an educator from Strasbourg, and his wife, Clarice; Bruno, a naturist from Marseille; Frederic, a French policeman; and a few other hard-core naturist hikers. When I announced that I had just come from a week at Cap d'Agde, the French naturists in the group scrunched up their faces and looked at me as if I'd just unleashed some sort of sulfuric hell-fart. Bruno shook a finger at me and said, "*Ce n'est pas le naturisme.*"

Most of the hikers were from France or Italy, but there were two Germans, Andreas and Mathius, who didn't say much, or maybe more accurately, they didn't speak much English and I don't speak any German. Karla and Stuart, a UK couple who lived in Munich, also joined us.

Then there were the first-timers, the people who stumbled across the NEWT website while googling keywords like "nudism," "naturism," and "hiking": Maarten, an insurance company executive from Holland; Roberto, the dapper attorney from Rome; Maria-Grazia, a health care worker from a small town in northern Italy; Gus, an actor from England; and Conxita, a documentary filmmaker from Spain. Conxita was making a film about the hike so, between us, we made up the press corps of the expedition.

The trail narrowed and we began zigzagging up a steep incline in a series of rapid switchbacks. It was a serious ascent and the moment when I began to realize that I was exerting myself at altitude—about 1,500 meters (approximately 5,000 feet) above sea level—and it was getting hard to catch my breath, I looked at Maarten, who seemed incredibly fit for an insurance executive, and said something about not being accustomed to the altitude, which explained why I was gasping for air like a beached whale. He just smiled and said, "I'm from the Netherlands. I live below sea level." And then he bounded up the hill like some kind of mountain goat.

I shut up and kept trudging.

Eventually we climbed above the mist into brilliant sunshine and a clear sky. The birds were chirping, the air was warm, and the moment of truth was at hand. I joined Roberto and a few other hikers and stripped down to boots and sunhat. I thoroughly blasted my skin—yes, all my skin—with spray-on sunblock and then the hike resumed.

I'd never hiked naked through a forest before. In fact it's safe to say that I'd never hiked anywhere naked other than to the bathroom or the fridge. But there is something remarkable about hiking naked, or "free hiking" as it's sometimes called. I quickly realized that skin is an amazing thermostat. I didn't get cold—as long as I kept moving my body stayed warm—and I didn't get hot. Normally when I hike up a mountain, I work up a serious sweat, but without clothes to trap the heat, my skin easily regulated the temperature. I walked for hours, up steep inclines, really working hard, and didn't break much of a sweat at all. Granted, we were hiking in what I consider the ideal temperature for uphill exertions— around 68 degrees Fahrenheit. The other thing about hiking naked is that it feels good. It really does. Once you get past the awkwardness of being out in nature with your genitals exposed—thinking about the flora and fauna judging you as you stroll by, or worrying about thorns, thistles, nettles, bees, spiders, venomous snakes, and other critters with a taste for human flesh—then the raw physical sensation of being in the woods or on a mountainside naked is extremely pleasant. Sort of like skinny-dipping in fresh air, or what the great American poet Walt Whitman called "air baths."

Whitman described his version of outdoor nudism, writing, "An hour or so after breakfast I wended my way down to the recesses of the aforesaid dell, which I and certain thrushes, catbirds, &c., had all to ourselves. A light south-west wind was blowing through the tree-tops. It was just the place and time for my Adamic air-bath and flesh-brushing from head to foot. So hanging clothes on a rail near by, keeping old broadbrim straw on head and easy shoes on feet, havn't I had a good time the last two hours!"[44]

And that's pretty much how we did it. The home base for our daily air baths was a rustic Austrian farmhouse that was called a "hut" for some reason. This was a three-story hut with ten bedrooms, six bathrooms, a large communal kitchen, and a view of a spectacular and verdant valley where I wouldn't have been surprised to see Heidi tending to her flock of goats and looking for her grandfather. Fresh-baked bread was delivered every morning from the restaurant next door and fresh milk was procured from a farm down the road.

Everyone shared rooms and I bunked with Harry, the sound engineer from Belgium. I realized that—not counting one-night stands—I hadn't shared a room with a stranger since my college days, but Harry turned out to be an ideal roommate. He's in his early sixties, yet has the lean build of someone who rides bicycles a lot, which it turned out is what he does for fun. He is also smart, funny, and has an infectious laugh. Like a lot of the people on the hike, Harry is a longtime naturist, someone who used to take his children to nudist camps on their family vacations. Their one family vacation in the States involved a trip to Disney World in Orlando and then a stay at Cypress Cove, a famous nudist resort in Kissimmee, Florida.

I asked him if his children, who are now grown, still practiced nudism. He shook his head sadly. "My son is involved with bike racing, but my daughter sometimes works as a nude model. Maybe that's her way of being naturist."

One thing about the NEWT experience is that the nakedness doesn't end when the hiking does. For many of the participants the fun part is that they don't wear clothes the entire time. There was always a naked Frenchman or a half-naked Italian woman or a nude Englishman hanging out in the kitchen or drinking beer outside, and Harry was no exception. He'd put on a little sweatshirt in the morning and at night, but otherwise he never wore clothes in the house or on the trail.

Dinners in the hut became a team-building exercise, with various people chipping in to help make them happen. Of course all it took was for a vat of rice to get burned and for me to make a watermelon and feta cheese salad* before the French declared a culinary coup d'état and took over the kitchen. In my defense, the people who initially poked the watermelon feta salad with a fork and said, "Mark? What is this?," eventually devoured it.

But having the French in charge of the cooking seemed like a natural solution and the quality of the food improved

---

* Ideally this salad also includes fresh mint, which the local Austrian grocery stores didn't have.

immediately. Harry and I, who are both predominantly vegetarian, were lucky as Vittorio, the soft-spoken librarian from
northern Italy, took over cooking vegetarian dinners. He had
packed his Fiat Panda with supplies, including three or four
large jugs of red wine and enough olive oil to last a month.
When I suggested we go into town and buy some pasta, he
looked at me and said, "I have twelve kilos of pasta in the car."

Watching a brigade of naked people cooking dinner—
with big pots of water boiling and pans of hot oil spattering—
is a completely unique experience and I found myself chewing
my nails with anxiety when Vittorio decided to make vegetable
tempura one night. I guess it wasn't the first time he'd faced
a skillet of hot oil in the nude, because if he got burned, I
didn't hear any screams or cursing.

Of course if someone had been screaming, I'm not sure
I would've understood them. Communication wasn't always
easy or clear in the hut. Several of the French speakers only
spoke French, the Germans German, and the British English,
and although most of the Italians spoke a little English, even
they had trouble communicating. One time Maria-Grazia was
talking to Roberto and me, and when I asked for a translation,
Roberto shrugged and said, "She speaks an Italian I don't really
understand." But there were a number of people who were
multilingual. Pascal spoke good English and German, and
Conxita was fluent in four languages. Official announcements,
like the planned hour of departure for the next day's hike,
were announced in English, and then various people would
take turns translating. The overall effect was chaotic but fun,
like we were part of some naked United Nations task force.

. . .

The organizer of NEWT and the driving force behind the Naktiv* movement is Richard Foley, a British expat living in Munich and author of the books *The World Naked Bike Ride* and *Active Nudists: Living Naked at Home and in Public*. Richard has a compact and powerful build, with strong legs that propel him up and down the mountains with relentless energy. Imagine the Energizer Bunny as a naked hiker and you'll get an idea of what he's like. He has a broad, friendly smile and a good sense of humor, which is an important quality to have when you've invited a bunch of naked strangers to live together in a hut for a week.

Richard isn't a naturist or a nudist; he's a "Naktivist." Which isn't about posing nude for PETA or taking off your shirt to protest the patriarchy—that's a different kind of naked activism. Naktivism is about getting naked and going out and doing things. It's the opposite of lying on the beach and sunning your buns. Would it surprise you to know that Richard has written a manifesto?

The Naktavist manifesto is built on three main themes. The first one is pretty basic: to support and encourage naked activities everywhere. It's the belief that "being naked is okay in all contexts." Although Richard clarifies that not everyone has to be naked all the time if they don't want to be. Which I think is generous of him.

The second part of the manifesto is a call "to educate society that the naked human body is acceptable in all contexts." This is an appeal for basic human freedoms. If you want to be naked, you should be able to be naked, and Naktivists are urged to demonstrate "how healthy and non-shameful the

---

* Yet another portmanteau of "naked" and something, in this case "active."

naked human body is." Richard wants to show that nakedness is a "positive action with beneficial mental and physical aspects for the whole of human society." Of course this requires an "attempt to disassociate society's automatic linking of sex and violence and the media with nudity." To his credit, Richard understands that's a big task.

The third part hits at the political agenda. Simply put, the Naktiv manifesto is a call "to decriminalize the naked human body. . . . there should be no law of any land which may be misused by the loud and righteous minority to dictate how anyone else chooses to dress."

As far as manifestos go, it's a pretty good one.

I sat down with Richard in the hut kitchen to talk about the Naktiv movement. He was naked, as he generally was the entire week, and sat at the table with a mug of tea. Conxita set up her camera and I suddenly felt like we were having a proper press conference. I'm fascinated by how people get into nudism, so I asked Richard how he first discovered he liked being naked. He thought about it for a moment and then said, "I guess my first experience of nudity would have been my mother taking me to a nudist club when I was very young."

"So you're a second-generation nudist?"

"Well, kind of. It wasn't particularly active. I went several times with my mother to a club. She was going with this big scriptwriter and got to have a bungalow in a London nudist club. So we went there for a few weekends and they packed me off to the swimming pool. And basically, that was that for a long time."

"So where did this desire to return to nudism come from when you were an adult?"

"When I was about forty, I suppose, a special time of life, I was realizing that my activities in the mountains, because I had been quite active scrambling and walking and a little bit of climbing, were quite curtailed through work and family life. I was sort of looking for a way to get back into the mountains a little bit and I came across Stephen Gough's rather epic trip from Land's End in Cornwall, in England, all the way through the length of England and Scotland going right out to the top."

Stephen Gough is a former Royal Marine who has served more than six years in prison, off and on, for public nakedness. Known as the Naked Rambler, he has appeared in court naked, walked out of prison naked, and stripped midflight on an airplane. And "Naked Rambler" is no misnomer. Depending on whom you talk to, he is an inspiration, a martyr, or an annoying nutjob.

Richard continued. "It was an extremely impressive achievement, although he had a lot of trouble on the way. I was thinking about nudism a little bit at that time as well, so I thought I'd try some naked hiking myself. I started on my own. Started walking completely naked in the forest barefoot, no rucksack, almost pure naturist if you like, classic naturist."

"How'd that work out?"

Richard laughed. "I very quickly found, with all the thorns in my feet, and the stinging nettles and the bees and the thirst and the hunger and the 'I wonder where I am now,' that this is pretty stupid. And so it seemed to make much more sense to combine my previous knowledge of mountaineering—again, take a rucksack, you put your food in it and your map and your compass, and you put your boots on. You wear a sunhat and you're prepared for eventualities and it made an awful lot more sense. You could get a good day's tour in."

"And so then, how did you make the leap from that to starting the NEWT?"

"I was looking for some kind of a trip, perhaps a little bit like Steve Gough, which wasn't quite so epic because I didn't have that much time. You know, I had commitments to my family and work and all sorts. So I had to think of something that was smaller scale. And I decided to walk across the Alps naked. I started in Germany, walked across the thinnest bit of Austria I could find, and down the other side into Italy. This took me a week. I did it on my own, taking my tent with me. And it was fun, you know, it was fine. Anyway, I wrote it up, put it on my website as an adventure that I had done, and I got a little bit of feedback from it."

"And that was that?"

He shakes his head. "During the following year, I had various people write to me and say they'd love to do this trip with me if I did it again. I was thinking, 'Well, I've done it once, it was quite fun. Maybe it would be interesting to do it with other people.' I wasn't sure; I hadn't really been out hiking with anyone naked before. It was a little bit new to me as an idea, because I wasn't actively part of any club at that point. So we went on the second trip with seven of us and that was also quite fun, and it was interesting to see the reaction of other people when you're in a group rather than when you're on your own as a single male. Now it seems to have become a bit of an annual tradition. Every year there's more and more people who join, particularly now that we use a hut as a base rather than a tent. And I encourage women to join because a mixed group is much better when you're outside."

A mixed group is essential to Richard's mission of educating the public about nudity.

Richard sipped his tea and continued. "I think a single male, like a single male in a nudist club, is always regarded as a bit of a predator. A single male who is out naked hiking is regarded with some suspicion. But if you have a male and female couple, or a group of fifteen people, three or four who are female, perhaps, and a couple of dogs, the impression that everyone else gets is completely different, it's far more relaxed and you can get into much more natural conversation with people. It's almost like diplomacy, you know."

"And you're proving your point to the public."

Richard nodded. "Yeah. I think most naked hikers will tend to steer towards places where there are fewer people, or no people, which you can't guarantee. But at the same time, the more people you do see, the more people actually realize they've seen or met a naked hiker and survived to tell the tale. And it's actually perfectly okay and it's mildly amusing, perhaps. There's no big deal about it."

I had seen a variety of responses to our naked hiking group on the trail; some people were delighted, laughing and smiling, totally amused by the parade of nudists. Of course they could've been making fun of us—I don't speak German. And then I noticed a father turn his children away so they wouldn't look at us, which I thought was a strange thing to do. I recounted this incident to Richard.

He nodded. "There's one in a hundred that is actively against it. This is the vociferous minority I'm talking about, the ones that you hear about because he might be prepared to make a complaint of some kind. Everyone else is all . . . 'That looks a bit strange or unusual, but perfectly harmless. Why bother making a fuss about it?'"

I realized that this kind of diplomacy—a sort of "lead by example"—was exactly why Richard organizes the NEWT hikes and makes it clear to participants that there will be media attention and photography. So I asked, "Is there a political aspect to what you're doing?"

Richard pondered that for a moment before speaking. "The NEWT, for instance, is not a protest march, right? We're just a walk in a nice environment. That's what we're doing. Naktiv as such, it might be a little bit more active in terms of like publishing a manifesto and generally having a few points to make about nudity being acceptable in different environments, or anywhere, at any time."

I asked Richard what inspired him to form the Naktiv movement. Richard leaned back in his chair and scratched his head.

"Anita and Wolfgang Gramer did a lot of writing on naked activities in German, which is where 'nackt' and 'active' comes together. And I was inspired by their writings and their examples of their naked hiking and their naked cycling and naked poetry reading in Berlin, and all sorts of things like this. And they wrote this book called *1, 2, Frei!* [*1, 2, Free!*],[45] which is a classic, I think, for this new kind of paradigm of naked and active. And I thought, well, I could anglicize the word and slightly adopt it and hopefully not plagiarize it so much as . . . what's the word I'm looking for?" He looked out the window for a second, then said, "Pay homage to. To prove this idea that they've essentially focused. And so that was when naktiv.net was born, if you like."

"This was what? Ten years ago?"

He nodded.

"Are you doing anything on the political front?"

Richard shook his head. "I'm not really politically moti-vated. People like APNEL, which is a French organization, are very active in trying to change the law in France, for instance, where they can make being naked in public explicitly not a crime. Whereas at the moment, I think, I believe it is explicitly a crime in France. And in England, it's specifically not a crime to be naked in public. Whereas in the past, there used to be a law in England called indecent exposure. If you were naked, you would just be collared on that one and that was the end to it."

"But that's pretty enlightened compared with the States."

"That could still happen in the UK, but if you get a decent enough lawyer, that actually knows the law rather than knows what he's told in the pub, then he'll be able to quash that instantly."

Which made me wonder why the Naked Rambler keeps getting put in jail.

"I mean, I think that's one of the things that Stephen Gough has got slightly wrong in that he goes head-to-head with people. I don't know how familiar you are with what he does. But he tends to walk through the middle of the village naked, and maybe two or three villages are okay and the fourth one, you know, someone objects and he gets arrested and he's put in prison, and then he goes to the court hearing and he refuses to get dressed for court. So the judge gets upset from lack of respect, blah blah, and it goes on and on and on." Rich-ard shrugged and continued. "But it's not my life, he's doing what he has to do. And, as I said, I can respect his strength of character to stick with it, but not the implementation."

I agree with everything he's saying. Gough could be viewed as some sort of politically motivated flasher, and yet he's a folk hero for a younger generation of naturists. I wondered if Gough will have a lasting influence on when and where to be naked.

Richard considered that. "Well, in the naked and active part of that, yes, definitely, because you're doing something and young people want to do something. They don't want to sit around on deck chairs for the entire afternoon reading the paper, which is what the old-school nudist clubs do, right? They cater to the retiree population largely . . ." Richard leaned back in his chair for a moment and then said, "That's obviously an unfair generalization. But as a general broad-brush statement, it probably holds true. I think the naked movement, if you like, can learn a lot from the gay movement and how extremely successful it was. Because it's not only—you have to remember—it's not only that being gay is now acceptable, right? It's enshrined in law. You can't discriminate against someone for being gay in a job environment, in the army, you know, anywhere. It's illegal to do that and that's how is should be with nudity as well. You shouldn't be able to turn around and say you can't have this job because you go naked hiking or because you go naked swimming or something like that."

This statement reminded me of the previous night's dinner when there was an informal poll asking each of us if we could tell our friends or coworkers or employers that we'd been on a naked hike. I was surprised by how many people felt that they would lose their jobs, or get in some kind of trouble, if they told the truth.

Richard finished his tea and looked at Conxita and me. "Shall we get back to hiking?"

Richard has the unenviable job of trying to please a group of hikers with varying levels of fitness and diverse reasons for coming to NEWT. Some, like Bernard, the seventy-two-year-old Parisian, are superhikers who can motor up and down the mountains with apparent ease; others just want to get some fresh air and sunshine and be naked. I was just enjoying the incredible mountain air, which, for an Angeleno, was so clean and smelled so good it seemed unreal, like it was the kind of air that they only served in Michelin-starred restaurants.

The first day we went about ten miles at a fairly decent pace. I struggled to adapt to the altitude, but mostly it was an excellent hike. I wished that my wife had come along, not because she would enjoy being around a bunch of naked people, but because she is an avid hiker—she hiked the John Muir Trail years before Cheryl Strayed made it popular—and the scenery, the super-alpine Alp-iness of it all, would've blown her mind. Or maybe, after visiting three countries over the past month, and being naked around everyone but my wife, I was just getting homesick. One thing was certain, I no longer felt strange or awkward about being around naked people. At least, not when the naked people were as friendly as this group of hikers.

Despite my complete enjoyment of the ten-mile hike up and down large Austrian mountains, some of the superhikers complained that the route wasn't sufficiently grueling, so the following day Richard took us on what many of us came to call the Ursprungalm Death March.

We left early in the morning and drove in a caravan of six cars for more than forty minutes, winding through rich green valleys, around small towns like Mandling and Radstadt, past shuttered ski resorts dotting the sides of mountains, up through mountain passes, back down into another valley and then up another mountain. There wasn't a lot of traffic on the roads, although we did pass several cyclists who were getting a serious low-gear workout.

Eventually we arrived at the trailhead, a large gravel lot that was packed with cars like a mall at Christmastime. There were clusters of hikers standing around, families, little kids, grandmas and grandpas, teenagers, college students. They were all fully dressed and didn't look like they'd be stripping down and joining us anytime soon.

The scene called for tact, so we set off on the trail with our clothes on. We ascended rapidly, toiling up a steep incline. After we put about a quarter mile between ourselves and the parking lot, it was time to strip. This happened quickly and without a lot of discussion. Once Richard's shirt and pants are off, that's the signal that it's time to get naked.

As I slipped out of my shorts, I received a text message from my wife. She was in Los Angeles and getting ready for bed. Her text read: Have a great hike! I replied: Sweet dreams!

It turned out that this part of the trail was a fairly popular hiking destination for Austrian families. Just as we disrobed we began to encounter large numbers of hikers. It's one thing to be naked with a bunch of naked people in an area like a nudist resort or nude beach where you're expected to be naked, but it's totally different to be naked around people who are fully dressed and aren't expecting to encounter a troop of nudists. Interestingly, I didn't find myself getting as embarrassed as I thought I would be. There were a lot of friendly smiles and good-natured laughter as we passed and—perhaps because there was a number of attractive women in our group—a lot of people reaching for their cameras.

The main trail ended at a scenic *gasthaus* that overlooked several beautiful lakes. One of the things I found surprising about hiking in the Alps was the number of taverns plopped atop mountains. It seemed like there wasn't a trail that didn't end at some scenic little restaurant where hikers could have a seat, a strudel, a beer, or a big plate of cheese and bread. Needless to say, I'm a fan of the Austrian *gasthaus*. Every trail should have one.

We dressed as we approached the *gasthaus*—Richard felt we should respect the people who were eating and drinking there—and then we made a turn that sent us up a small goat trail. Once clear of the pub, everyone stripped again, the French being particularly adept at the clothing change as they were wearing what they called "hiking kilts," but what were really miniskirts for men. I'd never seen anything like them before.

We made it to the summit in time for lunch, then set off again after twenty minutes, which brought howls from the French hikers, who like to sit and enjoy their food. Richard assured them that there would be another stop in a little while—and in retrospect, I think he suddenly realized how much ground we had to cover before it got dark and knew we needed to move—but they weren't happy about having to eat quickly.

We traversed a ridge dotted with several large patches of snow. You might think it would be weird to walk naked through snow, but it isn't when the sun is shining and it's warm out. Roberto looked at a large ice field that ran down the side of the mountain and said, "If you slip, you slide all the way to Vienna."

The trail ascended and descended multiple times, wrapping around one side of a mountain and then cutting back

across to the another—the word "serpentine" comes to mind—
and the overall effect was disorienting. Of course the scenery
was magnificent. Jagged mountains rose in the background on
almost all sides, the sky was blue, the sun was hot, and there
were streams and ponds caused by snow melt running across
the trail. If the von Trapp family had skipped past us holding hands and singing songs, I wouldn't have been surprised.
Though they might have been.

The first five hours of the hike were thoroughly enjoyable. We would stop for periodic rests while Karla and Stuart
took photographs and I quickly learned to spot clumps of
soft lichen to sit on.

At one of these breaks I was astonished to see Bruno,
the naturist from Marseille, open a thermos and pour himself
an espresso. The smell of hot strong coffee mixed with the
clean mountain air caused me to salivate. The French hike
with style. If he'd pulled out some cheese, a baguette, and a
cold bottle of crisp Sancerre, I wouldn't have been surprised.

As the day wore on, I noticed that many of my fellow
hikers were starting to show signs of sunburn and I heard Dr.
Grenier's voice saying, "They should give you combat pay."
So I put on some clothes. I wasn't the only one. As the snow
patches increased in depth and frequency, other people began
to throw on layers.

We were a little past the halfway point in the hike when
my knee began to exhibit signs of falling apart. With each
descending step I felt a sharp pain shoot through my right leg
and, well, there was nothing I could do about that. I could
take a step up without a problem, but that wasn't going to
help. I had to go down the mountain.

Ironically, I thought I had prepared for this trip. I had trained for this alpine adventure by hiking up to the Griffith Observatory in Los Angeles twice a week for a month, a regimen that I quickly realized was like training for a marathon by jogging around the block a few times. But I wasn't the only one hurting. Casualties were mounting, water was running out, and, although I wouldn't describe the situation as dangerous or life threatening or anything like that, people were definitely getting cranky. My knee began to swell, which is never a good sign, but I persevered. I was touched by Bernard's offering to carry my pack and Vittorio's offering me one of his hiking sticks. I thanked them, but declined. These dudes were ten and twenty years older than me. I would tough it out, do a gut check, see what I was made of, keep a stiff upper lip, and other heroic wilderness survival clichés. Besides, it wasn't like I had to saw my arm off with a Swiss army knife—which I didn't have—or eat one of my companions. My knee was swollen. I would live. I refilled my canteens from a spring and we trudged on.

My phone peeped to tell me I had a new text message. My wife, who'd just arisen from a good night's sleep in Los Angeles, had texted: How was the hike? My reply: Still fucking hiking.

A little over nine hours after we started, we made it back to the parking lot.

People were uncharacteristically silent when we returned to the hut; everyone was exhausted and even Richard, who was generally chatty, was quiet. I think Richard felt a little bad about the hike being so demanding. Not that it was his fault—he'd never hiked that trail before.

I didn't have anything to say to anyone about anything. It wasn't just my knee that was swollen; my body ached all over. My elbow hurt and I had a gash on my right hip that was oozing blood. How these things happened, I cannot say. I went to the refrigerator and grabbed two beers. I washed down three Advil with the first beer, then sat outside staring off into space as I sipped the second.

Stuart had an app on his phone that kept track of our adventure, but the stats tell only part of the story of the Ursprungalm Death March. We walked thirteen miles and climbed 2,400 vertical feet in a hike that took just over nine hours to complete. According to Stuart's app, we burned 4,125 calories.

...

Richard's passion for naked hiking has turned into a major problem in his marriage. "My wife thinks it's disgusting," he said. "She told me she'd rather I have an affair." They were beginning to go through divorce proceedings. I could see that talking about this made Richard unhappy, but it made me curious. With all the societal and marital pressures not to hike, why did he keep doing it? What motivated him?

Richard looked off into the distance, considering the question, then turned to me. "I got this thing called vitiligo when I was fortyish, which makes your skin all blotchy. And it's not a skin problem, per se, it's a systemic problem. You can tell because it's mirrored on both sides. I'll show you, you can see that there on my wrist."

He put his wrists together and, sure enough, there was some mottling and discoloration on his skin. I looked closer at his face and saw that what I had assumed was just sun- and windburn was more evidence of his condition.

"I've got it all over—can you see that?—blotchy on both sides, mirrored. Anyway, it disfigures you, basically, visually. And you're kind of walking down the street and you see people looking at you strangely, you're not sure that they fancy you or whether they think you're a bit of a weirdo or you just . . . you're being stared at strangely." He shifted uncomfortably. "And I think that being naked has helped me deal with that in a more positive way because I'm less concerned about what other people think. I'm probably still concerned about what other people think as a person, you know, but I'm a bit less concerned about it than I used to be. So this kind of disfigurement is something I just think, 'Well, that's how I am, that's how I look. Get over it. That's just me.' It's something other people have to deal with. You know, I don't need to wear makeup to cover myself up to make myself look a different color or clothes to hide behind."

His skin condition is subtle, you wouldn't really notice it unless you were looking for it, but I can see how it would color his self-perception. I asked him if he felt some acceptance from practicing nudism.

He nodded. "Yeah, yeah. In that respect, I think it has given me confidence. I think you get that being an ordinary naturist, if you like, in a club. You know, you can say, 'People accept me.' And I've got it through my naked hiking. Some sort of a positive benefit for me personally, in that respect."

. . .

Although the next day's hike was an easy one, I was not confident that my knee would make it. In fact a few of us needed a rest, so while Richard led the hard core out on what he called "a leg stretcher," I puttered around the hut.

On their way back from the hike Richard passed the little restaurant next door, the Mandlberggut—which is also apparently a schnapps distillery known for making a hay-flavored spirit—and asked the proprietor if she would host a group of naked diners. Soon enough, picnic tables were set up outside next to the distillery tasting room and there were twenty naked people sitting around drinking beer and eating pizza. It was an amazing thing to see. The owner of the restaurant, an attractive Austrian woman in her early forties, and her teenage daughter waited on us and there was nothing strained or unnatural in the way they behaved, nothing that showed any hint of discomfort or embarrassment. In fact, they seemed to be enjoying the experience as much as the naturists and, a few weeks later, they e-mailed Richard and welcomed him and his group back any time. It was great to see, as if Richard's manifesto had come to life, nakedness normal in any context. And that includes a large group of naturists out to dinner.

In fact at one point Andreas, one of the German hikers, stood up and put on his shorts to go to the bathroom. The idea of putting on clothes to go to the bathroom was surreal enough, but the fact that he unknowingly stood in front of a glass partition while he slipped on his shorts, essentially mooning the entire restaurant, well, that was funny.

It's one thing for the restaurant staff to be cool with a bunch of naked people, but how did the naked people feel? I mean, you're the one who's exposed. When I was eating lunch in Cap d'Agde it was different. Almost everyone was naked, so that became the norm. But to be naked in an environment where everyone else is wearing clothes, where the expectation is that you are dressed? Doesn't that make you feel weird?

I asked Richard about it. "I'm much more relaxed about it. I'm much more comfortable with the idea that—and maybe this would be similar to someone that was gay that was coming out, you know—I feel much more comfortable about saying I'm a naked—I hike naked. And I have every right to enjoy that experience."

"But what about a place like this?"

"The informal rule I have is on tarmac you get dressed, which basically includes all towns and villages and so forth. And I regard every *gasthaus* or mountain hut as being owned by those people and it's their space, right? So what they say goes. Now when we're out hiking through wild mountain territory, that's open public space, so I have every right to be there and dress in any way I chose. And when I go into someone else's home, or their house, I expect to abide by their dress criteria, if you like, or their rules, whatever they might be. It is more about respecting other people's place, space, and environment. This is one argument I've had in the past where people have said, 'You just want everyone to be naked all the time.' Well, I don't want that. I want everyone to have their own choice."

One of the interesting things that happened when I injured my knee was I suddenly didn't feel like hiking naked. I know that a pair of shorts isn't going to offer me any real protection, I understand that, and yet being totally exposed while my leg hurt was just not happening. The clothing offered a kind of psychological protection if nothing else. It was too bad, really. When I was feeling spry and energetic I had really enjoyed scrambling up the mountains in the buff; it was way more fun than sitting by the pool at a resort or walking on the beach in Spain or France.

Now I just wanted to keep up and enjoy the scenery and the company of my fellow hikers, and I hoped my knee didn't totally give out. In some ways it was interesting to be wearing clothes, like I was the control group in an experiment, because it really was different. As soon as we began an ascent, I worked up a serious, shirt-drenching sweat. That didn't happen when I was naked and, trust me, it wasn't particularly pleasant to walk around in sweat-soaked clothes.

Later, Gus, the one-man-show writer and performer from England, and I stood outside the hut watching birds flit and swoop around the field feeding on insects. It turned out Gus was an amateur bird-watcher.

"I wish they'd slow down. I can't make them out."

I looked up at the sky. "They look like swallows."

Gus looked at me like I'd just said I'd shit myself. "Those aren't swallows."

"They look like swallows."

"Well, they might look like swallows to you, but they're not."

"Are they larks?"

Gus burst out laughing. "Larks? Do those look like larks?"

"They could be."

"They're definitely not larks."

I think I heard his teeth grind.

"Barn swallows?"

"No." He shook his head in disgust. "They're probably house martins."

"That's a band."

Gus was fully agitated now and began to swing his arms wildly in the air. "Yes. It is the name of a band. It's also the name of a bird. Those birds. That one there. House martins."

I couldn't resist provoking his bird-watcher rage. "Looks like a swallow to me."

Gus grumbled angrily and said, "Why were you wearing clothes today? These are supposed to be naked hikes."

Before I could say anything Richard jumped to my defense. "People hike in whatever makes them comfortable. There's no problem with that."

Gus turned and skulked back into the hut mumbling about house martins.

...

The last day we hiked up from the hut along a wide, easy trail that looped through a valley to a small lake. Richard insists on mountain safety, and on every hike someone had to be the last person, the "tail-end Charlie" or, as the French called it, the "defense." If you are moderately awake and can count to twenty, it's a pretty stress-free responsibility. The job is to make sure everyone is accounted for when the group gets to a rest stop or fork in the trail. Because I was still treading gingerly on my leg, I accepted the assignment, or as Pascal so exuberantly shouted, "USA in defense!"

Pascal is another longtime naturist. He's a tall and ruggedly handsome Frenchman in his early fifties who, like Harry and many of the naturists on the trip, wears a big beaming smile most of the time. He also has a fondness for Americana and wears a baseball cap that says I HIKED THE GRAND CANYON and a T-shirt that says FBI in giant letters. These were souvenirs from an RV tour of the States he took with his wife and kids a couple of years ago. I asked him if this hike was his summer vacation.

"No. We're going to go naturist camping next week and then we're going to Croatia."

Croatia is famous for having many naturist beaches and nude campgrounds along its coast and is a common destination for European naturists.

"Do you always take naturist vacations?" I asked.

He nodded. "Yes. This is what we like to do."

"When did you start being a naturist?"

Pascal thought about it. "When I was eighteen I went to a naturist camp. I have been doing this ever since."

"Were your parents naturist?"

He shook his head. "Oh no. Not at all. They are very Christian. Super religious."

"So you rebelled?"

Pascal stopped on the trail and looked at me like I was the first person to ever suggest this. "Maybe." He laughed. "Maybe so."

I know that Pascal and his wife have teenage children and I wondered if they were still naturist or if they'd started wearing clothes like Harry's kids. Pascal thought about it for a moment and then said, "They are teenagers so they're not so naturist anymore. They have textile friends and this creates a problem."

For some reason the trail was busy that day with groups of chubby middle-aged churchgoers out for a day of prayer and communion with nature. I can guarantee that they didn't expect to commune with our kind of nature. The first Christian group we encountered actually turned away from us, facing the mountain in an act of shunning. I've never been shunned before and seeing the group turn away from us baffled me. It made me wonder what they would've thought if they'd come across the medieval Turlupins of France, devout Christians who thought that the truly faithful didn't need to wear clothes. Of course I know the answer. They would've done what the medieval Christians did: denounce the nudists as heretics and burn them at the stake. I grumbled something about religion and hypocrites to Richard, who laughed. "Not a God-fearing man, are you, Mark?"

"I only fear His followers, Richard."

As the hike wore on we passed several other church groups and thankfully their responses weren't as severe. Mostly they looked at us like we were aliens from another planet. Their jaws would drop and their mouths would hang open like someone had flipped a switch in their heads. Once the initial shock of seeing a dozen or so nudists wore off, they looked down or looked up or looked anywhere they could but at the dangling man bits traipsing past. Not all of them were so horrified. Some cast quick peeks and grinned.

We hiked down a trail until we came to a tranquil little lake. I sat under a tree while a few people went swimming or lay out in the sun. The superhikers decided to continue up the mountain. It was the first time in the week that we'd splintered off into different groups.

Richard joined me under the tree, and we ate our lunch and watched Gus stand by the lake and rehearse his one-man play *This Way Madness Lies*. His promotional material calls it "a raw and humorous tale of going mad."

I turned to Richard. "How long do you think you can keep doing this?"

"Naked hiking?"

I nodded.

Richard looked off at the lake, where Gus was now waving his arms and bowing to an imaginary ovation. "Until I drop, if I can."

The warm sun and sheer exhaustion from a week of alpine hiking seemed to settle into our bodies, and soon no one was saying much of anything. It was deeply pleasant, only the sounds of the bubbling stream feeding the lake, the insects buzzing, a few birds chirping in the trees, and a mad actor rehearsing his play.

Sex and the Single Nudist

Most people would think that twenty naked adults living together in a mountain hut for a week would lead to some kind of sexual something or other. A bit of hanky-panky. Maybe an orgy. At least a furtive booty call out by the barn. But if anything happened, aside from some minor flirting, it was incredibly discreet. Maybe that's because most everyone was married or had a significant other, or perhaps everyone was too exhausted from hiking. Whatever the reason, the only sound I heard at night was in my room, and that was the sound of two very tired men swatting at the long-nosed Austrian mosquitos called *mücken** while trying to sleep.

People didn't even talk about sex. Maybe bringing the subject up might, you know, bring the subject up, so it was best left unspoken. But I can't really say, because nobody really said. Although on our last evening at the hut, Harry and I were standing outside watching the sunset when Maria-Grazia came out dragging her suitcase. She was driving back to Italy that night, but that's not why I did a double take. She appeared to be transformed. I almost didn't recognize

---

* A great name for a heavy metal band.

her. Harry laughed and said, "You see someone naked for a week and you don't think anything of it, and then she puts on a cute dress and some makeup and you think, 'What an attractive girl!'"

And he was right. Here was someone I had eaten dinner with in the nude, whom I had hiked with in the nude, watched doing naked yoga on the grass outside, and I never once thought of her as a sexual being. Which is odd because she is a very nice-looking woman. But something had changed and it wasn't her. Maria-Grazia was still Maria-Grazia; she'd just put on some clothes. What changed was my perception of her. Naked she was just another naked person among a group of naked people, but in a sundress and sandals, she was suddenly sexy.

How did this happen? Was it the clothes that suddenly made her attractive?

Diana Crane, a sociology professor emerita at the University of Pennsylvania, writes, "Clothes as artifacts 'create' behavior through their capacity to impose social identities and empower people to assert latent social identities."[46]

Which is true. We all know that "clothes make the man." We send a message to the world about who we are, what we desire, and what we aspire to be by what we wear, whether it's a uniform, a business suit, or a backward baseball cap. But asserting latent social identities is one thing; going from naked and irrelevant to sexually attractive by putting on clothes is another. It seems counterintuitive.

Italian philosopher Mario Perniola, in his essay "The Glorious Garment and the Naked Truth," writes, "In the figurative arts, eroticism appears as a relationship between clothing and nudity. Therefore, it is conditional on the possibility of movement—transit—from one state to the other. If either of these poles takes on a primary or essential significance to the exclusion of the other, then the possibility for this transit is sacrificed, and with it the conditions for eroticism."[47]

That's more like it. The act of taking off your clothes is erotic because it is the "transit" between one state of being and another. Which probably explains the enduring popularity of the striptease: it excites the imagination. It's not what you wear but what we imagine you look like in the act of taking it off and what we'll be doing once you do take it off that is arousing. In other words: it's all in our head. Maria-Grazia's transformation wasn't something she did; it was Harry and my imaginations being sparked by her wearing clothes.

Dr. Gloria G. Brame, a clinical sexologist, says pretty much the same thing in a *Cosmopolitan* article titled "How Clothes Make Sex Hotter" when she states, "Staying partially clad builds anticipation and makes sex feel spontaneous."*

Which could explain why the swingers at Cap d'Agde got dressed up in the evening. When it's time to swing, you slip into your sluttiest clothes, whereas if you're standing around with a bunch of naked people, the mystery is gone. If there's nothing to take off, no erotic "transit" to spark the imagination, well, the whole thing goes limp.

When the week of free hiking was finally over and we'd cleaned up the hut, Pascal and his wife were kind enough to offer me a ride to Salzburg in their Chrysler minivan. There was construction on some of the tracks through the mountains

---

* She also advises her readers: "Blindfold him with his tie. Blocking his sight heightens his other senses, and not knowing your next move will drive him insane (in a good way)."

and the railroad had contracted a bus company to link the stations, but the idea of a long bus ride to a short train ride to a taxi to the hotel seemed less appealing than door-to-door delivery in the relative luxury of Pascal's minivan. Conxita, the Spanish documentarian, was also catching a ride. She had a flight back to Edinburgh that evening, while I had a whole day to hang out in Salzburg before going back to Los Angeles via Berlin.

Conxita and I dumped our luggage at my hotel—the hip and friendly Hotel Auersperg—and then strolled downtown in search of lunch.

I think Walt Disney was thinking of Salzburg when he built Disneyland. The city center straddles the Salzach River and is clean and quiet and beautiful in a way that's almost a cliché of a picturesque European town. It could be the well-preserved baroque architecture or the narrow cobbled alleyways or the overall greenness of the valley and surrounding mountains, but whatever the reason, I got the sense that I was on a Euro-fantasia movie set: manicured, quaint, and unreal. No wonder it was named a UNESCO World Heritage Site in 1997.

Preternaturally gifted composer Wolfgang Amadeus Mozart lived here and they don't let you forget it. They've got a Mozart museum, the house where Mozart lived, the house where Mozart was born, and Mozart's face on chocolate bonbons, T-shirts, key chains, rubber bathtub duckies, and multiple statues around the city. I'm surprised they don't pipe Mozart through the streets twenty-four hours a day.

Although I was only spending the night in Salzburg, my visit coincided with the Salzburger Festspiele, an annual music and theater festival. There was a full slate of concerts, performances, and parties that weekend and it brought the people of Salzburg out into the streets. That these hearty Austrians showed their civic pride by wearing traditional clothing struck me as charming and more than a little goofy—I can't imagine that a modern Salzburger would normally wear a dirndl or lederhosen when going out on the town. But there they were, imposing latent social identities en masse.

Conxita and I strolled across the river, ending up at an old cinema that had been converted into a restaurant and scenester hangout called Republic Café. We ordered a couple of Aperol Spritzes and leaned back to check out the scene. Coming from the hipster epicenter of Eastside Los Angeles, I have to say that Austrian hipsters are pretty conservative-looking. No tattoos or obvious body modification were evident, but there were a lot of polo shirts tucked into lederhosen and Timberland loafers without socks.

Conxita has an effervescent and distinctly Catalan personality—she's open, friendly. She sports a pixieish haircut and is undeniably good-looking, and her voluptuous naked body attracted a lot of attention on the trail. Like me, she was not a naturist or nudist—her first day on the trail was her first day being naked in a nonsexual social nude environment—but unlike me, she seemed to take to it with real gusto and surprised herself in the process.

"Are you going to start running around Edinburgh naked?"

She laughed. "You've obviously never been there."

Which is true.

"You don't have to answer this if you don't want to, but I was curious if anyone hit on you while we were in the hut."

She looked at me, slightly perplexed. "Hit on me?"

"You know . . . made sexual advances?"

She burst out laughing and shook her head. "I have a boyfriend."

"That doesn't always stop people."

"No." She shook her head. "They were all gentlemen."

Although I knew she was shooting a documentary film, I wondered what made her go on the hike in the first place. Conxita thought about it and said, "It was like an anthropological experiment because I'm fed up of this kind of desk life we are supposed to have, you know, under these little fluorescents, eight hours and go home. And I hate that. So I'm really supportive of people like Richard."

"But you'd never done anything like this before. Weren't you nervous?"

She nodded. "Once in the plane I realized where I was going and then I start to have the tachycardia, but it was too late. And once I was there, it's like okay there's no way back; I have to do it. And I was very impressed at how nice they were. I didn't feel pressure at all."

Which I have to say was pretty much my experience of the Naked European Walking Tour. I was very apprehensive when I first arrived and left feeling like I'd made a bunch of friends.

"And what was it like the first time you undressed in front of everyone?"

"I felt shy, you know, because I didn't know anyone and there's the body thing, but then I think the attitude was so relaxed and everybody was so friendly and it was hot as well. So once I jumped in the lake I thought, 'Look, they've seen me now, so no way back.'"

"Did you have conflicting emotions about it or did it make you happy?"

"I feel really happy that I did that actually, because I think it was beautiful. It was a very challenge experience. I will recommend it even to my mother-in-law, you know, because I think people live ignoring the body. And if you have your belly, your double chin, you're big, you're small, it's fine. Be friends with that. So for me it was an opportunity to be friends with my body."

We encountered a lot of different people on the trail and I had noticed that Conxita had gotten a lot of long looks from men and women, so I asked her, "Did you ever feel like you were being looked at or treated as a sexual object?"

She shook her head and laughed. "I never had the thought of I'm going to be raped in the shower. No, thank you."

"Did you find the experience had changed you in some way?"

"Yes. I felt really kind of proud and kind of sexy, like, 'Yeah, I can do this.' For some days I felt really empowered."

Which is pretty much what I thought. Even if they were attracted to Conxita, no one could act aggressively sexual, as it would've made all the women in the hut—and possibly some of the men—uncomfortable. Except for Cap d'Agde and its swinger scene, this has been my experience of non-sexual social nudism. Sitting around the pool at the Desert Sun Resort or the Hotel Vera Playa Club is like being in one of those Victorian drawing room comedies and sex is the elephant in the room that no one wants to mention for fear of spilling their tea.

But why shouldn't they? Aren't humans sexual animals?

I think Ruth Barcan gets it exactly right when she says, "In a kind of circular logic, nudism had to seem non-sexual in order to attract women and it needed women in order to prove it had nothing to do with sex."[48]

Because if nudism isn't about sex, if it's just about personal freedom or positive body image or not having a tan line, then it's somehow safe for men and women to enjoy being naked together in a social situation and that makes it somewhat more palatable to the public at large.

A good illustration of the conflict between our animal impulse to be sexual and the rigid nonsexual rules of social nudism is the battle between longtime nudist Catherine Holmes and the Maryland Health Society (MaHeSo), a nudist resort and campground in Davidsonville, Maryland. Holmes had a long-term lease on a cabin at the rustic resort and became concerned about reports of swinging activity. Blow jobs were rumored to have been administered in the pool—although I'd imagine that would require some kind of snorkel or scuba gear—and people were allegedly hooking up in the woods. Although Holmes hadn't seen any of these activities herself, the hearsay was enough for her to seek a restraining order and unspecified damages against the resort, claiming that the nature of the club had changed. "It used to be sexuality and nudity were two totally different things," she said.[49]

I'm not saying she didn't have a case. After all, in its list of rules the resort states clearly that "Violence, overt sexual behavior, questionable conduct with children or any other behavior that offends or embarrasses others is not permitted."[50] But the club revoked her membership and Paul Blumenthal, the attorney for the resort, argued that the complaint was "completely and utterly devoid of any specific facts."[51]

Apparently the judge agreed and her claims were denied.

And so Catherine Holmes did what any red-blooded anti-swinger pro-nonsexual social nudist would do: she barricaded herself in her cabin and posted anti-swinger signs on her windows.

The standoff lasted five months before the resort got a court order to evict her and she was forced to move.

One of Holmes's complaints about the perceived sexualization of the resort was that many of the men wore cock rings. Vicky Jarboe, president of the board of directors for MaHeSo, responded by saying, "Yes, my husband wears a cock ring, along with probably 16–20 other men here. What's wrong with that? We've got 80-year-old men here wearing cock rings. She's pulling at straws."[52]

There's a joke in there somewhere.

Historically, positioning nudism as nonsexual is a way to short-circuit any morality police or politicians who might try to quash a group of consenting adults from enjoying themselves without clothes. It eases the fevered imaginations of the funwreckers who want to enforce their idea of what's appropriate or inappropriate. Why shouldn't a group of adults do whatever they want with whomever they want as long as no one gets hurt? I mean, seriously. But even Gay Naturists International, a men-only homosexual nudist organization, has nonsexual codes of conduct on its website: "Our goal is to promote healthy, legal, non-sexual nude recreation. While GNI knows sex is natural, sex is not equated with naturism."[53]

The opposite of this, and definitely unsafe for your average nonsexual social nudist, is the erotic, nonprofit ecological organization started in Norway called Fuck for Forest (FFF). Modern-day merry pranksters, the dreadlocked and tattooed members of FFF are eco-activists who use sex and pornography to promote an ideal of nudity and free love in harmony with nature. "Sex is often shown to attract us to buy all kind of bullshit products and ideas, so why not for a good cause? We think it is important to show a more liberal relationship to our bodies, as a contrast to the suppressed world we live in."[54]

FFF engages in nudity and public sex acts to bring attention to its point of view, which is summed up in its manifesto as "War and nature destruction is normalized, while public lovemaking and nudity is considered offensive and criminalized."

Unlike the nonsexual social nudist activism of the Naktivists, FFF's version of free hiking includes having group sex in trees and filming it. Or oral sex in parks. Or a three-way in the streets of Berlin. Basically they have sex just about anywhere you can get two or three or four naked bodies together. As they say, "It is a nature [sic] right to be naked and have sex, anywhere."

I admire the sense of playful in-your-faceness that FFF exhibits, but its members are also environmentalists with an organization involved in projects in Brazil, Peru, Costa Rica, Slovakia, and Ecuador. As they say, "Sex has in this world become a tool for marketing. But usually it is just used to sell us crappy products and ideas, not giving the true honor to sexual energy at all."

Organized social nudism isn't really in a position to honor sexual energy. Throughout its history too many nudists have been arrested or stigmatized, clubs shut down, and nude beaches closed. Nudists have a tenuous relationship with society and one that might break down if nudists were suddenly fucking in the trees. That's why they have so many rules about nonsexual behavior; they don't want to give their enemies any ammunition to shut them down for being immoral or obscene or a threat to public decency.

David Wraith is a writer and founder of Sex Positive St. Louis, who sometimes organizes events like nude bowling night. Because he is a self-described voyeur and exhibitionist, he had a slightly different take on nudism than your average AANR member. "There are those that say that nudism is absolutely not about sex, and I think that's kind of bullshit, honestly. I don't think it's all about sex, but I don't think you can say that anything is absolutely, 100 percent not about sex."[55]

While I agree with Wraith that it's difficult to have anything in the modern world that is "100 percent not about sex," I have to say that my experience so far has shown me that, while they might not be celibate, nudists are trying really hard not to be sexy. But then I wonder if they're not overthinking it. Can you spark the erotic imagination without clothes?

Trends in Genital Topiary

When you look at photographs of nudists from, say, the 1920s and compare them with photos from the 1950s, they look pretty much the same. The human body didn't evolve, there were no radical advances in hairstyles, no sci-fi growth of wings or gills or antennae. Naked people frolicking in the fields of Germany in 1924 look pretty much like naked Americans or French or British people frolicking in their respective fields in 1955. Photographic technology changed, going from a somewhat diffuse black and white to kooky Kodachrome, but without the whims and whatnots of style, the fads and flair of fashion, to give a sense of time or place, people look the same.

Flip through a current issue of *N* or any other nudist publication and you quickly realize that things have changed. There is a noticeable thickening of bodies—the obesity epidemic appears to have hit American nudism especially hard—and there is a distinct change in hairstyles. Which is not to say that braids or bobs or ponytails are different; it is pubic hair that has gone missing. Like time-lapse footage of a disappearing glacier, the curly covering on our genitals has slowly receded until it is now almost nonexistent. I don't think we can blame this on climate change.

But I'm not surprised. It's not just nudists who are trimming, shaving, and Brazilian waxing their mons pubis; as Ashley Fetters reported in the *Atlantic*, "Today, it's all but commonplace for women to go to extreme measures to get bald, pre-pubescent nether regions . . ."[56] Fetters quotes a study by Indiana University and Kinsey Institute researchers that discovered nearly 60 percent of American women between the ages of eighteen and twenty-four and half of women between twenty-five and twenty-nine prefer to have hairless genitals. The researchers say this phenomenon is described as the "new norm."[57]

Of course not everyone is trying to make her vulva look fresh-faced. The Indiana University study found that "women's total removal of their pubic hair was associated with younger age, sexual orientation, sexual relationship status, having received cunnilingus in the past 4 weeks," and other factors. I think frequent oral sex is probably reason enough for a shave, but compare those figures with a 1968 survey of Australian nudists where 10 percent removed all of their pubic hair, 50 percent trimmed their pubic hair, and the rest did nothing to their pubic hair.[58]

The pubic hair paradigm has been flipped on its head.

While the study only looked at women's pubic hair, or lack thereof, in the nudist world it's not just the women who are going hairless; there is some serious manscaping going on.

When I was getting ready to go to my first ever nudist resort, I thought that I should do a little manscaping experiment on myself. I didn't want to spoil my first nonsexual social nude experience with a crotch that looked like Rip Van Winkle's beard. I did a little research and was encouraged by the fact that men's magazines—*Esquire*, *GQ*, and *Men's Fitness*—have all published articles and advice about manscaping.

Apparently, it feels good and the ladies love it.

I will admit that a part of me wondered if these articles weren't just product placement for companies like Gillette and Panasonic to sell body hair trimmers to insecure dudes. But was I an insecure dude? If I'm being completely honest, yes, I was not so super confident in my physical appearance that I thought strutting around a nudist resort was going to draw oohs and aahs from the other guests. I didn't think I would wow them with my manly endowment. I was just hoping they wouldn't all point and laugh. So when the articles promised that if I trimmed off an inch of pubic hair, my penis would magically look an inch or so longer, I thought it was worth a try. I mean, from a graphic design standpoint it makes sense, and besides, who wouldn't want the confidence boost an extra inch can provide? At least that's what the magazines said.

I bought a trimmer and went to work. It wasn't as difficult as I expected. The various attachments provide protection from nicks and cuts and, well, the hair just kind of falls off. I had intended to do a light trim, but once I was into it, I just kind of went for it. Like I said: it was an experiment.

Later that night my wife looked at me and said, "Oh, honey. What did you do?" She said this in the concerned, sympathetic voice you might use when a young child draws on his face with an indelible marker.

While I might have overdone it with the trimmer, I was nowhere near being a smoothie.

"Smoothies" are men and women who prefer to be completely hairless from the neck down and are not to be confused
with blended fruit drinks. "Smoothie" is the common term for
what's technically an acomoclitic naturist, a person who pre-
fers to have hairless genitals, the nudest of the nudists. Serious
smoothies will shave or wax all their hair, not just their pubic
hair. They claim that taking off this last layer of covering will
"promote the classical aesthetic ideal of a smooth and hairless body."* It is part of what they call the "smooth lifestyle."

As the "Smooth Naturists" section of the EuroNaturist.
com website proclaims: "Pubic hair serves no useful purpose
in humans and there are good reasons for going smooth."
While I don't want to get in a debate on the utilitarian or
decorative aspects of body hair, let's look at the "good reasons
for going smooth" they put forward: "It looks and feels great!
It is cleaner and more hygienic, especially for women. The
smooth skin is more sensitive and it enhances sexual pleasure
in many ways!"[59]

While I raised an eyebrow about the hygiene comment—
"especially for women," really?—it is refreshing to see a nudist
organization talking about sexual pleasure.

I had seen several men and women who were smoothies
when I was at Vera Playa and Cap d'Agde, but I didn't know
they were part of a movement. Or that the movement had
special clubs and events to promote mutual glabrousness.
If fact, being smooth means you might have a very active
social schedule. The World of the Nudest Nudist (WNN),
a smoothie club in the Netherlands, offers "weekly evenings

---

* There are Dutch and British versions of the "Smoothie Club." Here I quote
from the Dutch website (www.wnn.nu).

in saunas and swimming pools, summer meetings all over the country, weekends in a naturist hotel in Germany, nudist cruises in Croatia and our yearly International Smoothy Days at Flevo-Natuur, a naturist campsite centrally situated in the Netherlands."

Smooth and Cut Naturists (SCN) is an organization in the United Kingdom that promotes not only hairlessness, but also circumcision for male smoothies. As it says on its official website: "SCN is of the firm opinion that to be smooth (ie without any body hair), and for the male to be circumcised, forms the perfect combination (especially when nude) with so many distinct advantages." The SCN is also into hygiene, which makes me wonder if it's also not some kind of germaphobic nudist club. Maybe it's just me but I think the circumcision requirement is strange, but the club defends it by saying, "We at SCN firmly believe that the circumcised penis is aesthetically more pleasing for various reasons—hygiene and looks (as naturists) being just two—particularly when it is not surrounded by what we, as smoothies, consider to be unsightly pubic hair. It is this extra requirement that makes SCN unique."[60]

...

Pubic hair has an oddball history. First the U.S. government wouldn't allow magazines to show any, and the art directors of *Sunshine & Health*, *Modern Sunbathing*, and many of the dozen or so nudist magazines that sprang up in the late 1950s and early 1960s would have to pose models to hide their pubis or simply airbrush pubic hair out of the picture entirely. As censorship relaxed, magazines like

Playboy and others began showing glimpses of pubic hair. My favorite magazine of this era is *Jaybird Happening*, a kind of flower child nudist skin rag that showed freaky, free-flowing, uncoiffed genital hair in abundance. The magazine merged the nudist lifestyle with the pro-sex hippie movement of the late 1960s, and routinely showed naked men and women goofing off in various locales and posed in what are known as "spread shots." *Jaybird Happening* was pretty much a celebration of free-range pubic hair.

A study by researchers at George Washington University used *Playboy* centerfolds as a timeline for the evolution—the researchers called it "Evulvalution"—of female genitalia and pubic hair. They found that, up until the late 1980s, almost all the models featured in the magazine had natural-looking pubic regions, but in the 1990s things began to change, and nowadays the majority of *Playboy* bunnies have partially trimmed or shaved pubic regions. According to their study, as the "appearance of centerfold models' genitalia was becoming increasingly deviant from a natural female appearance, we hypothesized that pubic hair would appear partially or completely removed among the majority of the sample."[61]

Why did this happen? Some people claim that the arrival of the Brazilian wax in our hemisphere introduced it and the television show *Sex and the City* popularized it. That may be true, but I think the simple answer is: online porn.

Porn stars shave their pubic hair off for the simple reason that it provides the viewer a clear and unobstructed sight line to the actors' genitals while they're acting. A cleanly shaved vulva is the face, if you will, of the porn industry. I think this is done to distract the more discerning cinephile from the wooden quality of the acting and the simplistic script.

Shaving your mons pubis does have a historical precedent. It was primarily done by courtesans and prostitutes to control lice. Of course, a prepubescent pubic area wasn't considered erotic back in the day, so to bring the sexy back early professionals would wear a pubic wig called a merkin. In an ironic twist, contemporary Hollywood actresses—who are, we must remember, young women living in this day and age—have been having to wear merkins while playing roles in period films like *The Reader* and television programs like *Boardwalk Empire.* I imagine that if *Downton Abbey* had explicit sex scenes, they would need a merkin or two to keep things historically accurate.

Maybe nobody has pubic hair in Hollywood—which, let's be honest, is in the business of infantilizing women—but they are slaves to fashion like everyone else, and fads and styles, much like influenza, eventually run their course.

It's ironic that men and women are spending so much time and money grooming a part of their body that they are reluctant to reveal. It doesn't make sense to me. Unless the smoothies are right and being hairless just makes everything a little bit sexier. But I guess I'll never know, because the pendulum of pudendum coiffure is swinging back to the style of early naturists. In a recent *New York Times Magazine* article, Amanda Hess wrote about a recent resurgence in wild and woolly pubic hair: "there's something refreshingly retro, delightfully expressive and confidently grown-up in getting back to nature."[62]

I'm putting my clippers in the garage.

There's a Reason Florida Is Shaped Like a Penis

I was driving a rented Yaris* along a two-lane road through the scrubby central Florida woods when I looked up and saw a small plane skywriting the words JESUS LOVES U in puffy white letters against a vibrant blue sky. I wondered if this was unusual. Do they write religious messages in the sky every day or was today a special occasion? Maybe Florida is just a place where unusual things happen. Earlier that day I'd been at a truck stop and saw a food product called Alligator Bob's Smoked Alligator Jerky. The packaging claimed it was the original recipe. Which apparently meant it contained pork. I've never had pork jerky but I'm guessing that pork and alligator pair well. Not that I tried any.

A sign at the freeway rest area warned motorists to look out for venomous snakes on their way to the bathroom. We don't have these things in California.

I had left the Gulf Coast beauty of Tampa and was headed in the general direction of Lake Tohopekaliga, toward

---

* Toyota's answer to the Kia Rio and Honda Fit.

the center of the state. The road wound through flat country-side, past trailer parks, the occasional farmhouse, churches, Walmart Supercenters, and lots of new and expensive-looking housing developments. The fancy homes had weird structures jutting out into their backyards, like they were wearing futur-istic backpacks. These turned out to be massive screened-in porches, large bug-proof living rooms that were evidence of sweltering nights spent hiding from biblical swarms of blood-thirsty mosquitos. Maybe what they mean when they say this is a God-fearing country is that they're afraid of mosquitos.

A billboard on the side of the road informed me that a fetus's heart starts beating eighteen days after conception. An interesting fact, but I'm not sure what they're selling.

Florida is called the Sunshine State for a reason, and in February the weather is seriously pleasant—not too hot and not too humid—which might explain why there are so many nudist resorts in the state. According to the AANR, there are at least a dozen nudist resorts in Florida and even more non-landed clubs. Some of them, like Sunsport Gar-dens in Loxahatchee and Cypress Cove in Kissimmee, are well-established resorts that draw snowbirds from all over, including a surprising number of Canadians and Europeans who spend the winter months living the sunshine-filled good life in their RVs or rented homes.

And then there's the Pasco County phenomenon. Just north of Tampa, on the Gulf Coast, Pasco County is the only place in the United States where you can find five clothing-optional resorts and a surprisingly large number of nudist communities in one place. Maybe it's some kind of skin-happy vortex or a harmonic convergence that makes people in this area want to take off their clothes, but whatever the reason, there are a whole lot of nudists in Pasco County. The communities have names like Caliente, which boasts of being the "Hottest Party on the Planet," and Paradise Lakes Resort, "Where you are free to be yourself," or you could "Be a 'Bare' in the Woods" at the Woods RV and Park Model Resort. Some, like the Oasis and Lake Como Resort, don't have slogans. They are more discreet.

A nudist community is a place where you can be naked twenty-four hours a day, seven days a week, three hundred sixty-five days a year. You can mow your lawn, pick up your mail, go to the clubhouse restaurant, play some tennis, drink a beer with your neighbors, and never have to put on any textiles. Imagine never having to do laundry again. *That should be a slogan*. If you somehow manage to get bored at your nudist community, you're only a short drive from the beach. But it's hard to imagine you would be bored. For example Caliente resort offers daily yoga, tennis, water aerobics, and something called "cardio pump" that might be an exercise class or, given the age of the residents, a CPR refresher, along with Spanish lessons, happy hour, karaoke, and much more. There are even real estate agents who specialize in selling homes and condominiums to nudists. Florida is second only to Alaska in miles of coastline, and with its warm, sunny weather it's basically a recipe for a clothing-free paradise. Except for the biblical swarms of bloodsucking insects.

But I hadn't come to the middle of Florida for a cardio pump or to go house hunting in the buff; I'd come because the small town of Kissimmee in central Florida is where I'd find the American Nudist Research Library.

I turned onto the aptly named Pleasant Hill Road and soon found myself pulling into the driveway of the Cypress

Cove Nudist Resort and Spa, considered by many to be one of the best nudist resorts on the East Coast, and home to the library.

Cypress Cove's motto is "Away from it all, but not far from anything," and it's no exaggeration. The resort is a short drive from Walt Disney World, Universal Studios, and Sea-World in Orlando. Like a lot of nudist resorts, this is a family place, a couples-only resort, and single male visitors need special permission to stay there. And, similar to my earlier experience at the Terra Cotta Inn, when I first called to get a reservation I was denied, but I appealed to Ted Hadley, the owner of Cypress Cove, and explained my desire to visit the library. Ted couldn't have been nicer or more understanding—he probably figured a writer who wanted to go to the library probably wasn't a dangerous swinger—and gave me permission to visit.

I followed a yellow line painted down the middle of Sun Cove Drive, past a crowded section of RVs, until I reached the main office at the intersection with Suntan Drive.

As I checked in, I learned that the resort was established in 1964, which meant it was celebrating its fiftieth anniversary, and I was given a special commemorative pin to prove it.

Steve, a friendly young man and a "third-generation nudist," gave me a tour of the resort in a golf cart. He drove the cart casually, bouncing over a grassy field to show me the large lake for kayaking, paddle boating, and swimming—although Steve warned me that the water might be "cold this time of year." There was an area with bungalows and mobile homes where many of the year-round residents lived, an RV park with full hookups, a campground, and the "Villa Hotel" rooms where I was staying. For fun I could go to the horseshoe pits, pickleball courts,* two swimming pools, a fitness area, a spa, and two different restaurants: Cheeks Bar and Grill, which was sandwiched between the pools, and the Lakeside Restaurant and Scuttlebutts Lounge.

There is a ramshackle charm to Cypress Cove. The mobile home residents show off their individuality by landscaping their small lots with spinning plastic gewgaws, flower beds, topiary, and exotic plants; there are bird feeders, antique-looking streetlamps, oversize nude statues, and the occasional garden gnome. Most of the residents seem to drive golf carts— I even saw one that was designed to look like a Mercedes-Benz—and at dinnertime, you have to pass through a gauntlet of the electric buggies as you walk toward the restaurant. The lake and surrounding woods are beautiful and the residential area is compact, so that you get the sense that there is a lot going on, even if it's mostly people sunning themselves or stretching out in a hammock with a book.

My room had been recently remodeled and, except for the naked Australians drinking beer at the picnic table directly outside the front window, looked like a stylish suite you might find at a hip boutique motel in San Francisco.

The library is normally closed on Mondays, and naturally the only day I could be there was a Monday, but I had arranged a special visit with Bob Proctor, one of the volunteer

---

* The International Federation of Pickleball describes the sport as "a simple paddle game played using a special perforated, slow-moving ball over a tennis-type net on a badminton-sized court."

librarians who runs the place. I told him I'd be easy to spot: "I'll be the guy wearing clothes."

The library is housed in a bungalow right next to one of the swimming pools. I was standing there trying not to feel too ridiculous in my khaki pants and T-shirt when Bob and another library volunteer named Jim pulled up in a golf cart. Bob was wearing only a T-shirt, and, except for his hearing aids and some faded tattoos, Jim was completely naked. Was I expecting the librarians at the American Nudist Research Library to be wearing clothes?

Not really.

Although the library isn't that big, the collection is impressive. There are nudist magazines from France like *Solaire Universelle de Nudisme* from the 1950s, an extensive collection of magazines from the *Freikörperkultur* in Germany, a few in Spanish, and then almost every nudist publication in English from the 1930s to present day, from classics like *Sunshine & Health*, *American Sunbather*, *Health & Efficiency*, *Sundial*, and *Suntan* to more eclectic magazines like the Australian magazine *Tan*, *New Zealand Naturist*, *Jaybird Safari*, and *Nudest*, the magazine for Dutch smoothies.* Most of the magazines had been collected and hardbound by year, although more recent publications were stored in loose cardboard racks.

Looking through the old magazines, I was struck by the articles they published. A quick read of the table of contents of, say, *Sunshine & Health* from March 1945 and you'll find articles on the exact same subjects you might find in a current edition of *N* or any other contemporary nudist publication.

---

* See the chapter "Trends in Genital Topiary" for a closer look at the smoothie phenomenon.

There was "Why I Am a Nudist (Part Two)," "Let's Eat Health-fully and Like It!," "Analysis of the Nature of Obscenity," and "Is Going Naked a Sin?"

It seems that when it comes to the idea of men and women taking their clothes off and socializing, society still has the same old hang-ups.

One of my favorite discoveries was the reader-submitted photos published in *Health & Efficiency* in the 1940s. They were typically pictures of naked young women in natural settings, studying flowers, walking in the woods, or gazing off into the middle distance by the seaside. The photographs were given captions like "Tribute to Grace," "After the Bathe," and "The Lily Pool."

The library contains hundreds of old photographs of nudists, some dating back to Sky Farm in 1932 and the origi-nal American League for Physical Culture nudist camp in 1930. There's also a collection of nonfiction titles about nud-ism and a smaller section of fictional titles with nudist themes.

As I browsed through the collection, Bob sat on a towel and worked on his laptop. He's got a big smile and a sweet demeanor, and with his graying beard and glasses he looks like a friendly history professor. Bob's a former pilot who now grows papayas in his garden, teaches Apple computer classes to his fellow retirees, and, when he's not volunteering in the library or enjoying nude recreation, maintains a collection of more than one thousand beer bottles and cans and offers seventy different recipes for Jell-O shots on his webpage.

Although Bob had only been living in Cypress Cove for "six or seven years," Jim was an old-timer. He'd been com-ing since 1964 and was somewhat notorious for, as he said, "bringing a different girl every time." Jim is tan and trim and has a full head of windswept hair that makes him look like one of the original members of the Beach Boys. With his bangs, tattoos, and mischievous grin, I'm not surprised the ladies like him. Back in the day, Jim and his girlfriend wanted to live in Cypress Cove full time, but the owner wouldn't let them until they were married. Like I said, it's a family place.

By 1984, Jim was living here full time.

The library opened in 1979 and then expanded in 1996. A large chunk of the room is taken up by a state-of-the-art digitization device. Volunteers perform the tedious task of scanning every page of every magazine in the collection. It's an ambitious project and they still have a long way to go, but the goal is that someday every piece of nudist history will be available online for scholars and historians, even amateur ones like myself.

Knowing that I was traveling alone and being, as I said, a very nice person, Bob invited me to join him and his wife and some of their friends for dinner at the Lakeside Restaurant.

"I hate to see people eating alone," he said.

I quickly agreed.

The Lakeside Restaurant and Scuttlebutts Lounge is, as you might expect, right next to the lake. The interior is large, with tables on two levels surrounding a dance floor in a wide U shape. There is some kind of entertainment every night and a small stage acts as the focal point for the dining room. The entertainment that evening was a singer doing karaoke versions of "hits from the '50s and '60s."

I joined Bob and his wife, Mitzi, at the table along with several of their friends. There was a couple, snowbirds down from "a little town just outside Toronto"—when I said, "I really like Toronto," the snowbirds looked at me as if I'd just announced that I was freshly released from an insane asylum—and at the far end of the table, another couple, a man whose name I didn't catch and his wife, a tan woman with a quick laugh who went by the nickname "Ro." I was told that she knew everything about everyone at the resort.

The Canadian husband flagged down the waiter and ordered a pitcher of beer. His wife looked at the waiter and said, "And don't forget my dildo." This, I realized, might become a unique dining experience.

Suffice to say that everyone at the table except me was older than sixty-five, but they were tan and happy and ready to party. They were also, I should clarify, clothed at dinner. When the pitcher of beer arrived, I was shown how the dildo—really it was more like a plastic cylinder that had been frozen—could be inserted into the pitcher to keep the beer cold. Ingenious, practical, and potentially kinky.

Bob and Mitzi both recommended the eggplant rollatini, so I ordered that and a Goose Island beer.

As I sipped my beer, the evening's entertainment began. The singer was a portly man in, I'm guessing, his early thirties, wearing saggy black pants and a black shirt. Ro looked at the stage and clapped her hands together. She turned to the snowbirds and said, "Look at how much weight he's lost!" Which made me wonder just how big he was before this miraculous weight loss. A prerecorded band started playing. The singer picked up the microphone, scrunched up his face in a rictus of well-rehearsed emotion, and began to croon.

I wasn't surprised to hear the hits of Elvis Presley, Tab Hunter, and Sam Cooke. I wasn't surprised to see dozens of couples taking a spin on the dance floor. What surprised me was that most of the men weren't wearing pants.

They weren't naked, exactly. They wore Hawaiian shirts and sandals—or, for a few of the fashion forward, shoes and socks—but their genitals were free to swing in the breeze. The women were not so free with their bodies. They wore dresses or blouses and shorts; there wasn't even much cleavage on display. I ate my rollatini and drank my beer, enjoying watching the dancers as they swayed and twirled to passable versions of the Everly Brothers' "Cathy's Clown" and Del Shannon's "Runaway," the men enjoying their anti-textile freedom from the waist down, their penises swinging to the beat like fleshy metronomes.

Free Beaches

In the American Nudist Research Library there's a small wooden sculpture of the German philosopher, economist, and revolutionary socialist Karl Marx. Although there is no historical or anecdotal evidence I can find that Marx was a nudist, he is depicted standing naked, his beard wild and unkempt, his belly jutting out over his penis. He's holding a book in one hand, the other raised in a revolutionary fist. Naked Karl Marx looks like he means business.

A small plaque attached to the base reads: DONATED BY LEE BAXANDALL.

Lee Baxandall was a writer whose work ranged from translating plays by Bertolt Brecht to editing a collection of writings by Wilhelm Reich and the anthologies *Marx and Engels on Literature and Art* and *Radical Perspectives in the Arts*.[63] His writing appeared in magazines and periodicals as diverse as the *Nation, Partisan Review, Liberation, Journal of Aesthetics and Art Criticism*, and the *New York Times*. Ironically, despite his highbrow preoccupation with the intersection of the arts and dialectical materialism, his biggest-selling book is *Lee Baxandall's World Guide to Nude Beaches and Recreation*.

How does a socialist become a nudist? Imagine if Fidel Castro had suddenly turned the whole revolution thing on its head and changed Cuba into a clothing-optional paradise. Actually it's not hard to imagine that there would still be some kind of embargo, what with American culture's fear of naked people.

Baxandall was born in Oshkosh, Wisconsin, in 1935. His childhood seems normal enough, but as he grew older he became "bored and alienated by Oshkosh."[64] He was an Eagle Scout, a member of the high school debate team, and class president, which is pretty much the résumé of your average all-American go-getter, but it was the Scouts that introduced him to skinny-dipping, which, honestly, is something I didn't know the Boy Scouts did. I can't imagine that there's a merit badge for nudity. But if there were, what would it look like?

Baxandall attended college at the University of Wisconsin at Madison, earning a BA in 1957 and his MA a year later, and appears to have gotten into all the trouble that a young, rebellious, and highly intelligent young man might get into. He fell in with a radical crowd; cowrote and directed an antimilitarism play,* cofounded a left-wing journal called *Studies on the Left*, and "smoked unusual cigarettes."

In New York, Baxandall was a part of the intellectual bohemian lifestyle, editing books on sex and left-wing politics, writing plays and articles, meeting Che Guevara in Cuba, and protesting against the Vietnam War. To escape the heat of the city, he and his family—his second wife, Roz, and his son, Phineas—spent their summers on Cape

---

* *The Boy Scouts in Cuba*, cowritten with Marshall Brickman and Danny Kalb.

Cod in Massachusetts, skinny-dipping at the nude beaches at Long Neck and Brush Hollow.

It's easy to imagine Baxandall settling into a job as a theater critic or tenured college professor, but career trajectories don't always go smoothly. When local authorities on Cape Cod decided to close the beaches to skinny-dipping, Baxandall suddenly found a cause that was close to his Boy Scout heart.

As nudist historian Cec Cinder writes, "Nude sunbathing and swimming in the ocean seemed to him a heritage from, and extension of, his fondly-remembered, idyllic, Wisconsin boyhood."[65]

The neosocialist former Eagle Scout channeled his revolutionary zeal into something more concrete than liberation theory; he wanted to skinny-dip, and to continue to do that, he'd have to fight the powers that be.

Baxandall formed the Free the Free Beach Committee, collected signatures for a petition, and wrote letters to the editor, and when all of these efforts failed to persuade local officials, he had the American Civil Liberties Union of Massachusetts file a lawsuit.

He lost.

I'm not sure it's that unusual for a socialist activist to become a naturist activist. If you think about it, Marx's critique of capitalism is not so different from the early naturist's desire to live naked and free from the demands of bourgeois society, to take control of the means of production. They may not be the same thing, but they are connected by a similar impulse for a better life removed from the stresses of capitalism and the conformity demanded by consumer culture.

Like many of the nudist movements throughout history, there was a serendipitous synchronicity unfolding among nudists in the late 1960s and early 1970s, only this time it was in the United States. At the same time Baxandall was fighting to "Free the Free Beaches" in Massachusetts, Bay Area nudists in California were forming the Committee for Free Beaches. Their goal was to "establish a number of beach sites along the Pacific Coast that will be free from irrational restrictions." Or as they declared so eloquently, "Our point of view is that the most logical and wholesome way to enjoy swimming and sunbathing is in the nude."[66] By 1967 they had turned San Gregorio beach, south of San Francisco, into an informal nude beach just by showing up in numbers and enjoying themselves.

It's interesting to note that Baxandall and the Free Beachers weren't members of the American Sunbathing Association (later the AANR) or any organized nudist group; these were freelancers, people who just liked to frolic on the beach without any official affiliation to anything other than surf, sun, and textile-free fun. I'm guessing that most of the participants were less radical socialists and more just young people imbued with the groovy spirit of the times.

The 1970s brought on acts of civil disobedience by nudists, most notably Chad Merrill Smith's arrest for lying naked on a beach near San Diego. Smith was violating section 314 of the California Penal Code: "Every person who willfully and lewdly, either 1. Exposes his person, or private parts thereof, in any public place, or in any place where there are present other persons to be offended or annoyed thereby."[67]

Smith was found guilty, fined $100, and put on probation. But he soon discovered that this conviction would force him to "register as a sex offender pursuant to Penal Code section 290." Smith didn't think he was a sex offender; he hadn't been lewd, he didn't draw attention to his nakedness, and he didn't have an erection. So he appealed, eventually taking the case to the California Supreme Court, where, on June 13, 1972, he won.

In an opinion that expressed a unanimous decision by the California Supreme Court, Justice Stanley Mosk wrote, "By parity of reasoning, we cannot attribute to the Legislature a belief that persons found to be sunbathing in the nude on an isolated beach 'require constant police surveillance' to prevent them from committing such 'crimes against society' in the future. Lacking that belief, the Legislature could not reasonably have intended that section 314, subdivision 1, apply to the conduct here in issue."

The court decided that being naked didn't constitute lewdness; if you wanted to be lewd, you had to make an effort.

It was a crucial decision for skinny-dippers and brought more people to the beach, which, paradoxically given Smith's acquittal, brought more police to the beach to write citations for indecent exposure. In fact the decision brought a negative backlash from law enforcement and local authorities, and in Malibu, Santa Barbara, and farther up the coast, traditionally informal nude beaches were faced with closure.

Nudists in California realized that, despite the supreme court ruling, they needed to organize to protect their right to swim in the buff, so in 1973 a group of like-minded individuals created BeachFront USA with Cec Cinder as acting president.

One of the first battles for the Free Beachers was over the Los Angeles City Council's decision to close Venice Beach to nude swimmers. As in most beach closures in the United States, the city council was pressured by a combination of the moneyed interests of real estate developers; the outrage from concerned citizens and religious figures like Cardinal Timothy Manning, the archbishop of the Los Angeles Roman Catholic Archdiocese; LAPD chief of police Ed Davis's concerns about public morality; and vote-pandering by members of the council itself. Church groups organized a letter-writing campaign to put pressure on local politicians and the public debate grew contentious. In a letter to the *Los Angeles Times* on August 20, 1975, Chief Davis announced he was canceling his subscription to the paper because "You are the Paul Revere of the oncoming avalanche of libertine behavior."[68] Which, considering he was complaining about the *Times'* "constantly attempting to condition us to a dramatic new set of moral values," including "strong editorial support of homosexuality, marijuana and many, many other forms of behavior recently socially proscribed in our country," shows a strange understanding of what Paul Revere was actually up to.

The city didn't even consider a compromise that would have made a small section of Venice Beach clothing optional. Not long after that, the county board of supervisors followed and nudity in Los Angeles was banned, including "any portion of the breast at or below the upper edge of the areola thereof of any female person." Which made openly breast-feeding babies a misdemeanor.

Over the years there have been dozens and dozens of battles fought for the right to skinny-dip on an American beach. The popular Mazo Beach on the Wisconsin River, just northwest of Madison, was the only legal nude beach in that state and was closed to nude recreation on weekdays by the Wisconsin Department of Natural Resources in March 2013. That means you can still be nude on the weekends, although that too appears under threat. The shutdown was due to complaints of drug use and sexual activity at the beach and in the nearby forest, which is kind of ironic, as nudists also complained about drug use and sexual activity at the beach and in the nearby forest.

Another example of encroachment on nude beaches happened just north of Santa Cruz, California, in 2010 when park rangers put up signs at the traditionally clothing-optional Bonny Doon Beach saying NUDITY IN THE STATE PARK SYSTEM IS PROHIBITED. Which doesn't mean local nudists put their clothes on. As Rich Pasco of the Bay Area Naturists said, "A fifty-year tradition cannot be extinguished by a simple sign."[69]

And in 2013, Lighthouse Beach on Fire Island in New York was closed to nude swimmers after having been an unofficial clothing-optional beach for decades.

Most of the time, the nudists ended up on the losing side, but that's not always the case. There are some success stories.

When the Travel Channel did a roundup of the world's best nude beaches, Haulover Beach in Miami was ranked alongside nude beaches in Brazil, Crete, Australia, and Jamaica as the world's best. But, for the most part, those other beaches are off the beaten path, in isolated areas. What makes Haulover Beach unique is that it is in an urban park, a public clothing-optional beach that was approved by local authorities in 1991 and is administered by the Miami-Dade County Parks, Recreation and Open Spaces Department. According to the Lifeguard Ocean Rescue Service the beach attracts approximately 1.4 million visitors annually.

I wanted to see this fabled stretch of sand, so I booked a flight to Miami.

I have to admit that I'd never really been to Miami. I usually end up changing planes there to get to the Dominican Republic or Nassau or some place like that and I was curious about the city. I wondered if a typical Miami resident would go to Haulover Beach or if they even knew about Haulover. So I arranged to meet the journalist and longtime Miami resident Juan Carlos Pérez-Duthie for lunch at Versailles, a restaurant that calls itself "The World's Most Famous Cuban Restaurant." Famous or not, it's probably the biggest Cuban restaurant in the United States and it is a rite of passage for presidential candidates from both parties to come here and meet with Miami's influential Cuban community. The dining room is massive and airy, with plush green curtains and ornate mirrors that give the place a Las Vegas vibe. Yet the mosaic tile floors and the tables and chairs are pretty much the same as you'd find in any diner anywhere in America. All of which lends the restaurant a funky charm. I instantly liked the place.

Juan Carlos is lean and lanky. With a handsome face framed by meticulously trimmed facial hair and red rectangular glasses, he looks like a tropical hipster intellectual, which I suppose is exactly what he is. Today he looks slightly sunburned, as befits someone of Puerto Rican–Scottish descent. Perhaps we are related.

I ordered a Midnight Sandwich,* some mashed fried plantains—because I love plantains—and a guanabana shake while Juan Carlos ate the oddly named *vaca frita de pollo*, or "cow fried chicken," and recounted his early days visiting Haulover Beach.

---

* Traditionally called a *media noche,* the sandwich consists of a sweet Cuban roll with ham, roast pork, Swiss cheese, mustard, and pickles.

"A good friend of mine used to live nearby, so it was convenient for us to go. I remember Haulover had two sections, one straight, one gay, divided only by a lifeguard's booth. People walked back and forth."

I wondered if it was a cruising place. He nodded. "People were checking each other out, but no more than on a regular beach where you're supposed to keep your pants on."

Remembering it, Juan Carlos laughed. "But after the sun set and the lifeguards and the families left"—he raised an eyebrow—"things could get frisky in the water."

"What was the straight side like?"

"On the straight side . . . the first thing that struck me was the number of families and the elderly people naked, going into the water, hanging out while speaking different languages, sunbathing. Many burned to a crisp."

He shook his head as he said it, as if the biggest tragedy of coming to the tropics was getting an overdose of sunshine and burning your skin.

As I ate my sandwich I became alarmed that they had forgotten the pickle and for me, someone who likes pickled vegetables of all kinds, the pickle in a *media noche* is the best part, but before I could ask the waitress, Juan Carlos continued. "On the gay side . . . strangely, those with the best bodies did not take their clothes off. They wore skimpy briefs."

"Were you a nudist or were you going for the gay scene?"

"I usually kept my bathing suit on, though swimming au naturel felt really good. Better for me was talking to the people gathered there."

Haulover Beach has a reputation for being a friendly, sociable place. I watched as Juan Carlos speared a plantain and popped it in his mouth.

"Like two middle-aged men who had been dancers at Cuba's famous Tropicana club. And they had pictures to prove it. They visited every week, always bringing a sun umbrella, chairs, and coolers filled with refreshments. They also came equipped with big pots holding food. More surprising to me than seeing them naked was the amount of food that they brought . . . a big chunk of roasted pork, black beans and rice, yucca, bread. They always offered us something." He took a sip of his Coca-Cola and then laughed. "Once they brought a bucket of Kentucky Fried Chicken. We may have had a few thighs."

After a *cortadito*, Juan Carlos and I said good-bye, and I headed off to find this urban oasis of nudity and handsome Cuban men with pots of roast pork.

Whenever I think of the words "Miami Beach" my brain almost always follows it up with the "chicks with dicks" line from the Cornershop song "Lessons Learned from *Rocky I* to *Rocky III.*" * But I didn't notice any signs of overt transvestite fetishism as I drove up Collins Avenue and made my way past the art deco hotels and hip and happening hot spots that give way to a charming small-town main street mixed with surreal canyons of ritzy high-rise condominiums. I motored through North Shore and Surfside, until I crossed over a bridge and found myself turning left into the parking lot at Haulover Beach Park.

Haulover Beach is one and a half miles long but only the final quarter mile is designated as clothing optional. I parked in the parking lot and walked through a tunnel under the road toward the beach.

* From the 2002 album *Handcream for a Generation*.

The beach was hidden behind a tall hedge of scrubby sea grape with entry paths cut every thirty or forty yards. The sea grape acts as a screen between the city, the busy street that runs alongside the park, and the relative tranquillity of the beach itself. I found a cut in the hedge and walked out onto the beach. I don't want to oversell it, but the beach is beautiful. Classic postcard pretty. Coarse white sand that appears to be made out of trillions of tiny broken seashells stretches out to turquoise-colored water that shifts to a deeper blue green before it hits the horizon and a deeper blue, the blue of the sky, takes over. Look to the right and the high-rises of Bal Harbour and North Shore smoosh together like they're in a crowded elevator. Turn to the left and there are even more high-rise apartments and hotels. You can feel the money-grubbing encroachment of real estate developers pressing in on the park like the sharks that I'm guessing aren't far offshore. That the city of Miami chose to save this pristine urban beach from development is nothing short of a minor miracle in this day and age.

I crunched along the sand until I reached a sign warning me that BEYOND THIS POINT YOU MAY ENCOUNTER NUDE BATH-ERS. I did encounter a few, but they weren't bathing. Mostly people were sitting under umbrellas enjoying the breeze. A family was having a picnic. Kids were kicking a soccer ball around. An old man stood naked in ankle-deep water looking out at the horizon.

I sat down in the shade of the lifeguard station—I couldn't see any divide between gay and straight but I wasn't there to take sides. The air was cool and smelled fresh, the sun was warm, and that combined with the sound of the surf put me into a kind of meditative trance. No wonder people come to Florida and take off their clothes. No wonder they never want to leave. They've been hypnotized by the sheer hedonistic pleasure of being here. When the air and sun and sea feel this good, why wouldn't you want to experience it with every inch of skin you've got? And why should Miami residents have to drive hundreds of miles or hike into some out-of-the-way spot just so they can take off their clothes and swim?

...

Equally beautiful, but on the opposite end of the spectrum in terms of accessibility, is Black's Beach near San Diego, California.

On May 31, 1979, Russell Cahill, the director of the California Department of Parks and Recreation, wrote a memorandum that stated that the official policy of the department would be that "enforcement of nude sunbathing regulations within the State Park System shall be made only upon the complaint of a private citizen" and even then "citations or arrests shall be made only after attempts are made to elicit voluntary compliance with the regulations." This memorandum made Black's Beach, in the Torrey Pines State Park just north of San Diego, one of the first quasi-legal nude beaches in the country. It's a law similar to Amsterdam's tolerance for cannabis. It's not exactly legal, but it's not necessarily illegal either. It all just depends on the situation.

I wanted to visit Black's Beach, so I grabbed a beach towel and hit the road.

Black's Beach isn't easy to get to. I tuned my GPS to the coordinates provided on the website of the Black's Beach Bares, a volunteer organization that promotes clothing-optional recreation on the beach, and, a few mind-numbing hours of freeway driving later, made my way past the campus of the University of California at San Diego to the Torrey Pines Gliderport at the top of a three-hundred-foot cliff overlooking the Pacific Ocean.

A gliderport is just what you think it is. A strong breeze blows in from the ocean and up the cliff face, creating the lift that keeps paragliders from making human-shaped craters on the beach below. I guess it's as good a place as any to jump off a cliff, and there were numerous people hurtling themselves into space with billowy parachute-wing contraptions strapped to their bodies. The gliderport isn't fancy, but it does house a snack bar, a gift shop, and an office with—I'm guessing here—body bags and tools for scraping people off the rocks below. There are windsocks and wind speed gauges arrayed to help the "pilots" figure out if it's safe to jump off the cliff. And a cluster of Porta Pottis stood at the ready in case the thought of plummeting to your death caused any would-be pilots an unexpected movement of the bowels.

The trail to the beach is posted with several warning signs. Unlike Haulover Beach where the signs warn you that you might encounter nude sunbathers beyond this point, these signs warn that the cliff is unstable and that you shouldn't get close to the edge. The warning is no joke: in 2010 a fifty-seven-year-old man leaned against the base of the cliff to take off his shoes and was killed by falling rocks.

The path to the beach, which *Surfer* magazine accurately calls a "danger sign–spiked goat trail," is steep and consists of a series of irregular and rough-hewn steps that switch back and forth at random intervals as you descend the crumbling cliff. As I negotiated the slippery sand and loose gravel on my descent, I couldn't help but notice that the people passing me on their way up were panting, sweating, and not looking all that happy about what amounts to a thirty-two-story trudge back to the top. Not that I blamed them. Just last year a friend of mine, a man who seemed to be in peak condition, had a heart attack climbing up this trail.

I made it to the bottom and walked out onto a seriously beautiful beach.

Black's Beach is big and open, almost two miles of soft sand, and that Saturday afternoon was one of those triumphant days that make California the envy of the world. The sky was blue, golden sunlight reflected off the waves, a fresh breeze was blowing in off the ocean; there were surfers riding waves in the distance, paragliders drifting along the cliffs above, and right there on the beach, three naked women—the lithe and blond California girls celebrated in song—doing cartwheels on the sand.

It was awesome.

I started walking up the beach, reconnoitering, looking for a suitable spot to lay my towel. Unlike the anxiety I sometimes felt at nudist resorts, I was happy to be here. It was simply too pretty to be nervous about being naked.

Even though there were a lot of people at the beach, it was big enough that it didn't feel crowded. I stopped to watch as a young man, wearing only dreadlocks, swirled an unlit fire torch around his head like a drunk majorette in a Fourth of July parade. He was lucky that it wasn't lit because I don't think he'd have any hair left if it had been. Next to him, his topless girlfriend practiced her hooping routine. They both seemed serious, focused on what they were doing, as if they'd tried to join the circus but had been rejected because they lacked the requisite circusing skills and were desperately working on their act.

There were naked people being active everywhere I looked, swimming in the ocean, tossing a Frisbee, throwing footballs; there was even a nude volleyball game in progress. Of course there were a few older nudists sitting under umbrellas or lying on towels, but mostly it was all very young and Naktiv. Not only were the majority of the naked people younger, but it was a mixed-race crowd, the typical melting pot you'd find in any public space in California. Perhaps Black's Beach skews that way because it's just not that easy, or that safe, to get here.

I sat on a towel, stripped down, and began applying layers of spray-on sunblock. While I might be getting more comfortable with being naked in public, I am still terrified of getting sunburned. Fully protected from solar radiation, I walked out into the surf. As the frigid water slammed against my naked body, I thought of an episode of the television show *Seinfeld*. It's the one where Jerry's buddy George Costanza tries to explain to his girlfriend that his penis looks small because he'd just been swimming. Take a dunk in the freezing Pacific and, trust me, if you have a penis, you will have empathy for George.

I sat back on my towel and let the sun warm my body. It was then that I noticed something unusual. Unlike nudist resorts with their rules about public displays of affection and sexual activity, there didn't seem to be any such restriction on Black's Beach. There were couples making out on the sand, embracing in the surf, flirting along the shore; naked people were cavorting everywhere I looked. A man with a fantastic Mohawk and pharaonic goatee combo lay on a blanket with his girlfriend and looked to be practicing sexual positions. They weren't actually having sexual intercourse, not in the way a Kinsey researcher might define it, but, seriously, do you have to rehearse doing it doggie style on the beach?

There was also a decent amount of gay cruising, buff young men walking back and forth on the beach chatting with other buff young men who were walking back and forth on the beach. Instead of feeling uncomfortable witnessing naked people express themselves in a sexual way, I felt relief. I find the ultrarestrained nonsexual social nude interactions of people at nudist resorts to be somewhat unnerving.

Which is not to say that it's always harmless romantic fun. The Black's Beach Bares website has posted warnings about a few weirdos who frequent the area. According to the website, the modus operandi of the creepy is to set their towel near a young couple and pretend to read a book. What the French would call a *voyeur*. There are also, apparently, some exhibitionists who just like to walk around and let people see them in all their naked resplendence. These things seem like a kind of normal level of creepiness, if there is such a thing as a normal level of creepiness, but the website singled out one man in particular, a "Robert Goulet look-alike," who apparently "has some sort of penile implant that he pumps up." He then waggles his faux boner while standing in the surf. And, lucky me, he was there on Saturday, flailing his pumped-up dick in the air. Although to be honest, he looks more like Elliott Gould.

But ultimately, the beach was refreshing. The lack of nudist dogma, the freedom to actually kiss your wife or husband or girlfriend or boyfriend, the idea that a couple could make out or a weird dude could pump up his dick, made it seem human. No wonder Baxandall and his Free Beach comrades were so passionate about setting sections of beaches aside for nude recreation.

Baxandall returned to Oshkosh to run his family's printing business and used it as the base for his continued activism. In 1980 he published *Lee Baxandall's World Guide to Nude Beaches and Recreation* and he founded the Naturist Society (TNS), an organization that welcomes anyone interested in preserving nude recreation in the United States. For years the AANR had been the sole organized voice for nudists. Baxandall saw TNS as an antidote to AANR's private club mentality and its conservative politics. He published a magazine with the terrible name *Clothed with the Sun*, later renaming it *Nude & Natural.* *

Baxandall created an organization that was inclusive of all sexual orientations, races, and religions. Mark Storey, a member of TNS, summed it up: "In the Naturist Society they tend to be left-leaning. Lee wasn't a full-blown Marxist, but he had that kind of leaning. It was a grassroots, change-the-world kind of thing."

One way of changing the world is to get people to change their perception of their own bodies. In other words, to accept themselves as they really are. In 1997 TNS offered up this definition of naturism: "A way of living in greater fidelity to nature, with a norm of full nudity in social life, the genitals included, when possible and appropriate. We aim to enhance

---

* It's now just called *N.*

acceptance and respect for one's self, other persons, and the biosphere."

TNS continues this riff in its official literature: "The Naturist Society views clothing-optional recreation as essential to body acceptance. Through clothing-optional recreation, participants, be they individuals, couples or families, learn to appreciate the diversity of body types and gain a better understanding and acceptance of their own bodies."

You start accepting diversity of body types, you'll start accepting diversity of races and sexual orientation, and soon you're breaking the conformist mold that corporate capitalism tries to put you in. Baxandall had a lot in common with the French anarchist Émile Armand; they both believed you could change the world by taking off your clothes.

Baxandall decided that the naturists couldn't just sit back and wait until beaches got closed, they needed to be proactive, they needed to talk to lawmakers and get some public land set aside for nude recreation. To that end, he founded a spin-off of TNS, a nonprofit, all-volunteer political action organization called the Naturist Action Committee (NAC).

That the NAC can boast a 90 percent success rate against anti-nudity ordinances around the country is kind of astounding. Especially given its adversaries.

Take, for example, a case in Wharton County, Texas. In December 2003, the county commissioners considered a ban on strip clubs and other types of "sexually oriented businesses." To craft these laws, local governments often turn to templates provided to them by right-wing Christian groups like the Community Defense Council* and the

* Formerly called the National Family Legal Foundation.

Alliance Defending Freedom.* In the Wharton County case, lawmakers would have made it illegal for any business to allow "activities between male and female persons and/or persons of the same sex when one or more of the persons is totally nude, semi-nude or in a state of nudity." Which is pretty much exactly what nudists do at nudist resorts.

The NAC intervened and convinced the county commissioners to revise the bill, rewording it to protect the interests of naturists.

In 2002, in Wilmington, Vermont, a local real estate developer—aren't they always the bad guys in these stories?—was planning to build a subdivision of luxury homes adjacent to the Harriman Reservoir. For some reason the developer didn't believe that wealthy retirees would want to share the expensive lakefront with the skinny-dippers who had traditionally used the reservoir. Initially the developer put an anti-nudity ordinance on the ballot and, despite efforts by the NAC, won. But as skinny-dippers were cited—and learned that citations came with a yearlong ban—locals became disgruntled. The NAC mounted an effective grassroots campaign and got the ban rescinded.

These are small victories, to be sure, but even if you aren't a skinny-dipper I think it's reasonable to allow others to do

---

* A self-described "servant ministry building an alliance to keep the door open for the spread of the Gospel by transforming the legal system." This is the same group that fought for Arizona's odious SB 1062, a bill described as "protecting religious freedom" when in actuality it would have allowed people to discriminate against homosexuals and minorities and then hide behind "religious freedom." Fortunately the governor of Arizona vetoed the bill before it could become law. The Alliance Defending Freedom's senior counsel, Doug Napier, said, "Freedom loses when fear overwhelms facts and a good bill is vetoed. Today's veto enables the foes of faith to more easily suppress the freedom of the people of Arizona." Which is, you don't need me to tell you, utter hogwash.

it, not just because it's the right thing to do, but because of equal protection under the law, the right to life, liberty, and the pursuit of happiness, you know, stuff like that. That's the battle Lee Baxandall was fighting. Sadly, Baxandall suffered from Parkinson's disease and was forced to retire in 2002. He was subsequently elected to the American Nudist Hall of Fame in 2004,[70] and he died in 2008.

In an interview Baxandall said, "A country that lacks nude beaches is not a civilized country."[71] And that rings true to me. Just look at Europe, the birthplace of Western civilization, where every beach is top-free and nude beaches dot the coastline. Skinny-dipping is pretty much the norm in the Greek islands, while Spain, France, Italy, and most other countries have official and unofficial beaches where nudism is permitted. There's even a nude beach called Ursetvika* in Norway that's inside the arctic circle.

But read the Naturist Society's current list of official nude beaches in the United States and you'll find less than ten. That's because the U.S. Parks Department and local officials are still playing Whac-A-Mole with skinny-dippers. Religious groups lump nudists in with pedophiles and sex offenders, developers build condominiums next to nude beaches and see them as threats to their investment, and prudes and moralists apply political pressure to ban nudism. Even a site as secluded and difficult to get to as Black's Beach comes under attack from conservatives from time to time. But then this kind of fundamental fear of people who prefer not to wear clothes has been plaguing nudists since Charles Crawford and the Fellowship of the Naked Trust first dropped trou in 1891.

* Near Saltfjorden, about an hour's drive east of Bodø.

The Dark Secrets
of Lisa Lutz

When I first started writing this book I asked some of my friends if they'd ever been to a nudist club or a nude beach, or if they'd had any kind of nonsexual social nude experience. A few admitted that they had gone to a nude beach or were naked at Burning Man—one of my friends and his wife went to a nude beach as a rehearsal for Burning Man—but except for one female friend, who it turns out is a bit of a nudist, most people had either no experience of social nudism or had tried it once and never did it again. I heard a lot of stories about teenage skinny-dipping in lakes and quarries and backyard pools, and a few tales of going topless at rock festivals. My favorite story was from a female friend who was taken to a nudist club on a second date. Which is one way to break the ice. But for the most part, people tried some version of nudity and then put their clothes back on and kept them on. However, there was one friend who had a story.

Lisa Lutz is the author of six novels in the Spellman series, beginning with *The Spellman Files* and ending with

The Last Word. She's also cowritten the novel *Heads You Lose,* the children's picture book *How to Negotiate Everything,* and *Isabel Spellman's Guide to Etiquette: What Is Wrong with You People.* She is a very talented and funny writer and, as it turns out, has harbored a dark secret from her childhood.

She lives in the country in New York and I live in Los Angeles, so we sat down at our laptops and Skyped about her past.

"All right. So tell me, was this some sort of child abuse or something? What happened?"

"Right." Lisa heaved a sigh. "Well, I don't . . . Okay . . . my mom married her second husband when I was about six and they got really into the seventies. I mean they were just fully entrenched in it."

For me, personally, the seventies was about the birth of punk rock, the Sex Pistols and Talking Heads, and the rise of New German Cinema and filmmakers like Werner Herzog, Rainer Werner Fassbinder, and Wim Wenders, all of which were major obsessions of my late teens and early twenties. But I do remember my father, in particular, trying to be part of some kind of hip and happening seventies scene. He would eat fondue and drink sweet Portuguese wine while sitting on a flokati rug with his girlfriend. She wore striped bell-bottom pants and those peasant blouses that were so popular at the time. They would listen to James Taylor and Creedence Clearwater Revival records. Sometimes they would drive downtown in his exotic sports car to meet their friends. Maybe they went to a disco. It wouldn't surprise me.

I wondered if Lisa had experienced a similar childhood.

"My mom wanted to disco dance, and they'd have friends over and then they'd bring an instructor over. So they had disco dance lessons in our house, which was, to me . . ." She paused before continuing. "I was that kid that was always embarrassed of everything and everyone around me. And so this was just the height of embarrassment. I remember we weren't allowed to watch them but we could hear the music and hear the instruction."

"That does sound embarrassing."

"There's a lot of things. I'm not saying they did, but my parents could have had key parties for all I know with the way they were. They just were into it."

"And nudity was part of that?"

"My mom was naked a lot around the house. And then after a while my stepdad was naked a lot. And they would . . . they would try to talk to me about how you're supposed to be comfortable with your body. And I remember learning the basics of sex at a freakishly young age as well."

I asked her to clarify what, exactly, a freakishly young age is.

"Like freakish, I mean . . . And this wasn't—my parents didn't do it. There was some book that was like a sex book, *Where Did I Come From?* I remember my mom's friend reading it to me—and I couldn't have been more than four—and being mortified. But the thing is, I remember that. That is really one of my first memories ever in life. And so I was just . . ."

Her voice trailed off as she collected her thoughts.

". . . I think that they were trying really hard to be this new modern type. And so they were naked in the house."

"That's it? They were indoor nudists?"

Lisa groaned. "They had these friends who lived in the Hollywood Hills. A guy named Harvey and his wife and they had a swimming pool. So my sister and my stepbrother and I would go over there and we all swam naked."

"Were you a teenager by this point?"

"None of this went past, I would say, age nine. So that was the first time of seeing other people naked. It was the first time I saw fake boobs. And I didn't understand that they were fake. I just thought, 'Wow, they're just so, like, round and big.'"

I could see where breast augmentation might traumatize a young girl. They traumatize me and I'm an adult.

Lisa continued. "I liked this woman a lot. She was very nice to me. She was the second wife of this doctor. They were a part of the whole thing. And we did that a lot."

I wondered if that was it, just an innocent backyard skinny-dip, but there was more to her story.

"We would take vacations, I remember, as a family. We went to Miami to visit my grandmother. And then one day we took off to the beach. But it was a nude beach. I mean my grandmother wasn't with us and I don't know if anyone told her. And this was the first time it was just sort of complete naked people everywhere. I was just sort of like, 'What are we doing?' The beach thing, it really bothered me."

"Why do you think it bothered you so much?"

"I don't know. I think some people are nudists and some people aren't. I think this is a fair statement. When I was a teenager I had a friend who didn't look awesome naked. Let me just put it that way. She was a big girl, but she was naked all the time. You came over to her house, I mean you were lucky if you got her in a towel. And to this day I just think that's her thing. She doesn't like the feeling of clothes. Whereas, I am . . . People have joked that I go to bed in a suit. But I like the old-timey pajamas. If I'm woken up in the middle of the night for a fire, I want to be able to run outside and be able to wear that for the next two days to two weeks if the whole house burns down."

"Because you were sensitive about your body? Or what people thought about your body?"

"During this time I absolutely was comfortable wearing a swimsuit. Which I can't say is the case, you know, these days. I liked swimming. I liked that stuff. I just didn't see why everybody needed to see me completely naked. And I found something very strange about my parents' extreme openness about sex. Because it didn't end there. I mean . . . I guess she'll never read it . . . but you know my parents liked to explain everything to me even if I didn't want them to explain it. I remember walking through the living room and my dad was watching some sort of very soft-core porn. There was, like, some topless nurse. And I'm just like, 'Okay, just keep walking.' And they stopped me and said, 'Lisa, are you confused? Do you want us to explain this to you?' And I'm like, 'No, I'm fine.' And someone apparently on the screen was having an orgasm and they were trying to explain an orgasm to me. And I just felt like, 'I don't care.' You know, I kind of had this sense of 'I'm a kid. I don't need to know this shit right now.'"

I can empathize with her parents. After all, this was a time when *The Joy of Sex* was a bestseller and people thought it was healthy to talk openly about sex and reproductive health; the feminist revolution was in full swing, pocket calculators were replacing the slide rule, and the microwave oven was introduced. It was also the era when running naked across a sports field or through the streets or basically anywhere there was a crowd of people became a fad known as "streaking."

It was especially popular on college campuses and an "epidemic" of streaking broke out. The climax of the streaking sensation was 1974. That year saw the world record of 1,574 simultaneous streakers recorded at the University of Georgia on March 7. On April 2, at the Academy Awards, a man famously streaked across the stage flashing both a peace sign and his penis, and by May, Ray Stevens's classic novelty song, "The Streak," was number one on the *Billboard*'s Hot 100. The sexual revolution of the 1960s was being assimilated into mainstream culture, and being naked and running free was as popular as it ever got.

Lisa agreed. "I think they were trying to be really open. I'm sure that they read some book or some article or something that suggested it was, you know, good for kids or whatever to let them know what's going on. But this phase literally stopped, like stopped sharp, when I was ten. And while my mom was still naked around the house my dad wasn't. It's like they sort of were aware that once they had kids that were going through puberty, this was maybe weird. And so it stopped completely. And then later I found that my mother could be very prudish about sex, at least in terms of the idea of me having sex. Even though I wasn't having sex, they were always thinking I was up to something. And I think part of it's just because they spent so much time talking about it when I was little."

"When you became older then they got uncomfortable with their own sexuality," I suggested.

"That's what it seemed like to me. I really don't know what happened. I mean I know that my mom, like my friend who was a naked person, she just didn't care. I don't know what that was about. Even in a women's locker room you can see different levels of comfort in being naked. You know?"

"It's certainly true in the men's locker room. Did your parents ever take you to like a nudist camp or a nudist resort or anything like that?"

"Oh yes. So aside from the nude beach, we once went on this vacation where . . . I can't remember the details. But it was like one vacation was changed so we just took a road trip. Now mind you, this road trip my mother didn't come on. So it was me, my stepbrother, my stepdad, and that guy Harvey and his son. I was the only girl. And at some point we all decided we wanted to go swimming. I didn't know what that meant. And Harvey and my dad heard of some nudist-colony-type place where you could get a day pass and go swimming. And so once again I'm like, 'Are you kidding me?' And, you know, we went and I remember when we drove up. There was this older naked couple—now this could be just some crazy memory that's just gotten twisted over time. But I swear when we drove up I saw this old couple standing side by side. The man was holding a pitchfork and they looked like the nude version of that painting. You know what I mean?"

"*American Gothic.*"

"It looked exactly like that but they were naked. And I'm just like, 'Oh my God.' And then we went and we swam and it was just like . . . it was a weird day. We just spent several hours there swimming. Everybody around us was naked. And then we left."

"And when you were naked at these places, how did that make you feel?" I apologized for sounding like a therapist.

Lisa heaved a sigh. "You got used to it on some level, but I didn't like it. And I think if they tried to push it at a certain point where I developed my resolve it wouldn't have happened. I think once age nine or ten rolled around, you know, it wasn't going to happen at all."

I asked her if she would feel weird if she saw people skinny-dipping in her pond in Upstate New York.

"It's one of those things that I really wish I understood more. But I'm not really bothered by it. Like when my friend decides to be naked. It's more for me a curiosity. Like 'Wow, how are you that comfortable where you just want your clothes off all the time?' I also wonder, 'Why does it feel that much better to you?' Because it just doesn't to me. But I don't know . . . how I would have turned out otherwise. But I think that I had a general sense that my parents were really not normal. So I think anything that they chose to like, I was immediately skeptical about."

"Did you ever share this information with your other six- and seven-year-old friends?"

"No. I have two childhood secrets. It's this and that we showed dogs, which I find more embarrassing by miles."

The Fall of Nudist Clubs

When you look at brochures and websites for American nudist resorts, you almost always see pictures of happy young people smiling at the camera, good-looking couples holding hands, and—in what I think of as a classic promotional shot for nudism—a full-body photo of an attractive young woman with an impressive derriere walking away from the camera toward the beach or swimming pool. The message seems to be that a nice ass, wordlessly urging you to follow, is the best way to sell nonsexual social nudism. The models in these photos—and let's just admit that these are models doing a job and not your average nudist—are projecting a lifestyle of health and vigor and youthful sexuality. The smiling men and women playing naked shuffleboard in the brochure for Bare Necessities' nude cruises, the topless women chatting in a garden, the physically robust couples artfully arranged around a pool—these images lead you to believe that going to a nudist resort would be an awesome thing to do: fun, exciting, maybe even sexy. But in my admittedly limited experience—I can't go to *every* nudist resort in the world—the people sunning themselves at your average nudist club are not young and energetic models; follow the beautiful buttocks in the brochure and she will lead you to a bunch of sun-ravaged retirees sitting around a pool. Which isn't a terrible thing, don't get me wrong. For the most part the people are friendly and fun; they just don't look like the nudists in the brochures.

This disconnect between the glamorized image portrayed in nudist advertising and the reality of nudist clubs is one of the reasons that organized nonsexual social nudism as practiced by landed nudist clubs and promoted by organizations like the AANR is in sharp decline. According to AANR's own numbers, since 2008 membership is down as much as 30 percent and continues to fall. Which is not to say the number of nudists in the world is declining, just membership in the AANR and its affiliated clubs.

Nicky Hoffman, head of the Naturist Society, has an idea why this is happening: "The whole lifestyle will just disappear unless we attract a younger crowd. The problem is, most of these resorts aren't geared to young people. They've become like retirement homes; they've sort of calcified."[72]

Or as one of the young nudists quoted in the same article put it, "It's not that I have anything against old people. I just don't really want to hang out with them at the pool."

This slippage is not limited to the United States. Membership in British Naturism has plummeted from a high of 18,500 to around 10,000 members in the last decade.

There are a number of theories being floated as to why organized nonsexual social nudism is suffering such a drastic decline. Some people, like British Naturism spokesperson Andrew Welch, think it's a branding issue. "I'm not sure in the twenty-first century that people are as keen to say, 'I am an -*ist*,' as in naturist. It sounds too ideological, too fanatical, too eccentric."[73] Others point to Facebook groups and nud-ist-specific social sites like Richard Foley's Naktivist "Nook" (Naked Online [is] OK), which provide ways for the nudist community to engage with each other without becoming dues-paying members of an organization.

One of the problems is visibility; even people who enjoy being naked don't know about organizations like the Natur-ist Society or AANR. As Mark Storey said, "If you go to any nude beach in North America—and I've done this I don't know how many times—I just walk there with my wife. We walk around and say, 'Have you ever heard of Naturist Soci-ety? Have you ever heard of American Association of Nude Recreation?' Maybe one out of ten's heard of AANR and no one's heard of TNS."

Some of the problems stem from the actual membership of the clubs themselves. There is an unintentionally funny com-plaint on the consumer advocate website RipoffReport.com that tells the story of a young couple going to a nudist club for the first time. In the complaint, a young man tells how he and his girlfriend felt "watched" and then, after they had kissed in the hot tub, how he was reprimanded by "some old gray haired man." Of course as any experienced nudist knows, the old gray-haired man was merely reminding the newbies of the rules—public sexual behavior will not be tolerated. But then Bret did the unthinkable: he got an erection. "As we made our way toward the lounge and pool area, we were confronted by about seven people on golf carts who asked us the reason we were there, and questioned us about the hot tub and about my erection. I couldn't believe this! They insisted that we pack up and find another resort to visit. My girlfriend was in tears and scared to death when they surrounded us on golf carts. Who did they think they were talking to us like that?"

I can understand both sides of this. Bret and his girlfriend are young, they're on a romantic getaway, and they're just doing things young people in love do, like get naked in a hot tub. Meanwhile the older nudists have worked for a long time to be nonsexual, and are worried that even something as innocent as kissing might cause some kind of kerfuffle in the local media and change the perception of the club and, consequently, of them and their lifestyle. They're just protecting what they've built up over the years. And they're old and cranky.

There are a couple of other stories on the Ripoff Report website complaining about being kicked out of nudist resorts, and they all involve accidental erections. Of course the flip side of this issue is that many younger women don't feel comfortable going to nudist resorts because they don't want to be eye candy for a bunch of old men. And, seriously, does anyone want to see an accidental erection from an old geezer?

Or as Mark Storey puts it, "Why in the heck would I pay five hundred dollars a year to sit in a chlorinated pool, sitting next to this gross guy drinking bad light beer, when I can go to the beach and go bodysurfing."

This generation gap is the principal reason that clubs and the AANR are in decline. That and the fact that people get old and die. Which isn't to say that the AANR isn't making an effort to reach out to young people. It has a program called Gen Next that offers a "young adult" membership fee and student discounts to nudist clubs and resorts. AANR is trying, and despite this, its membership is dwindling.

There is a theory that young people have been so bombarded by images in the media, the Photoshop-perfect actresses and models with their flawless bodies, that they don't even like to shower in the gym anymore in case someone sees their imperfections. And while there's some truth to that, I don't necessarily believe that advertising has shamed the impulse to be naked out of young people—I saw a lot of young people without clothes around the pools and on the beaches in Spain and France and on Black's Beach in San Diego. Maybe this new generation has its own ideas about what nudism and naturism can be.

One of the most interesting nudist groups that's sprung up recently is Young Naturists America (YNA), an organization whose mission is "To impact the world in a positive manner!" and whose mantra is "It's all about the love!"[74] Unlike a typical nudist organization, the YNA is also about environmentalism, social responsibility, top-free equality, and body acceptance; and while many resorts are couples only and exclusive, YNA presents a refreshingly inclusive attitude. It has many of the usual prohibitions against sexual behavior in a socially nude setting, but also requires mutual respect and open conflict resolution. Which means that members probably wouldn't ride around in golf carts hassling young men with boners. In addition to the rules, the group has a set of "ideals." These include: helping others in need, giving back to the community, mutual cooperation with other nudists and naturists, and "No discrimination of anyone as long as they abide by the rules (regardless of sex, race, sexuality/sexual preference, body art/piercings, body type and so on . . .)."

The YNA has chapters in New York, Oregon, New Jersey, Southern California, and Kansas City. It is also connected to a small network of affiliated nudist clubs scattered across the country.

Felicity Jones is one of the founders of YNA. She's a twenty-five-year-old activist and blogger who has had her naked body painted in Times Square, and has been arrested for a nude art performance on Wall Street. In other words, she is not shy about being naked. Lithe and attractive, the Penn State graduate lives in New York City and, because of her job, uses Felicity Jones as her *nom d'nue*.

"Honestly I grew up doing a lot of the things other kids do, just without clothes and a lot less hang-ups about my body," said Jones. "For most of my childhood I spent almost every weekend of every summer at a nudist club called Rock Lodge in New Jersey. It was my home away from home."

I wondered if her family practiced nudism at home.

"My regular home was a house in suburbia. My parents weren't really into home nudism so we didn't really hang out naked there, plus there were always neighborhood kids coming over. But it obviously wasn't a big deal to see each other naked in the house."

It reminded me of Pascal, the French naturist I hiked with in Austria, who was concerned that his teenage children had become textile. This is not uncommon. At the naturist resort in Vera Playa, most of the teenagers wore as many clothes as they could pile on. I asked Felicity if she went through a time when she was a teen where she felt like abandoning the nudist lifestyle and if she had any thought on why this happens.

"I think it's at least partly because of just the general awkwardness of puberty and dealing with changes in the body. For some I think they are more influenced by their peers outside of the club and/or don't want to hang out naked with their parents anymore. If there aren't any other teenagers at their home club, then they are definitely unlikely to stick with it. Teenagers want to go where their friends go. If I didn't have a best friend at the club where I grew up, I most likely would've stopped going. There weren't any boys my brother's age, so he stopped. But now in his twenties he's come to YNA events. He's still comfortable with it and everything, he just doesn't seek it out. A lot of times people don't return to it in their twenties either because there still aren't others their age, or their significant other isn't into it (very common, I think), or they're busy pursuing activities they can't do at their local nudist club. Some will go back when they have kids."

I asked Felicity why she thought nudist clubs were in decline.

"Well, the thing is, nudist clubs/resorts are not adapting to the times. It's like we're using Twitter and e-mail while the nudist world is still writing letters. They're not changing their marketing strategies, if they're doing much of any marketing at all. With AANR it's the same sort of issues. I think there's a bit of a disconnect between AANR and its members. If people don't see a reason to become a member, they won't. AANR clubs/ resorts have also been the ones selling a lot of the memberships, and some even require an AANR membership to join. So if the clubs/resorts are losing members, so will AANR."

"Is the YNA working like the youth wing of the AANR?"

"No. We're not affiliated with any of the big orgs. We're our own thing. We have found there's no lack of interest in naturism among young people . . . The media likes to report on how naturism is dying because there are no young people involved in it blah blah blah. But it's not true. There will always be interest in naturism. It's just a matter of reaching young people, having the right image and good marketing."

I wanted to know more about the genesis of the organization. I mean, in this day and age, when nudists are stigmatized and people have to use pseudonyms, why even start an organization? It seems daringly old school.

"Young Naturists America was founded by myself and Jordan Blum in 2010. It was Jordan's idea actually, and then he met me and asked me if I wanted to team up so we did. He also grew up going to naturist places with his family, and he had noticed that the movement seemed to be lacking the sort of values it started with. We believe it should be based on acceptance, but that just wasn't there anymore."

I have to admit that reading the rules and ideals of the YNA reminded me of the original vibe of early naturists like the German naturist pioneer and health food fanatic Richard Ungewitter—minus the anti-Semitism—and the clean-living Durville brothers from France. The early naturists were nature lovers, environmentalists before there were environmentalists; they were antitobacco, -alcohol, and -industrialization. You won't find much talk about recycling or climate change at your average American nudist club, but the YNA is making these issues the heart of its mission.

"We hope to keep growing, expanding, and bring naturism into the twenty-first century. There's a lot we could and want to do, but we're also limited by funds and just trying to break even right now. We launched an official membership about a year ago, and it's been growing steadily since then. We currently have maybe four-hundred-plus members."

I like that the YNA is approaching naturism from an environmental, social justice angle, but I think what's really resonating with young people might be the idea of body acceptance that it promotes.

"Absolutely it's beneficial for body image. I find that a lot of women my age won't try naturism *because* of their body image issues. But naturism is a great antidote to all the messages they get from the media that they're not good enough, too fat, too wrinkled, too old, etc. As well as the body shame most people grow up with. We find that many people resonate with our body-positive philosophy and message of acceptance. Body image issues have become more and more rampant, so people today really see it as a societal issue that needs to be addressed."

It must be frustrating to be the leader of a youth movement promoting healthy body image and environmental consciousness and have to use a pseudonym. Isn't this the kind of thing we hope people will get into?

"It's a valid concern, especially for certain professions, like teaching. I see stories all the time about teachers who get fired because their old modeling photos surface online. And not even nude modeling, but in bikinis or lingerie! I've heard of maybe one or two stories of people being fired specifically for being a nudist. It doesn't seem to happen too often. Maybe because most people hide it if they think it can get them fired, and also hide it even if it wouldn't. The fear might be for naught but it's reasonable to not want to take that risk at all."

I remembered the German and Austrian hikers I met on the Naked European Walking Tour who were unable to tell their coworkers and employers what they did on their summer vacation for fear of losing their jobs. I asked Felicity if she saw that changing.

"I suppose there will have to be some cases where people get fired for it, and they know that's why, and they take their employer to court. And then they change the laws to make it impossible to fire someone for that reason. It's pretty silly, really. We're all naked in the company of others at some point. But it's all about image and perception. More people being open about naturism will help a lot too. And educating the public. The more people know about it and understand it, the better! In the age of the naked selfie and sexting and social media, this might also become a nonissue in the future. More and more people will have photos of their boobs coming up online, and maybe at some point no one will think anything of it. So then who cares about the photo of So-and-So on a nude beach."

Which is the first time I've heard a positive spin put on naked selfies and sexting. But who can say? I hope she's right.

There are other nudist groups that direct their energies to bringing young people into the anti-textile lifestyle. Florida Young Naturists has about two hundred members and is an example of a regional organization that is trying to promote nudism and naturism to the eighteen-to-thirty demographic by hosting a series of events and get-togethers, but unlike the AANR clubs, it's about active beach parties and yoga classes.

This active ideal is echoed in a group called Vita Nuda— "Join the Nude Revolution!" Vita Nuda is loosely affiliated with AANR's Youth Ambassadors Program. It eschews a socially conscious message or political agenda and instead takes a hip and relaxed approach to promoting the fun side of nudism, posting an open invitation on its website: "You don't have to be a nudist to enjoy the nude lifestyle, either. You can come and be a nudist for a weekend, a nudist for a day, or not a nudist at all. You could just be someone who likes to party naked. We won't judge ;).''

Vita Nuda promotes activities such as "Hooping, Poi, Body Painting, Dancing, Volleyball, Boating, Canoeing, Kayaking, Swimming, Aquaball,* Drum Circles, Etc." I always thought that Poi was a paste made out of boiled taro root and commonly eaten at Hawaiian luaus, but it is, apparently, a Maori performance art involving slinging weights and hoops in geometrical patterns. And what twentysomething doesn't want to swing his junk around inside a Hula-Hoop while a drum circle pounds a primitive beat?

The Northeast chapter of Vita Nuda, which is easily the largest and most active of its youth-oriented chapters, had been using Lighthouse Beach in the Robert Moses State Park near Babylon, New York, as its go-to nude activity center, but that beach has now been closed to nudists.

Both Vita Nuda and YNA are supportive of AANR-affiliated nudist clubs and both sometimes hold events at these landed clubs. As Felicity Jones said in an interview with NBC News, "For more places to close up is just not good for any of us."[75]

But things don't look so rosy for nudist resorts and the AANR. Young people don't want to be forced to join an organization or pay dues or day fees, and they definitely don't want to hang out with their grandparents in the buff; they want to be naked and active and around other young people. And it's fairly easy to imagine how the retirees in their golf carts would react to a Poi-swinging, Hula-Hooping, boner-sporting drum circle next to their barbecue. They would call the cops.

---

* I don't know what Aquaball is either.

World Naked
Whatever Day

I had just left a yoga class in Silver Lake and was driving
down Glendale Boulevard, when I noticed a large group
of naked people riding bicycles toward me. This pinkish
peloton was a mix of men and women, some wearing shorts or
bikini tops, some with swirly body paint covering their skin
(a few had the words "No Oil" scrawled across their torsos),
but mostly they were nude. It's strange enough to see people
riding bicycles in Los Angeles, but the sight of so many naked
riders made the traffic stop. People literally hit their brakes
and gawked.

I watched the riders pedal up the hill, smiling and waving, chiming bike bells and hooting. A few of my fellow
motorists responded by honking their horns and waving. I
flashed a smile and a thumbs-up, although I have to say I
didn't envy the men riding the bikes. Was it safe? Couldn't
you snag your nuts on the seat?

Although a wide range of body types was represented,
the cyclists had a uniform look. They were mostly young, in

their twenties and early thirties, and, oddly for Los Angeles, predominantly Caucasian.

I don't know why, but my first thought was that it was someone's birthday and they had asked their friends to go on a naked bike ride through the city to celebrate. I imagined they'd go home and eat cake and gelato after a lap around the Silver Lake Reservoir. That would be a memorable birthday.

Then I thought that it was some kind of protest, a pro-cycling, antifur, vegan advocacy collective vying for attention. The Lactose-Intolerant Legume League or Vegan Vigilantes against Vivisection.

And then they were gone, heading up the hill, turning right onto Silver Lake Boulevard, and riding out of sight.

It wasn't until the next day when I was reading the newspaper that I learned that they were part of a world-wide phenomenon known as the World Naked Bike Ride (WNBR).

The WNBR is the brainchild of Canadian Conrad Schmidt, a filmmaker, writer, and social activist member of the Work Less Party of British Columbia. The Work Less Party's motto is "Work Less, Consume Less, Live More." It advocates a thirty-two-hour workweek, which you would think would make it the ruling party of most countries. It would have my vote.

The WNBR began as both a protest against oil dependency and a celebration of the human body. The first WNBR day took place in 2004, in twenty-eight cities in ten countries, and as cycling and social activist groups from around the world sparked to Schmidt's idea, the ride grew. By 2010 the event had rides in seventy-four cities—places as diverse as Amsterdam, Mexico City, Thessaloniki, São Paulo, and Melbourne—in seventeen countries.[76]

As the organizers say in their mission statement, the groups were "connected by their determination to all be naked on their bikes on WNBR Day, riding in celebration, jubilation to deliver a vision of a cleaner, safer, body-positive world to the masses." They also added, "It's time to join hundreds of naked compatriots in a free, non-sexual, fun bike ride!"

There's that nonsexual thing again. What do they mean by that? Have you ever been on a sexual bike ride?

The WNBR doesn't really have much to do with nonsexual social nudism—it isn't really a nudist or naturist event—but anytime you have a group of people getting together without their clothes on, nudists will be drawn to it. As Mark Storey, a participant in the WNBR in Seattle, explained, "What happened was a bunch of nudists got involved, and the young people who got it started were being surrounded by a bunch of older naked guys."

This made some of the young people—who weren't necessarily into nudism—uncomfortable and has led to stories of WNBR organizers giving fake locations and start times to nudists so they don't co-opt the ride.

In 2006 the WNBR organizers clarified their mission statement by announcing that "While the ride does include and appeal to participants from social nudity circles, the ride is not focused on promoting social nudity directly as much as cycling."

So it's not about nakedness, it's about pedaling. Which I understand. As they say in their mission statement, a bicycle is "the unabashed vehicle of the revolution. By cycling naked we declare our confidence in the beauty and individuality of our bodies and the bicycles's [*sic*] place as a catalyst for change in the future of sustainability, transport, community and recreation." There is a logic to the WNBR's vision of using nudity to bring awareness of the positive attributes of cycling to a wider audience. Cycling promotes self-sufficiency and locavore consumerism, provides health and fitness benefits, creates community, and is good for the environment, and nothing gets the American public's attention more than a pair of naked breasts.

With the WNBR more focused on cycling and less on nakedness, another group sprung up. As Mark Storey explained, "We wanted to see what we could get started to actually get people to try some things that would require minimal money whatsoever, no jail time whatsoever, and no effort whatsoever."

Storey and his friends took a poll of other naturists to see what their favorite nude activities were. "Everybody picks swimming. But after that, hands down, it was walking and gardening. Not everybody can walk, but everybody can garden."

So they created World Naked Gardening Day.

"The first year we did some photo shoots at some public parks, cleaning things up, weeding. We just found a park early in the morning. A bunch of us got naked, cleaned up the park. Somebody took pictures. We got the thing off the ground, and then we kind of waited to see what would happen."

The concept is super simple. The first Saturday in May whoever wants to garden in the nude is encouraged to do so wherever they are. You can weed, prune, plant, mulch, mow, harvest, and hoe in the buff. Why, you ask? Because "our culture needs to move toward a healthy sense of both body acceptance and our relation to the natural environment.

Gardening naked is not only a simple joy, it reminds us—even if only for those few sunkissed minutes—that we can be honest with who we are as humans and as part of this planet."[77]

That was in 2005.

Storey continued. "It's been almost ten years and I'm still getting phone calls from radio people: 'What's your group doing?' I go, 'Trust me, it's not a group.'"

Because World Naked Gardening Day is intentionally open-sourced and unorganized—and for the most part conducted in backyards—it's difficult to say how many people around the world participate, but I admire the idea behind it. As Storey said, "We figured that if people tried gardening naked once, they would smile."[78]

I can see that it could be nice. Hang out in your backyard and do a little weeding, prune some flowers, maybe lay down some mulch. As long as you're not using electric hedge trimmers or a chainsaw, it sounds totally pleasant. But because my yard is essentially a rock-strewn cliff covered with giant agave, thorny euphorbia, and clusters of spiky haworthia, I don't see myself naked gardening; it would be like herding porcupines.

While tending to your backyard in private is probably a good introduction to nudism, those who do so are not engaging in social protest like the World Naked Bike Ride and others who use nudity to get attention for various political and environmental causes. A few examples are Breasts Not Bombs, an antiwar protest group founded by actress Sherry Glaser that uses "our feminine nature to wake people up, to cause a stir, to arouse people from their apathetic complacent slumber";[79] photographer Spencer Tunick, who makes amazing fine art photographs of large groups of naked people, but has turned his attention to climate change by posing naked people on a glacier in the Swiss Alps; and AnimaNaturalis, a group that in 2013 protested the fur industry in Barcelona's Plaça Sant Jaume by having members cover their naked bodies in blood and lie in a pile. There are dozens more grassroots political and social action groups around the world that use the naked human body as a way to draw attention to their message. Why? Because it's effective. As the old adage goes, sex sells. Even if it's not trying to be sexy.

Credit Lady Godiva as the first naked activist to expose herself in public. As the eleventh-century legend goes, she felt pity for the impoverished people of Coventry and asked her husband, Leofric, Earl of Mercia, to lower taxes. He refused and then, like a lot of married couples, they squabbled over the issue until he offered her a challenge he was sure she would refuse: if she rode naked through the town on a horse, he would lower taxes. We know how the story ends. Author Philip Carr-Gomm observed, "The power in the story lies in its alchemical nature, whereby she transforms the potential for humiliation into a moment of dignity and of pride for all the city."[80]

Two groups that have taken naked protest and turned it into something of an art are People for the Ethical Treatment of Animals (PETA) and FEMEN, a revolutionary group whose ideology is "Sextremism, Atheism, Feminism."

PETA has run successful advertising campaigns with actresses like Alicia Silverstone promoting vegetarianism or porn star Jenna Jameson touting the seductive, tactile joys of wearing clothes made from the poromeric fabric called pleather. The group is not afraid to mix sex and its message—NBC famously refused to air PETA's "Veggie Love" commercial during the Super Bowl because, according to Victoria

Morgan, an NBC Universal advertising standards executive, the ad "depicts a level of sexuality exceeding our standards."[81] I've seen the ad and it is steamy—promoting hot girl-on-vegetable action—and boldly claims that "Vegetarians have better sex."

I guess the network thought that millions of carnivorous football fans couldn't handle the truth.

But what PETA is most famous for is the use of nudity in street actions. PETA members have been naked in cages to illustrate the plight of industrially farmed animals, naked protesting the sale of foie gras, naked en masse to promote veganism, and naked protesting KFC's treatment of poultry. They started the "Running of the Nudes" in Pamplona, Spain, to try to prove to city officials that they could have a fun, tourist-friendly event without being cruel to animals. The running proved extremely popular, but didn't manage to dissuade Pamplona from continuing the Running of the Bulls, a chaotic dash through the streets of the city where drunk tourists run alongside bulls and try not to get their wineskins gored.

But PETA is not a nudist organization. Like the World Naked Bike Ride, it uses nudism and nakedness to draw attention to its social and political cause.

FEMEN has a more ambitious agenda. Founded in Ukraine but now based in Paris, it sees society as a male-dominated construct: "We live in the world of male economic, cultural and ideological occupation. In this world, a woman is a slave, she is stripped of the right to any property but above all she is stripped of ownership of her own body."

FEMEN has an excellent manifesto on its website where it articulates some of its objectives. (Keep in mind that English is not the authors' first language.) FEMEN would like:

- to ideologically undermine the fundamental institutes of patriarchy—dictatorship, sex-industry, and church—by putting these institutes through subversive trolling to force them to strategic surrender.
- to promote new revolutionary female sexuality as opposed to the patriarchal erotic and pornography.
- to instill in modern women culture of active opposition to the evil and of struggle for justice.
- to create the most influential and combat-effective women's union in the world.

I was with them until that last one, but then I'm a believer in combat ineffectiveness. Isn't it better to just, you know, work things out?

To bring these issues into the public consciousness, FEMEN activists disrupt politics as usual, religion as usual, and culture as usual by baring their breasts—often with slogans painted on their bodies—waving signs, and shouting. Like sweet honey to a fly, naked breasts invariably bring photographers and reporters, and FEMEN has been very successful at getting its message across. It calls these actions "Sextremism" and defines it as "female sexuality rebelling against patriarchy and embodied in the extremal political direct action events." Acts of Sextremism often come with catchy titles like "Get Out of My Vagina!," which members shouted at a meeting of the Spanish Parliament in Madrid on October 9, 2013, and "Fuck You, Putin!," which they greeted Vladimir Putin with as he met with German chancellor Angela Merkel in Hannover in August 2014.

You've most likely seen a picture of FEMEN protestors in the news, usually facedown on the ground being handcuffed by police.

FEMEN's ultimate goal is "complete victory over patriarchy," and I wish them well.

The World Naked Bike Ride and World Naked Gardening Day are trying to change the world in a slightly gentler way; they have some of the same goals as FEMEN and PETA, but the use of nudity is more, well, nudist than revolutionary. Mark Storey has a different take on nude protests: "Instead of thinking in terms of how much hassle we can cause people, I would rather try to look at civil disobedience in terms of how many smiles we can put on people's faces."

As Marshall McLuhan said so insightfully, the medium is the message, and in the case of naked protestors, the medium seems to be bare breasts. The breasts bring the attention of the public and news media, and the message—animal rights, women's rights, etc.—is embedded in the nakedness of the activists. I think there's something more than just our culture's obsession with nudity. It's not just casual titillation at work. A protestor without clothes is vulnerable; images of topless women tackled to the cobblestones bring out our natural empathy. By taking off their clothes, they appear to be putting it all on the line, putting some skin in the game, transforming "the potential for humiliation into a moment of dignity."

But what about the young naturists who might not have an overt political agenda? The people who like to be naked and outdoors but don't necessarily want to shout, "Fuck you, Putin!" Since they're not joining nudist clubs or resorts in appreciable numbers, where are they going?

To answer that I have to revisit Austria and the Naked European Walking Tour of 2013.

...

It was mid-July and we had spent the morning climbing to the summit of an Austrian mountain that overlooked the Obertauern ski resort. We had made the climb without clothes, as this was the Naked European Walking Tour, but now, as we sat on the summit and ate our cheese sandwiches, the weather began to turn. A cold wind kicked up and dark clouds moved across the valley toward us, the sky threatening to open up and drop rain or snow or sleet or something unpleasant on our heads. Most of us put on jackets or those thermal fleece things that hikers like to wear—I even put on my wool beanie—and we began the trudge down the mountain before the weather got even worse.

As I walked around a few patches of snow and felt the first drops of cold rain hit me, Karla, a British naturist in her thirties, ran past me. Except for a pair of boots, she was totally naked. She stopped and looked at a small pond on the mountain and turned to me. "Is that ice?"

I followed her glance and saw that the water on the small pond had indeed been frozen over by a thin layer of ice. I turned back to her and said, "Yes. Yes it is."

She nodded and said, "Thought so." And then she scampered down the trail.

Karla and Stuart* are the couple behind the website Free Range Naturism. Previously they had a website called Naked Munros, which chronicled their ambitious attempt to climb all 282 Munros in Scotland in the nude. A Munro is what they call a mountain that rises over three thousand feet above sea level in Scotland. This friendly moniker is a tribute to Scottish mountaineer Hugh Munro, who cataloged the peaks. It's a thing among Scottish climbers to try to "bag the Munros" by climbing all of them. It is not a thing among Scottish climbers to bag the Munros in the buff—in fact, it's illegal. But that didn't stop Karla and Stuart from bagging more than twenty-five summits and documenting their exploits by taking some genuinely beautiful nude-in-landscape photographs of each other. It doesn't hurt that they are both attractive and fit.

The day after the Ursprungalm Death March, I sat down with them over tea at the hut in Mandling, Austria, to talk about their nudes-in-the-wild project.

I propped my leg up on a chair, trying to rest my swollen knee. "How're you guys feeling?"

Stuart looked at his feet. "I feel kind of dead at the moment." It was true that everyone on the NEWT was walking stiffly and joints were creaking after the long hike. Even Vittorio's dog was tired.

"What made you take on the Munro challenge? I mean, climbing all of them with clothes on is difficult enough."

Karla, who's English, looked at Stuart as if something so specifically Scottish required a Scottish explanation. Stuart shrugged. "I grew up in Scotland, and everywhere in Scotland

---

* They've asked me to omit their surnames from this book.

you're near hills. So as soon as you're old enough, a lot of us start running into the hills, that kind of thing."

Which is understandable. But how does a person go from a casual hiker to a naked mountaineer?

"I quite often walk by myself and, you know, it would be a long hot day and you're coming down the mountains, no one else around, and you see this beautiful stream with rock pools, and I thought, 'Well, let's just get in.' So I stripped off, jumped in, and I thought, 'Oh, I rather like this.' And it sort of went from there, you know, just walking a little bit naked sometimes, but I guess it really took off when I met Karla."

Stuart has a whacky sense of humor and I wondered if that was a pun. Was Karla a nudist? Did Stuart get her into it?

Stuart continued. "The first time we went hiking together, we went with a couple of friends and they were going rather slowly, so we raced on to the summit. And Karla had such a wonderful idea. When we got to the summit she would take her clothes off. We'll take some pictures and then she'll put her clothes back on, and then the friends would turn up and be none the wiser. And the pictures turned out really quite well."

Karla looked over at Stuart. "We made a rule, didn't we?"

Stuart nodded. "We always made the rule that no matter what the weather, the very minimum would be the summit naked shots, which encouraged us to stay naked a little bit longer. Now it's quite a big thing in Scottish culture to try to complete the Munros. I've been doing Munros since in my early twenties, so every time I went out, I was usually trying to do another Munro. But you know, there's thousands of people every year who complete the Munros."

I pointed out that not many of them were naked because, among other things, the weather is notoriously windy, wet, and cold.

Karla laughed. "Sometimes it made us turn back before we reached the summit."

Stuart took a sip of tea. "I think we both had thoughts or urges to get into nature and lose the clothes, but the artistic photography side of it almost brought a kind of discipline to it, because we'd get to an interesting place, we'd take our clothes off."

"You weren't afraid of being caught?"

"We'd climb mountains and often be back quite late in the day, and so we thought, you know, we're the last people here, we'll walk down naked. You kind of got to be careful in Scotland because you get quite a bad reaction."

Karla joined in. "And then it was: get into the wilds, walk naked where we can, take interesting photographs."

Stuart agreed. "I just got bored of landscapes. You ideally need some item of foreground interest, which is like a rock. Well, it's actually best to have a naked body because a lot of what landscape photography is trying to get is the idea of being there. To have someone there, you could actually imagine being there."

Karla finished his thought. "But if someone's got clothes on for that picture, it is quite jarring, whereas if you can be nude in it, then it's sort of making a statement."

Stuart and Karla are both politically astute, and I wondered if there was a political component to what they were doing or if it was a kind of art-for-art's-sake endeavor.

Stuart put down his tea. "I think a lot of my personal rant is about how modern-day society really takes us away from our natural environment. We have gyms, we have straight walls and edges and stuff, and people, in different ways, are trying to get back to nature, whether it's drinking organic beer or sitting in their car watching the sea. Good art always evokes a strong emotional response and this is something that humans are kind of keyed into because it's where we've kind of come from, you know, the natural environment. So that's the statement from me."

I looked at him and thought, *He should write a manifesto*.

Karla added, "I believe that you have got so many different aspects to the human brain, that you should actually kind of exercise all the different parts of your artistic, engineering, mathematical, science, literature. And the whole is greater than the sum of its parts."

Stuart continued. "It was our intentions to do all the Munros as part of this kind of . . ." He hesitated and Karla finished his sentence.

"This kind of artistic nature project"—she glanced at Stuart—"that kind of came to an end when we had the problems with the media."

Their problems started when one morning Stuart's brother phoned him and said, "I'm looking at a naked picture of you in *News of the World*."

Stuart's response was "Why are you reading *News of the World*?"

News of the World is a now-defunct English tabloid that was part of Rupert Murdoch's media conglomerate portfolio. Like a lot of Murdoch's papers, it specialized in sex, scandal, and celebrity gossip and was ultimately shuttered when evidence of phone hacking and other illegal activities by its editors and reporters was revealed.

What the editors of *News of the World* did to Karla and Stuart was typical of the publication. Someone spotted their Naked Munros website and the paper pulled photographs off the site and published them without permission. Stuart found himself suffering the ignominy of being in the paper with a clip art lunchbox—"lunchbox" being British slang for the male genitalia—covering his crotch, and the photograph of Karla had been adorned with strategically Photoshopped daisies.

After that, the media descended on them in full force. Even Graham Norton, the Irish comedian who hosts a popular BBC television program, asked them to be guests on his show. As Karla said, "We were overwhelmed."

Stuart nodded. "Yeah, they picked us apart and, you know, when you get the gutter press saying they want to find out more about you . . . run and hide." He shifted and took a sip of tea before he continued. "We didn't speak to the press. We didn't go on the TV shows. We took our website down."

Which is pretty much the opposite reaction you'd get from an American couple who suddenly found themselves getting their fifteen minutes of fame.* But for Stuart and Karla there were real-world consequences that they didn't want to deal with. As Stuart pointed out, "She was in education, I was working in social care; we thought it might be a bit dodgy to keep it up."

When Karla, who is a computer scientist, was offered a job in Munich, they jumped at the chance to get away from the media circus in England.

* See: Kardashian, Kim; Hilton, Paris; Plumber, Joe the.

"Do you feel bad about having to take your website down?"

Stuart shook his head. "We changed the concept a bit. Which is good." He's referring to their new website, Free Range Naturism. "The old links now point there."

"And was there a reaction to the new direction?"

Karla shrugged. "We've gotten the same kind of reactions as beforehand. 'I can't believe you just stood there naked.'"

"And it's lost its novelty, which is kind of good," Stuart added.

As nudist clubs decline in membership, more and more young naturists are adopting Karla and Stuart's "free-range" ideal. People are starting to get naked in places where they used to not get naked, places where they could potentially be subject to arrest for getting naked. Besides the typical beach spots and "free hiking" in the woods, there are now naked nighttime bike rides through cities, guerrilla nudism in city parks, and what is possibly the mecca for youthful nudists, the "Playa" at Burning Man.[82]

In NEWT founder Richard Foley's book *Active Nudists: Living Naked at Home and in Public*, he chronicles dozens of naked activities from gymnastics on the beach to canoeing and kayaking, horseback riding, bike riding, gardening, and, of course, hiking. There are naked anglers, naked sailors, nude surfers, naked skydivers, and clothing-free tree climbers. Basically almost any sport you can do with clothes on you can do naked. There's even a traditional naked rugby game played on the beach in New Zealand.

Although they are not naturist or nudist by definition, Secret Swimming "is a worldwide community of underwater people who are passionate about swimming and discovering secret places." It operates like a kind of flash mob swim society that organizes dips "in the wildest places, rivers, streams, ponds, iced lakes, wild seas, reservoirs." Secret Swimming members find the swim locations and times via "secret maps" that are sent a week prior to the swim. If the photographic evidence on the website is any indication, many of these secret swims are actually secret skinny-dips, but that's not to say nudism is the point of the secret swims—swimming in secret is.

ActiveNaturists.net is a website started by three guys, one in Berlin and two living in New York City. Not surprisingly, they are all European. Kirill and Joe are German and Juan is from Spain. On the site they chronicle their adventures hiking in Upstate New York, performing capoeira on the beach at Sandy Hook, running trails in Pennsylvania, and taking a trip to the Burning Man festival. The website lists places to vacation nude and promotes a variety of activities from naked mud wrestling to nude waterfall climbing in Hawaii.

But ActiveNaturists.net isn't unusual; there are dozens of websites devoted to people who like to hike, bike, or otherwise frolic in the nude in the countryside. But what about nudists who don't want to leave the city? While it's not unusual to see people sunbathing in the nude on sunny days in parks in Germany, it's less common in cities like New York.

In New York City, the Outdoor Co-ed Topless Pulp Fiction Appreciation Society[83] puts a literary spin on urban nudism. Taking advantage of an enlightened New York City law that explicitly gives equal protection to men and women who desire to go top-free, they gather in public places like Central Park, take off their shirts, and read books, specifically pulp fiction. I can't tell if this is a liberation movement, a kind of hipster book club, or the greatest book marketing idea ever, but the accounts of their exploits are fun to read and the photos of lithe young women in the city are compelling.

Naktivist Richard Foley finds all this activity encouraging. "I think, generally, there are more and more people involved in naked activities all around the world and they get encouragement from sites like Free Range Naturism. And there're more and more sites just popping up all the time, you know, describing just how much fun such a simple activity is, you know, it's economically viable, it's environmentally friendly, it's fun, it's harmless. It's all this good stuff, really."

One of the more unusual things that Stuart has done is write a naturist-themed novel titled *Naturist, Red in Tooth and Claw* under the name Stuart Pitsligo. If it sounds like a horror novel, well, it kind of is.

I wonder if the Outdoor Co-ed Topless Pulp Fiction Appreciation Society would put it on its reading list.

"Naturist fiction is one of these things which you think, 'Oh, I wonder if there's any fiction about naturism,' and you have a look and it usually falls into three categories: a sort of comedy romp where someone experiences naturism for the first time, a murder-mystery set in a naturist environment, or some romance which is completely joyless. And so I thought, 'Let's do something different,' and I came up with this bit of zombie horror."

"Are the zombies naked?" I asked.

"It's the characters who are naturists, but they had to be naturists for them to get to the situation. It's set in the Scottish Highlands; there's a lot of our own experiences there. So I think I've promoted free-range naturism in the novel, but at the same time, I've done something completely new with the naturist fiction genre."

As one reviewer wrote on Amazon, where the book is available on Kindle, "If you love Nudists and Zombies this is the book for you!"

While the writing in *Naturist, Red in Tooth and Claw* isn't up to Stephen King's level, the book is a lot of fun and does have a clever and redemptive ending. And who knew there was such a thing as a zombie horror-naturist genre? As Stuart says, "It was an experiment."

. . .

What's happening is inspiring. As the old nudist clubs begin their slow fade into obscurity, young nudists are finding ways to be active and enjoy themselves without the need to be tucked away safe from public view. It's the opposite of the closeted nudist resort mentality.

And there's no telling where this free-range naturism will end. Stuart explained, "We did some paragliding in Scotland, but next year we're going to do some refresher courses for the Alps. We're going to learn to fly here and then . . . naked paragliding."

I can't imagine flying around on a paraglider without any clothes on. But then I can't imagine flying around on a paraglider with clothes on. Karla laughed. "We could be soaring above you the whole day going 'Ha-ha.'"

Funwreckers

The Chincoteague National Wildlife Refuge is set on a long spit of land off the coast of Virginia called Assateague Island. It's a kind of barrier island, part of the half-isthmus that separates the Chesapeake Bay from the Atlantic. It is famous for a herd of wild ponies and a lighthouse listed on the National Registry of Historic Places, and is reportedly a good place to dig for clams. There are miles of beautiful beaches, which, as you can imagine, might attract the occasional skinny-dipper or nude sunbather. Apparently nudity was semitolerated on the north end of the beach until 1985 when NO NUDITY signs were posted and the U.S. Fish and Wildlife Service park rangers began enforcing the new regulations.[84]

On a warm June day in 1989, a young woman named Jeanine Biocic was strolling along Chincoteague beach with a male companion. I'm not sure what prompted her decision—maybe it was the beautiful day, the beach, or her friend—but whatever the reason, she decided to remove her bikini top and "get some extra sun."[85] Her breasts came to the attention of a park ranger and Jeanine was given a summons for "indecency and disorderly conduct" as defined in the Code of Federal

Regulations 50, Section 27.83. It's a weird regulation, as it basically throws the jurisdiction back to the local authorities by saying, "Any act of indecency or disorderly conduct as defined by State or local laws is prohibited on any national wildlife refuge."

At her trial—to her credit Jeanine didn't deny that she was topless on the beach—she was found to have violated Accomack County's anti-nudity ordinance, which defines female toplessness as indecent "in order to secure and promote the health, safety and general welfare of the inhabitants." How the health, safety, and general welfare of the county's residents would be jeopardized by Jeanine Biocic's exposed breasts is, I guess, open to speculation. I haven't found any pictures of her breasts and can only imagine that they look like, you know, a young woman's breasts and not dangerous sea monsters.

She was fined twenty-five dollars for an "act of indecency." She appealed.

United States of America v. Jeanine M. Biocic was tried in the U.S. Court of Appeals for the Fourth Circuit on October 4, 1990. Jeanine and her attorney, John Patrick McGeehan, felt that the regulations in the park and the county were vague and violated her constitutional rights.

One of her claims was that the charges violated her "guarantee of personal liberty rights." This was rejected as the judges said, "No one would suggest that the First Amendment permits nudity in public places." Which is a very parochial view of the First Amendment. Why can't nudity be free expression? I mean, seriously. It is a kind of expression.

But the most interesting argument was her claim for equal protection. In other words, if it's okay for men to go topless on the beach, it should be okay for women, and if it's not, then that is gender discrimination. Jeanine lost, the court deciding that the gender "distinction here is one that is substantially related to an important governmental interest." Which makes it sound as if her breasts were a threat to national security. The court clarified what the important governmental interest was by saying it was "the widely recognized one of protecting the moral sensibilities of that substantial segment of society that still does not want to be exposed willy-nilly to public displays of various portions of their fellow citizens' anatomies that traditionally in this society have been regarded as erogenous zones."

So, essentially, if some random dude, like a park ranger, finds your breasts erotic in some way, then it's your responsibility to cover them. It's no longer your decision, but the dirty mind of a stranger, that decides if you're indecently exposed or not. Why the court didn't extend that ridiculous logic to men's nipples, I don't understand. If a homosexual man finds another man's nipples erogenous, then for God's sake don't expose them willy-nilly in public.

But what might account for a legal decision in Virginia gets a whole different interpretation when it comes to New York State. Hearing a similar case, the court brought some logic to the discussion when it said, "One of the most important purposes to be served by the equal protection clause is to ensure that 'public sensibilities' grounded in prejudice and unexamined stereotypes do not become enshrined as part of the official policy of government."

The New York court pulled a one-eighty on the Fourth Circuit Court of Appeals, which is why you can go topless in New York City, you just can't go bottomless.[86]

Law professor Ruthann Robson, in her book *Dressing Constitutionally*, looked at the *Biocic* decision and a similar case,[87] this one a bare-breasted protest in Rochester, New York. The case ended up in New York's highest court, where Judge Vito Titone argued that the "'underlying legislative assumption that the sight of a female's uncovered breast in public place is offensive to the average person in a way that the sight of a male's uncovered breast is not' is an assumption that replicated gender bias rather than confronting and eradicating sex inequality."[88] According to Robson, "Titone's concurring opinion stands as one of the most supportive judicial statements of the unconstitutionality of legally imposed gender differentials in required clothing."

There are hundreds of cases like these across the country. Nudists might think they're in a secluded location, strip down to enjoy an air bath, and the next thing they know a park ranger is creeping up on them. We live in a surveillance society; everyone is peeping at everyone else. Which is why a man sunbathing nude on his back porch in Georgia was cited for indecency and a dude hanging out naked in his own fenced-in backyard was arrested for appearing nude in public.[89]

Sometimes the nudists win, sometimes, like in Jeanine Biocic's case, they lose. But I don't really understand what the big deal is. Why is it against the law to be naked in public? In my interview with Mark Storey he said, "The Constitution doesn't give you the right to not be offended." Which to my mind drops an H-bomb on any legal argument against public nudity. Look at Spain: nudity is not against the law and yet you don't see nudists swinging from the Sagrada Família in Barcelona and you don't see sunbathers or skinny-dippers being charged with indecency or being labeled sex offenders. Is it because the Spanish just take a more responsible and mature attitude to living in society? In case you're wondering, the answer is yes. And their wine is good too.

So if the Constitution doesn't give you the right to not be offended, why isn't nudity legal everywhere in the USA? If a prude gets his or her nose bent out of shape by seeing a few naked people swimming at the beach, so what? Aren't we supposed to take a live-and-let-live approach to life? Land of the free and all that. Why do we have the right to keep and bear arms but we're not allowed to bare our bottoms? And statistically speaking, death by seeing a penis or a breast is extremely low compared with handgun fatalities.

Like a lot of people in Los Angeles I don't like rude drivers. I don't want to be cut off or honked at or flipped the bird or stuck behind someone going the speed limit in the fast lane. I find that behavior offensive and potentially dangerous. But should we throw them in jail? What about restaurants that don't put salt and pepper on the table? Or the women who wear short shorts and Ugg boots? Or that guy with the fake tan and the tight jeans who just seems like a total douche bag? We can all find things that offend us on some level. Bad table manners are offensive. If someone farts in an elevator, that is totally offensive. Do we throw those people into the legal system? What does it even mean to be offended?

In American legal philosopher Joel Feinberg's *The Moral Limits of the Criminal Law*, he defines offense by stating, "Offenses are usually unwanted emotional states and can vary greatly. Offenses include states of affront to the senses (e.g., an ugly sight, noxious smell, or grating sound); disgust;

revulsion; shock to moral, religious or patriotic sensibilities; shame; embarrassment; anxiety; annoyance; boredom; frustration; fear; resentment; humiliation; and anger."[90]

While offenses might be unpleasant, do they cause harm?

In 1859, British philosopher John Stuart Mill wrote in *On Liberty* "That the only purpose for which power can be rightfully exercised over any member of a civilized community, against his will, is to prevent harm to others."

In other words, as long as they aren't hurting anyone, society shouldn't have the power to tell people what to do. People should be allowed to skinny-dip in the ocean or play volleyball on the beach or hike in the woods or even mow their lawns in the nude because, while it might offend some people, it causes no harm. It seems pretty cut and dry, right? Harm is easily definable: you damage someone's person or property. And I think we can all agree that committing harm should come with criminal penalties. That's the pact society makes with itself to keep public order. The naked guys in the Castro should be able to shake their dicks at cars all they want as long as they don't cause traffic accidents. Because offense is different. Causing someone to be upset emotionally is not so easily definable, and since it's subjective—what offends some people will delight and amuse others—it's not fair to criminalize it, and it is arguably a right protected by the Constitution.

Case closed.

Like the Naktivist manifesto says, "Being naked is okay in all contexts." Let freedom ring. You want to take in a baseball game at Yankee Stadium in the nude? Please bring a towel.

Of course it's not that simple. Cases have been brought to trial, most recently an attempt to overturn San Francisco's ban on public nudity by saying nudism was protected expression under the First Amendment. That failed because, according to U.S. District judge Edward Chen, nudity is not protected speech because it is "not inherently expressive." Drop trou in public and go for a stroll and in all likelihood you will be arrested.

Since it seems, historically, that the people who are offended by nudity invariably cite some religious reasons to back up their claims, I wondered what the Bible said about nudity. So I went to Got Questions Ministries, a "volunteer ministry of dedicated and trained servants"[91] who answer questions from curious Christians like "How often should a married couple have sex?"* and "Can a Christian be a nudist?" The answer probably won't surprise you: "With few exceptions, the Bible presents nakedness as shameful and degrading." They drop several biblical quotes as evidence, like Isaiah 47:3: "Your nakedness shall be uncovered, and your disgrace shall be seen." Or this gem from Revelation 16:15, "Blessed is the one who stays awake, keeping his garments on, that he may not go about naked and be seen exposed!"

At least the Koran uses fashion as a reason to get dressed: "O children of Adam, We have bestowed upon you clothing to conceal your private parts and as adornment."[92]

The volunteer Bible scholars at Got Questions Ministries[93] conclude with this: "Naturist philosophy ignores the results of the fall. Even in 'asexual' contexts, public displays of nudity dishonor God by pretending an innocence that no longer exists. A Christian should definitely not be a nudist or participate in nudist activities."

But try telling that to Pastor Alan Parker and the clothing-optional congregation at the White Tail Chapel

---

* Twice a week, apparently.

in Southampton, Virginia. Pastor Parker delivers his sermons and performs weddings and other ceremonies in the buff, labeling the clothing requirements of most churches "pretentious."[94] And then there's the Christian Nudist Convocation, which hosts weekends of worship and Bible study at nudist resorts in Oklahoma, Tennessee, and Virginia.

Recently canonized Pope John Paul II might agree with the naked pastor. In his book *Love and Responsibility*, the pope stated that, "There are circumstances in which nudity is not impure. If someone uses it to treat the person as an object of pleasure—even if it is by bad thoughts—he alone is the one who commits an impure act."[95] Which gets us back to the park ranger giving Jeanine Biocic a ticket not because she was doing anything indecent, but because he had sexual thoughts about her breasts and his thoughts made her actions indecent.

It always comes back to sex. People generally have sex when they're naked so, ipso facto, if someone is naked they're having sex, even if they're just strolling through the forest by themselves. That scares people.

Mark Storey agreed. "A lot of people think if I want to sit here by myself, there's got to be some sexual deviancy or some sexual issue there. They just don't understand it. They don't understand the sexuality they think I'm engaged in."

In an article entitled "The Offense of Public Nudity" that appeared in *Nude & Natural*, Storey wrote, "Negative reactions to the sight of nude humans are learned behaviors. We are not born with an innate sense that nudity is bad, but acquire it through cultural conditioning."[96]

How did we get conditioned to look at our own bodies in a negative way? And why are we so afraid of human sexuality? Where did *that* come from?

For some historical perspective I turned to Mara Amster, chair of the English department at Randolph College in Lynchburg, Virginia. Amster has done a lot of research looking at the role of women and sexuality throughout history, and is currently writing a book examining seventeenth-century prostitution and its relationship to pleasure, pornography, and profit. She's also got a great sense of humor, a lot of really curly hair, and a PhD.

I told her what I was working on and how I was trying to figure out why our society has this idea that the naked body is offensive.

"When you first asked about it I was thinking about the Renaissance obviously, and England versus Italy, because I thought, well, the Italian Renaissance is all about the body, especially the male body. And in England, of course, it's completely opposite. I mean, there's no equivalent of the nude in English art at that time that I know of. But I'm not sure where that comes from necessarily, I have to say. Why do the Italians have such a different sense of the body? Both female and male nudes are everywhere. My sense is the body, for the English, just always remains full of fear."

Italian artists have created some of the greatest nudes in history. Think of Michelangelo's statue *David*—which is perhaps the most famous male nude of all time—or his fresco *The Creation of Adam* on the Sistine Chapel ceiling. Botticelli's *The Birth of Venus* is a classic nude and Titian's *The Bacchanal of the Andrians* is my kind of raucous summer picnic. But there are hundreds more, from da Vinci's kinky rendition of *Leda and the Swan* to the full-frontal pleasures of Giorgione's *Sleeping Venus*, and later, artists like Caravaggio and Bernini painted famous nudes. It took a couple hundred years for England to catch up, and William Etty, under the influence of the Italian masters, managed to crank out some nude paintings. Yet despite the fact that the men and women in Etty's paintings seem to always have their backs to the viewer, Etty was considered controversial.

What were the English painters afraid of?

"It's a distinct fear of female bodies and what the body can hold, what it doesn't show," Mara said. "There's really interesting links about venereal disease in female bodies, you know; you have to watch out for women because they might not look like they have a disease, but they have one."

Which made me think of the *vagina dentata*, the deadly toothsome female reproductive organ of legend.

Mara laughed. "They never say that per se, but it's—that's kind of in the background of it. My hunch is that this strong aversion to the body must have made its way over with the settlers and the Pilgrims."

It's hard to imagine the Pilgrims unbuckling their shoes, tossing off their doublets and breeches, and skinny-dipping on the cape, let alone what they might've thought of Lee Baxandall and his family invading beaches on Cape Cod.

Mara continued. "There's a wonderful section in *The Faerie Queene* where one of the female characters is stripped and her body is described in this horrific manner. I mean, she's a witch, which is important in some ways, I guess. She has a pig's tail and she has cloven hooves and she has the body of an old woman. I think the quote that Spenser said was something like, 'It was worse than I could have even imagined.' I'm always struck by that kind of horror at undressing, of what could be underneath those clothes."*

* *The Faerie Queene* is an epic poem published in 1590 by English poet Edmund

Mara explained further, "There's just this really strong drive towards keeping women covered. There's this great early sixteenth-century manual about how to be a good woman, and basically it says if you go out at all, you should be fully covered with only one eye showing. It's bizarre how the body is both flaunted so much in certain ways and then hidden so much in other ways. Really bizarre, actually."

I asked her to expand on that idea.

"I remember growing up and the beach we used to go to, there was a nude beach kind of connected to it, and there was always one guy who we would see jogging up the beach and it always felt really exhibitionistic and really aggressive. And then, of course, throwing it back on you, you're clothed and you're uptight and, you know, all of that stuff, or maybe it's just that clothed people feel that way . . . I mean, speaking as one of the clothed people."

"It forces the clothed people to think about why they're clothed, why they have to be clothed and what the clothes mean," I said.

"Which brings us back to the Puritans. I think feeling good is somehow seen as wrong, you know. Anything that does feel good seems to be taking away from God. I think we still feel guilt about feeling pleasure."

Which reminded me of the famous H. L. Mencken definition of Puritanism as "the haunting fear that someone, somewhere, may be happy."

Spenser. It's an allegorical work with knights and noble men and is considered one of the longest poems written in the English language, which might explain why I've never read it.

I asked Mara if she thought there was some kind of latent Puritanism in our culture that made people feel embarrassed or ashamed or sometimes offended and angry when they saw a naked person in public. She considered it for a moment and said, "I'm just thinking this morning, my daughter was running around outside and took off her shirt. She's running around in little shorts and I think of the pleasure kids take in being naked. And then it stops at some point because you can't do that anymore. At some age, I will be uncomfortable if she's running around without a shirt on."

I said, "Your social conditioning kicks in and her nudity becomes sexualized, or at least if other people are looking at her, you suspect that they're sexualizing it."

Mara agreed. "Yes, exactly right. I'm not going to want people looking at her in that way. But I think it's that whole idea that you can do that because you're a kid. And so for nudists, there's a sense that they haven't grown up yet. It's still this kind of primitive pleasure."

Our social conditioning is a strange cocktail of fears— fear of losing control, fear of microbial dangers hiding in the body, fear of being sexualized by others, fear that a naked person is engaged in some kind of deviant sexual behavior— mixed with a *j'accuse* of the nudist being an immature, non-conformist hippie freak who may or may not be mentally unstable, shaken and strained through an illogical legal system made bitter by a dash of Puritanism. All this fear of someone who wants to skinny-dip or hike in the forest in the buff? Have we really thought this through?

Mara said, "Going back to the naked jogger as being aggressive . . . you're forcing other people to think about their choices. And no one likes that."

Fashionista

On July 23, 1951, the *Singleton Argus*, a newspaper in Australia, reported on a nudist fashion show held in New York City. The fact that the event was called a nudist fashion show seems oxymoronic to me, but then there are nudist jewelry shows where naked models display belly chains and penis clips, so, okay, there was a nudist fashion show in New York. The paper reported that the clothes "had a minimum of buttons, zippers, and snaps." Which makes them sound like one of Diane von Furstenberg's wrap dresses. Or a bathrobe. The *Argus* went on to quote the "chic, suntanned Mrs. Norval Tackwood," wife of the Sunbathing Association's executive director, saying, "The clothes are all designed for quick and easy removal once the wearer is safely inside the nudist camp." Even better, "they can be slipped off in ten seconds." Because once you're safely in the nudist camp, why waste a precious second messing around with buttons?

One of the highlights of the show was an apron used to serve tea. As Mrs. Tackwood noted, "If a woman nudist gives a tea party she naturally has to wear an apron when she serves."

What is it about clothes and fashion that would make nudists want to display some style, even when they're supposed to be naked? Isn't the grooming of pubic hair enough?

I started wondering what fashion designers might think about nudism. After all, they make their living creating and manufacturing the textiles that make us textiles. In Montreal, Canada, there is a fashion design company called Against Nudity. The Against Nudity website claims that designers Louis Moreau and Thierry Charlebois "looked at fashion as if it had never existed." I'm not sure what that means, but their clothing apparently "thrives on the unconfined energy of its motherland: Montreal." Which, just keeping it real, is a city where you might want to wear something warm most of the time. I can see why they chose that name: they wanted to avoid frostbite.

I arranged an interview with Los Angeles–based fashion designer Erica Davies to ask her what she thought about nudity and why we wear clothes. She has worked with Richard Tyler, Sean John, Max Mara, and BCBG, and has her own label.

Erica met me at a little café in Silver Lake. She's petite and pretty, with light brown hair that was disheveled from the yoga class she'd just come from. Despite having just spent the last hour and a half down-dogging and sun-saluting, she looked stylish, wearing a sweater and scarf over her leggings. Erica announced that she was starving and ordered a cappuccino and croissant in her crisp Wales-meets-London accent.

I had been hoping to have some lunch and now I suddenly felt piggish about ordering a sandwich while the svelte yogini picked at a croissant, but then you see, that's how they do it; we hadn't even started talking about clothes and the fashion designer had me worried I was too fat. The waiter was not amused by my equivocations and muttered something under his breath as he spun away from the table to fill Erica's order.

I turned to Erica and asked what I thought would be my trick question. "So what does a fashion designer think about when you see a naked body?" I was sure her answer would be that a naked body needs clothes, casual wear for antiquing and gardening, maybe some stylish suits for the office, and some of those signature pieces that help you transition from the office to the nightclub—in other words, a wardrobe full of fashionable prêt-à-porter and things like that. But that wasn't her answer.

"You know it's funny because when I design, I always think of the naked body first. Because you have to kind of figure out how to fit that body. It was from Richard Tyler that I started to develop that. But at Saint Martins* their main concept is you always started from the female body."

Her coffee arrived and I managed to ask for the same thing. The waiter did not seem impressed that I had come to a decision.

Erica took a sip of her cappuccino before continuing. "It was funny because they always made you kind of look at the female body or a male body in a completely different way. Even before you've thought of the clothing you always think of what's underneath the clothing."

Which makes sense, but I was surprised that she designed a dress in the same way an architect designs a building: by studying the terrain. I wondered if this was common.

Erica nodded. "Richard Tyler worked that way. He would always kind of . . . study the client's body. Like he'd

* Central Saint Martins College of Art and Design in London, England.

have them come out in their underwear. And that's how he would start. Because he would never . . . he didn't really work with a patternmaker, he worked straight with his cutters. He would understand the female. How she was structured. And then he would cut into the fabric. I mean . . . he was genius."

Tyler is a long-haired Australian who lives in Los Angeles and has designed clothes for celebrities like Elton John and Cher, but is more notable for his elegant suits for men and women and red-carpet dresses for actresses Julia Roberts, Anjelica Huston, and many others. In 2006 he redesigned the uniforms for Delta Air Lines flight attendants and customer service representatives. I couldn't imagine Tyler looked at every flight attendant naked to make those dresses. But still, the fact that he based the cut of the clothing on the naked body was a surprise to me. "A nudist might say you can really only see a person, really see who they are, when they're not wearing clothes. Is that why he did it?"

Erica pulled off one of the ends of her croissant and popped it in her mouth. "I don't really know why he did it. But he felt that if he saw them naked and then put his ideas onto flat paper it would never translate. He could understand a woman's body, but he had to see it. He didn't take any measurements. He would work with his cutter. Just him and his cutter, because his cutter would study the woman too. It was unbelievable." She took a sip of her coffee and added, "He's the sweetest. He's such a charming man."

"Is that normal in the fashion world?"

"Most people drape. You know what I mean? Like they'll drape on a form, but it's still not the same."

What little I know about draping and fashion design comes from the television show *Project Runway* and watching the designers fret and frown over some bolts of fabric thrown over what looks like a pincushion shaped like a torso while the design instructor, Tim Gunn, puts his finger on his check, scrunches up his eyes, heaves a sigh, and uncorks his catchphrase: "Make it work." So for me, that was as close as designers came to the human body until the clothes had been sewn and the models would come in for a fitting. Apparently Richard Tyler simply dispensed with all that frowning and fretting over a stuffed torso.

"Do you design that way?"

"Whenever I start, like I'll always start with some kind of . . . I'll draw the body first, you know, then the clothes kind of come on top. Saint Martins did very interesting stuff about the female body. It's like if you don't study the human body, you can't really dress it. You know what I mean? When you do a piece of clothing, you know, the proportion, the silhouette, the way you cut it. If you don't study that body before you put it into the clothing it becomes like a sack. So the difference is if you study the body . . ." She paused and tucked a strand of hair behind her ear. "Then you're actually enhancing the form instead of just covering it. Trying to bring some body-ness out of that."

The idea of enhancing "body-ness" with textiles is fascinating to me and, I think, the opposite of what most fashion customers think about when they buy clothes. How many times have I heard people looking for clothes that cover up any perceived flaws in their waistline or bustline, their flabby triceps or cellulite-riddled thighs? Isn't it less about an individual body and more about some idealized version? But then, Richard Tyler was designing for a particular body, which was his unique talent.

My coffee finally arrived. I looked around and noticed that the café wasn't busy. The waiter saw me scan the room and gave me a nod, confirmation that I was simply being punished for my indecision. Which is fair enough.

Erica spent some of her childhood in Saudi Arabia, a country that knows a lot about covering a woman's body but not necessarily anything about bringing body-ness to the forefront; in many ways it's anti-body. But she didn't agree.

"For me, that was the first time I was, like, really interested in how people clothe themselves. Because you know underneath there was something completely different."

"What do you mean?"

"One day I was with four women and we were in the changing room and I looked. I was like, 'Oh my God.' They wore amazing heels and the most beautiful lingerie. So growing up there I was always fascinated with what was underneath."

And of course skin is what's underneath clothing.

"For me, like, less is more. I don't show a lot. So for me, it's the opposite again. I play with really sensual fabrics, like really soft fabrics, but I'll kind of cover the body a lot. For me, it's like when I see too much skin it kind of repulses me. It doesn't give me the feeling of sexiness."

Which is funny because you typically think of clothing that shows a lot of skin as sexy. It reminded me of Italian philosopher Mario Perniola's theory about the "transit" between being clothed and being naked and believing the erotic urge comes out of that. Wouldn't a fashion designer want to play with that transit? Wouldn't you want people wearing your clothes to show some skin?

"I think the new generations are becoming not so comfortable with being naked. And I don't know, I think it's kind of sad. You know, I love going to the Korean spa. I think it's something beautiful when you see a human body that's all different shapes and forms. It's not that I need to see it, it just makes you feel more . . . I need the rawness. Whereas I'll take a lot of friends there and they're so uncomfortable. It's interesting to see a generation of women who don't want to be naked in front of other women. It's so bizarre for me." She continued, growing more and more animated. "Women have changed. It's very interesting. They're becoming a little bit more uptight."

Which is something I've heard over and over. Kids in high school don't shower after gym class, people don't use changing rooms at public pools, people wear swimsuits in the private Jacuzzis at health clubs; no one wants to be naked anymore.

I asked Erica if she had any thoughts about this change in how people interact.

She nodded and flipped a strand of hair behind her ear. "I think there's so much advertising to be a certain way and I think that's a big, big problem."

I had been expecting her to deflect, to say that there were many factors involved in this cultural gymnophobia that's taking over. Because isn't that what fashion does? It creates a fear, it makes people afraid to look like they really look so they try to look like some ideal that sprang from a fashion designer's head. Isn't that why we're all neurotic body-obsessed eating-disordered weirdos? Isn't it all her fault?

Erica shrugged. "To me, seeing bodies is very freeing. If you want to clothe it, you clothe it. And if you want to be open or let it walk around, then that's what it is. When I'm on a beach, I hate having stuff on. I mean, to come to California and you can't go topless. It's crazy."

Brave Nude World

Nonsexual social nudism has a rich past, one that stretches all the way back to the earliest human civilizations; but with the current state of anti-textileness in flux, what does the future of nudism and naturism look like?

I guess that depends on whom you ask. On his website, Nick Alimonos, a writer and naturist blogger in Florida, takes an upbeat and optimistic approach when he writes, "Someday in the near future, no later than 2040, you will go to the beach and see more than a few people not wearing a bathing suit, or anything else for that matter. People will be able to get their mail in the buff, sunbathe their bare butts in their own backyard or skinny dip in their own pool, without fear of harassment, jail time, or offending anyone except hardcore church goers, who by that time will represent only a fringe minority."[97]

How does Alimonos think this change will occur? "Attitudes toward sex and nudity have been skewing left for hundreds of years, and like Moore's Law* of accelerating computer

---

* Moore's Law is named after Gordon Moore, one of the founders of Intel, who observed that transistors were getting more powerful at an exponential rate.

power, these changes are also accelerating. I mention computer power because history has shown, time and again, that the greatest catalyst for change is technology."

Somehow, through these super-powerful computers or maybe through some new kind of body image–enhancing app, he believes that "by 2100, bathing suits will seem as silly as the beachwear of the 1800's."

If you need a reminder, let's just say that the bathing costumes of the 1800s looked a lot like a prom dress with stockings.

Mark Storey doesn't take such a techno-optimistic view. He sees it differently. "California is becoming more and more Hispanic, and that's going to have an impact on cultural values. It's going to be a struggle for naturism because it just isn't a part of the Latin American culture."

I can see his point. Historically, religious groups and groups with more traditional values have been the adversaries of nudists. And the legal system often reflects those values. I wanted to get a broader perspective on the legal challenges nudists are facing nowadays, so I reached out to Bob Morton, chairman and executive director of the Naturist Action Committee, to see what he thought about the current, and future, state of nudism in America.

Morton is a big, burly Texan with a bushy gray beard and a look that indicates he doesn't suffer fools. He's got what they call gravitas. He is the man the NAC sends to testify to state legislative committees and city councils when it wants to bring some rational thought to the nudism debate. He's kept busy in his home state, as Texas has enacted "home rule" allowing counties to pass their own laws banning nudism.

I asked Morton if he'd always been a nudist.

He said, "I was born into a family that could never have been called 'nudist.' But unlike many other children, I was never indoctrinated to have body shame. As a youngster, I had heard vaguely of people called nudists. Despite my puzzlement that they should be forced to live in 'colonies,' my young mind was intrigued."

True to form for almost every nudist I've ever met, it was skinny-dipping that pulled him into the world of nonsexual social nudism. Or, as he said, "While I was in college, I was a regular at a local river bottom that was unofficially clothing optional, although I didn't know that term then either. It was there that I learned about the social part of social nudity."

I asked Morton if there were any typical or unifying reasons for the beach closures and nudism bans across the country. He responded, "Common threads exist among the various excuses for closures and bans, though few rise to a level of thoughtfulness that deserves the word 'reason.' There's no advantage to oversimplification, but in many recent instances, the problem has arisen when a public land manager attempts to impose his or her own personal prejudices and biases on the development and administration of policies and the conventions of enforcement. Contrast that to the persistent notion that 'public pressure' is responsible for clothing-optional beach closures. In fact, the general public is often on our side. For example, an opinion survey of California adults, commissioned in 2009 by the Naturist Education Foundation and administered by the prestigious Zogby polling organization, determined that 62 percent of Californians believe that the California Department of Parks and Recreation [DPR] should exercise the legal authority it already has to designate clothing-optional areas in state parks. Yet, Tony Perez, the DPR deputy supervisor for operations, decreed an end to clothing-optional areas in parks across the state, claiming there were large numbers of complaints about nudity at San Onofre State Beach, the state park unit he initially targeted for his nudity ban. When legally required to produce those complaints, DPR came up with just *one*. And that single complaint was from a woman who noted that her surprise concerning nudity at the beach could have been avoided if the department had simply put an advisory sign in place."

Seeing that nudists are stigmatized by society, Morton had an interesting idea about how to keep beaches clothing optional. "Perhaps we need to separate the activity from the labels we attempt to apply to it. Clothing-optional beaches are more popular than ever, but those on the beaches seldom call themselves naturists or nudists. In a 2006 Roper poll commissioned by the Naturist Education Foundation, 74 percent of American adults agreed that people should be able to enjoy skinny-dipping or nude sunbathing on beaches set aside for that purpose, without interference from local authorities. *Seventy-four percent.* We don't elect presidents with that sort of margin!"

Morton believes that some of the "problems" of nudism are overblown by politicians looking to curry favor. He had a pointed critique of San Francisco's ban on nudity.

"Anyone who examines the recent restrictions on nudity in San Francisco will recognize it as a power play by an ambitious local politician." Scott Wiener, Morton argues, "used his position to consolidate personal power, and he has used that power to strong-arm and persuade other local lawmakers."

But while there's a disconnect between politicians and the populace here in the United States, that's not necessarily the case in Europe. In April 2014, local authorities in Munich, Germany, approved six designated "urban naked zones" for nude sunbathing. These nude-friendly enclaves are located in several parks that run along the Isar River, which cuts through the heart of the city. While the naked zones are somewhat secluded, they are still in the middle of the city, not closed off from residents, and not a treacherous goat trail descent away from civilization. It's an enlightened view, to be sure, and not really surprising when you think of the popularity nudism has had in Germany since Richard Ungewitter wrote his book. I'm more surprised that it took this long.

I asked Morton to compare the new laws in Munich with San Francisco's ban and he did not hold back. "Scott Wiener is an opportunist, and it's fair to say that his success was not entirely of his own doing. Too many who were opposed to his heavy-handedness toward public nudity were also opposed to restrictions on lascivious behavior in public places, and that gift allowed Wiener to leverage the issue. Perhaps *die Münchner* on both sides of the matter are less likely to confuse nudity with lewdness. That's not to suggest, of course, that Germany is immune to ambitious and charismatic would-be leaders who ascend by repressing minorities."*

If Morton's polling numbers are correct, then a solid majority of American citizens believe that skinny-dipping should be allowed in appropriate and designated places. Maybe not in the middle of the city like the urban naked zones in Munich, but somewhere we ought to be able to carve out some land for skinny-dippers. It reminds me of the debate over marijuana legalization. More than half of all

* Yeah. He went there.

Americans want cannabis to be legalized for recreational use and, typically, the politicians are behind the curve. Marijuana laws and public policy toward cannabis are slowly changing, but will public opinion about nudity change? It's complicated and in so many ways more deeply connected to our own insecurities, our body image issues, and our fears of pleasure and sexuality. We take our nudity personally.

Caribbean Nakation

Anaked octogenarian strolled past the omelet station as if coming to breakfast without a stitch of clothing was just how she rolled. In any other situation you might be tempted to think that an Alzheimer's patient at a fancy nursing home forgot to get dressed for breakfast, but then this wasn't any other situation, this was the Big Nude Boat, a luxurious cruise ship filled with nudists. Like the cruise director said when we left port, we were welcome to enjoy a carefree environment. But while the little old lady without any clothes might feel carefree, I felt confused. Like I didn't know what was going on. Maybe it's because I hadn't had enough coffee yet.

The naked octogenarian walked back past the omelet station carrying a cup of coffee and a Danish—she was apparently taking her breakfast out by the pool—and the young Indonesian chef making the omelets looked up and couldn't help herself, she burst out laughing. It was a natural, unguarded reaction and it's not like the granny cared. She was oblivious to the stares. I laughed too and my wife—whom I had convinced to join me, promising that she didn't have to be naked in public if she didn't want to—gave me a nudge with her elbow. "We'll all look like that someday," she said.

It's a buzzkill, for sure, but she was right; we will all grow old and saggy, but I don't think we'll all grow old and saggy and strut our old and saggy stuff in the buffet line. And on the lido deck there was a lot of strutting going on, and the crew—predominantly Filipino and Indonesian men and women—needed some time to wrap their heads around what was happening. For them, the atmosphere had shifted. This was not a business-as-usual kind of a cruise. Everywhere you looked there were naked people in places where there weren't usually naked people. Aside from the lanyard with the key card that dangled from everyone's neck and the occasional pair of sunglasses or footwear, they were totally clothing free. There were naked people in the library, scattered around the pool, in the mini-mall, in the bars. It was not unusual to get on an elevator and find yourself squeezing in with six or seven or eight totally naked people. I will admit that it caused me moments of disassociation from reality.

I sipped my coffee and watched my wife spoon globs of sambal, an intensely spicy Indonesian chili paste, onto her scrambled eggs. She likes her food spicy and it's not unusual to see her mix two or three different salsas together to try to find some tongue-shredding sweet spot of harmony between the hot and the really hot. As I stuck a spoonful of oatmeal in my mouth, I overheard two of the ship's musicians talking at the next table. One of them, a muscular drummer, said, "I can't concentrate. I don't know where to look. This is the weirdest cruise I've ever been on."

The other musician, a singer-pianist, laughed and said that he found it inspiring. "I think I'm a nudist at heart. I wish I could come out and play with nothing on." Which was something he couldn't do because the cruise line had rules in place preventing employees from joining in and celebrating the "carefree environment." Which makes sense to me. I'd want the kitchen staff to have clothes on. For their own protection if nothing else. But the musicians could drop trou for all I cared. Everyone else was doing it.

That I had gotten my wife to join in, after her initial "no fucking way" reaction to going au naturel, is a testament to her courage and, perhaps, her yoga-toned physique. I assured her that even if everyone else was going to be naked, she didn't have to be naked unless she wanted to—and I bought her a couple of sarongs just in case—so why not bounce around the Caribbean on a luxury cruise ship?

She thought about it for a week or two and then finally decided to come along. She claimed that she felt obligated to go because I'd been required to purchase a double-occupancy stateroom.

"You paid for two people and I'd feel bad if we let it go to waste," she said.

I was happy she came. For starters, she is friendlier and more outgoing than I am. She genuinely likes people and they like her back. Perhaps it's because she's originally from Texas.

Like myself, Mrs. Smith* isn't a nudist. Which is not to say she's prudish; she just wasn't interested in seeing, or being seen naked by, other naked human beings. I think she convinced herself that wearing a sarong would be tolerable, even necessary, because she would be working undercover as my research assistant.**

---

* Not her real name.
** I did not assign her this task.

By the time we boarded the Big Nude Boat, I had been to a number of nudist resorts and thought I had a pretty good idea of what we might encounter on this trip, but I neglected to prepare my research assistant for the exuberant level of genitalia flashing that turned out to be commonplace on the cruise. It was a riot of penises of all shapes and sizes, a parade of low-hanging testicles, and a flash mob of shaved vulvas. As we strolled around the ship, she observed all of this and said, "Wow. Just. Wow."

And then she laughed.

Our itinerary would take us on a seven-day loop around the Caribbean, embarking and disembarking in Fort Lauderdale, with ports of call in the Bahamas, Jamaica, Grand Cayman Island, and a tiny island off the coast of Honduras called Roatán.

The ship was the *Nieuw Amsterdam*, built in 2010 by Italian shipbuilders Fincantieri–Cantieri Navali Italiani S.p.A., and registered in the Netherlands. It is a relatively fresh-faced seagoing vessel and is considered one of the flagships of Holland America Line. You can see why. The boat is impressive.

There are eleven decks and alcoholic beverages are available on each one. There's also a movie theater, a concert hall, a casino, a library, a spa, a gym, a culinary arts center, a shopping mall, jewelry stores, a couple of swimming pools, a basketball court, and an art gallery that featured the work of the late Thomas Kinkade, the self-proclaimed "Painter of Light."™

Perhaps most important for people trapped on a boat for a week, the unlimited food was good, although they could have done with a serious sommelier as the wine list was by-the-numbers. There were multiple restaurants ranging from a massive buffet on the lido deck to a pizza-by-the-slice kiosk, a sushi bar, a two-tiered dining room, a burger bar, an Italian restaurant, and a satellite of Le Cirque.*

The *Nieuw Amsterdam* isn't super big; at 936 feet in length it's considered a midsize cruise ship. It has a draft of 26 feet and the bow thrust is described as "3 units, 3400 bhp."** In addition to the two thousands guests the boat holds, there are 929 crew members. If only our public schools offered that kind of student-teacher ratio.

The first thing we noticed about our fellow cruisers, aside from the fact that they weren't wearing clothes, was that they were cruisers. We were one of the few couples who hadn't been on a cruise before, and the standard icebreaker seemed to be "What was your last cruise?" or "What's your next cruise?" or "How does this ship compare with other ships you've been on?" Surprisingly a lot of the people on the boat went on what they called "textile cruises" as frequently as they went on nude cruises. It was the cruising that mattered. And they were totally into it; they read cruise blogs, online cruiser forums, and cruising magazines. You can see why it could be addicting. It's a floating luxury hotel with twenty-four-hour room service and almost every kind of entertainment you could want. As my research assistant observed, "Where else can you unpack your stuff and your room follows you for the entire trip?"

---

* Pro Tip: I took a tour of the ship's kitchen and was talking to the executive chef about where the crew eats. He told me they had their own kitchen and their own Indonesian chefs. I asked if I could have the crew food in the main dining hall and, to his credit, he hooked us up with a fantastic Indonesian meal. Thanks, Chef Martin!

** No idea what a bow thrust is, but it must be important because it's mentioned in all the press materials about the ship.

Some of the more experienced cruisers decorated their stateroom doors with pictures, message boards, and balloons, not unlike the kind of decorations you might see in a freshman dorm. I'm not sure if this level of bedazzling is a personal statement—a declaration of their unique personality in a standardized corridor—or just a way to help them find their rooms after an afternoon spent downing Caribbean coolers and pineapple daiquiris.

Both Bare Necessities, the charter company, and Holland America offered a dense schedule of programmed entertainment and enrichment activities. A typical day might begin with a nude photography workshop or an abs class, a pastry-making lesson or something called a "Yellow Emerald Seminar," before making way for spa seminars, card player meetings, basketball games, ice-carving workshops, couples tantric massage classes, yoga, Ping-Pong tournaments, lectures by guest artists,* body painting, wine tastings, cocktail mixology demonstrations, and a course on how to maximize the effectiveness of Windows 8.

At the orientation tour of the boat, our guide suggested that we fold up the activity schedule and keep it in our pocket. An older woman in the back quipped, "What pocket?"

The nudists broke out into laughter and spontaneous cheering while the tour guide looked at his shoes and his face flushed crimson. Maybe he felt he'd committed some kind of textile faux pas, or maybe he was embarrassed by the fact that many of the classes and programs he was touting were thinly disguised sales pitches. I found this depressing,

---

* Photographer Jack Gescheidt talked about his TreeSpirit project and presented beautiful photographs of nude people climbing trees.

although I did enjoy peeking into "The Digital Workshop Powered by Microsoft Windows" lab to see the "techspert" hawking Microsoft products to a roomful of naked people sitting on towels. The corporate synergy is so pervasive that you can't even walk off the boat into a foreign port of call without first passing through a gift shop, a duty-free shop, and some kind of jewelry store, followed by another gift shop, ad nauseam. Which was weird because the boat itself was a floating corporate shill show with boutiques, clothing stores, jewelry stores, art galleries, photo galleries, knickknack emporiums, all throbbing to the unrelenting drumbeat of consumerism. I'll admit, it affected me. I found myself driven to consume massive quantities of alcohol. I would've broken down and purchased some jewelry if it would've made it stop, but then, that just encourages them.

In the evenings there were live theater shows and a variety of musical performers scattered at various bars and lounges around the ship. Depending on your interest, you could hear a piano and violin duo play classical music, listen to a female folksinger strum her acoustic guitar, watch a DJ nod his head to the beat as he looked at a laptop, or dance to a lounge band that bleated out hits from "The Way You Look Tonight" to whatever vapid filler is on the radio these days. Probably something by Robin Thicke. And, not surprisingly, there were men in Hawaiian shirts and shoes, pantslessly jitterbugging with their wives on the dance floor.

There were the theme night parties with names like "Heroes and Villains" and "Famous Lovers." While I have to admit that a number of the costumed and body-painted who paraded at these parties were inventive and impressive and fun—I'd like to give a special shout-out to the couple who dressed as Rocky and Bullwinkle—the theme nights really seemed to be an opportunity for guests to strut around in fetish gear. Watching a retiree in a see-through French maid's costume maneuver across the dance floor aided by her walker is, I have to say, an awesome sight and a raised middle finger to anyone who thinks senior citizens can't get freaky. That lady is my personal hero. But did the guy who looked like Kip from *Napoleon Dynamite* really need to wear a leather thong with a cutout so his penis dangled in the open?

...

The first port of call was a little spit of sand in the Bahamas called Half Moon Cay. The boat anchored just offshore and we took a tender, a small ferryboat, to the dock. We were required to wear clothes to and from the ship, and most of the cruisers dressed in shorts and T-shirts, things they could easily remove when they got to the beach.

Even though it was only 9:30 A.M. the man sitting in front of us was completely shitfaced. How he managed to get drunk *and* trim his beard into precise lines that stretched from ear to ear, making him look like some kind of riverboat gambler, revealed an impressive level of expertise. His beach excursion outfit consisted of black shorts and a bathrobe from the ship. This effortless resort look was crowned by a dented and dusty black leather cowboy hat. He boarded the tender and stood leaning insouciantly against the railings, looking every inch like an alcohol-blasted sophisticate on vacation. When the tender disengaged from the ship, he lost his balance and pinballed between the rail and the rows of benches, his arms flailing as he tried to grab something to hold on to. His wife looked at him and scowled. "Al! Sit down!"

He collapsed into a seat and proceeded to pull out an electronic cigarette. He took a puff and groaned. It was one of those outhouse groans that began deep in his boozy core and reverberated through the boat.

I'm guessing the level of nicotine was insufficient, because he pulled two more e-cigarettes out of his pocket and stuck all three in his mouth at once, sucking deeply.

His wife glared at him.

As the engines roared and the tender started to move, his head fell back and he looked up at the sky. He seemed lost in thought, perhaps musing on some existential question, before he proclaimed, "Ah, fuck it," and took another drag of his e-cigarette trio.

The Caribbean has some fantastic scenery, but there's a quality to the Bahamas that is hard to quantify, maybe because it looks like an idealized version of a tropical island, maybe because the area is just really fucking beautiful. The sand is white and soft, the water is aquamarine and clear, the breezes are balmy, even the sunlight looks unnaturally purified.

And yet, despite the physical beauty surrounding me, as the tender pulled into the harbor I began to feel vaguely unsettled. Was it the Holland America corporate flag that was flying from a flagpole on the island? Did my skin start to crawl when I realized the entire island is owned by Carnival Corporation, the parent company of Holland America, or was it when I saw the faux shipwrecked galleon planted on the middle of the beach and called Captain Morgan on the Rocks Bar? Will you be surprised when I tell you that they served cocktails featuring Captain Morgan spiced rum? Nothing says tropical paradise like a giant fucking billboard in the shape of product placement.

The subtleties of the corporate control at work were lost on the drunk. He began to shout at his wife, "It's so beautiful! I want to live here! I want to live here! I want to live here!"

She turned to him and said, "Shut up, Al."

Her attentions only seemed to encourage him, and he continued his drunken incantation until the boat docked and everyone began to file off, leaving him on the tender muttering about moving to the island. And, really, who am I to judge? Maybe living in an advertisement come to life would be really awesome.

From the nudist-on-a-cruise perspective, corporate ownership of the island meant that guests were free to cavort naked anywhere they wanted, and Half Moon Cay exploded in a riot of flesh tones as people shucked off their clothes.

Before we left the ship my research assistant had applied several layers of sunblock and sunscreen to her body because she is terrified of getting sunburned. It was a good thing she did because the early birds had claimed all the available umbrellas and mini-cabanas on the beach, so we decided to take a stroll down the glorified service road that had been designated a "nature trail," presumably so they could say they had one.

Although almost everyone else on the island was naked, we kept our clothes on as we trudged down a dusty path under the blistering tropical sun. I'm sure I'm making it sound more fun than it actually was to follow the trail as it looped through shrubby island flora too short to provide shade. We had gone only about a mile when the trail suddenly dead-ended at the beach, not far from where the majority of nudists were frolicking. We found two beach chairs shaded by a stand of Caribbean pine trees and sat down.

It's not like we were alone; there were several nudists around, including a guy who stretched out in the sand in front of us and began doing yoga poses—I'm no expert but his Warrior II looked pretty good—and a number of naked people walking back and forth on the beach. I drank from my water bottle, trying to wash the dust from the road out of my throat, and pointed out the obvious to my research assistant.

"The water looks pretty good," I said.

She looked at the aquamarine bay, the cruise ship looming in the distance, and pulled her legs up to her chest. "Don't let me stop you."

So I stripped down and waded out into the water. Once I was in waist deep I turned and waved.

She waved back.

I could see that she was nervous about getting naked in front of all these strangers, but I tried to be encouraging. I splashed around in the water—and believe me when I say that it was the most delicious water I have ever swam in—and called to her, "You've got to try it."

She waved again and took a picture.

"Seriously," I said. "It's amazing."

I knew she was wearing a swimsuit underneath her clothes and I thought that, at the very least, she might just come in wearing that, so I was surprised to see her take off her shirt and shorts, and then shimmy out of her swimsuit. She stopped for a moment and applied a layer of spray-on sunblock to her exposed breasts.

I wanted to shout some encouragement but figured that she probably wouldn't appreciate my drawing attention to her, so I just floated nonchalantly in the bay and watched as she tossed the sunblock onto the chair and skipped down the sand and out into the water.

When I talk to nudists and naturists about how they got started, they almost always say that skinny-dipping was the gateway to becoming a nudist. If that is true, if nude swimming is the gateway drug, then nude swimming on a beautiful day in crystalline water on a private beach in the Bahamas is like taking the best drug in the world.

I could tell my research assistant was suddenly understanding the pleasure of swimming without clothes. She could not stop grinning.

We swam for a while, then walked out and sat on our beach chairs. We let the dappled sunlight dry our naked bodies as other nudists sat around us and naked couples strolled along the sand. A warm breeze blew across the water and I was struck by the realization that it really was perfect. A nudist utopia. There's a reason that early engravings of Bahamian natives show them wearing nothing more than some shells around their necks. You don't really need clothes when the weather is this luscious.

And yet it wasn't real. It was a travel industry fantasy owned and operated by a multinational corporation. The bartenders and cooks all came from the ship, along with all the food and drink. No one lived on the island. The maintenance crew all lived on Eleuthera, a more populated island, about thirty minutes away by boat. They were shipped in on the days a cruise ship was in port. I wondered aloud if this kind of corporate-curated vacation experience was going to be the future of the travel industry. My research assistant reminded me, "It's not the future, it's right now."

But for the nudists, private ownership of the island gave them permission to do what they came to do, and in that regard, it was a beautiful thing. Even my research assistant admitted that it felt amazingly good to be naked on that beach. Which didn't mean that she was ready to be naked at the salad bar.

Back on board the ship, people were required to dress for dinner, and while for many that meant shirts and slacks for the men and dresses for the women, for others, evening wear was the chance for the dudes to break out the floral-patterned Tommy Bahama shirts and for the ladies to dress like cheap Vegas hookers. Skintight miniskirts and super-plunging necklines seemed as popular on board the ship as they were at Cap d'Agde, as did a kind of minidress that appeared to be made from fluorescent volleyball nets. I have to say that it was confounding at first. During the day, grandpas would wear macramé cock rings and lounge around the pool, while the grandmas typically wore a sarong or a cover-up at least part of the time, but at night everything changed, the men put on their Dockers and Hawaiian shirts and it was the women's turn to flaunt it. I should make it clear that this wasn't for any of the theme night parties, this was just the normal dining room attire.

I realize that we live in a world where older people are marginalized in the public consciousness. As far as Madison Avenue, Hollywood, and Silicon Valley are concerned, the old and the overweight don't exist. For sure they don't have sexual feelings. *That would be gross.* But here they were on this boat, wearing cock rings and see-through clothes, a bunch of grandmas and grandpas looking like they just stepped out of a really weird Beyoncé video. After I got over my initial shock—and I'll be honest, it's more of an aesthetic prejudice than anything—I thought . . . *Right on!* Let the old and the heavy get down with their bad selves. *Why not?* That's what nonsexual social nudism gives them. They get to feel sexy without having to be sexual. They get to expose their carnal nature, but the rules of nonsexual social nudity don't allow them to satisfy their urges in public. There's no risk. The pressure's off. Sexual contact and innuendo are forbidden, so you can dress up and pretend that you're a Vegas hooker without having to turn tricks. You can wear that dominatrix outfit or that weird penis thong with the suspenders that loop over your shoulders. Strap on that studded leather bandolier that criss-crosses your sagging breasts. It's all okay because it's fantasy. And it is definitely way sexier than that snowflake sweater you wear when the grandkids come over for Christmas.

What the ship's crew thought about all this, I cannot say. Holland America declined to let me interview the captain or any of the staff, and the few crew members I did talk to just smiled and said there was "no problem" and they hoped I was enjoying the cruise.

One evening in one of the cocktail lounges I asked a young Filipina waitress what she thought of all the naked people. She smiled and said, "Everybody is very nice." But there was a sly humor in her smile that told me she found the whole experience profoundly amusing. I took a sip of my Manhattan and said, "Have you ever worked on a nude cruise before?"

She laughed. "No. First time." And then she really started laughing and turned and walked away.

I will say that whatever concerns the crew members might've had about a ship full of naked people, they were always professional. If they gawked, they did so discreetly. For the most part, they acted like nothing was unusual. Even if they were just trying to avoid being run over by the naked people zipping around on their electric scooters.

The cruise director summed it up nicely in one of the introductions he gave before the evening's entertainment. "On most cruises people sit there with their arms crossed and wait for us to entertain them. But you guys? You guys are here to have a good time! I love you guys!"

He also said that he had made a conscious effort not to say that other cruises were "normal" cruises, because he didn't want the nudists to feel that he thought they were abnormal, but he wasn't sure what the right word would be. A man in the back yelled, "Textile!"

If the casino or the nightclub or the various musical entertainers weren't your thing, the ship offered theatrical shows every night. About half the people attended these shows naked, sitting on towels, while some came from dinner in the dining room. There was variety in the entertainment. I saw a fairly funny comedian; a cross between Blue Man Group and Stomp; the worst magician-comedian I have ever seen anywhere; a "Tribute to New York" musical extravaganza that opened with a song made famous by the band Chicago; and, best of all, a passenger talent show featuring a naked harmonica player and a man wearing only a T-shirt while playing a piccolo trumpet. I wondered if he was playing the small trumpet to make his penis look bigger.

But by far the most interesting diversion was the production of *The Vagina Monologues* presented as part of the onboard entertainment by an amateur group of Canadian actresses. *The Vagina Monologues* is a play written by Eve Ensler, in which a variety of female characters monologue about their vaginas. The play is sometimes performed as a solo act, sometimes with multiple actors; this production had six women taking on different monologues. I'm not a theater critic so I don't really want to dissect the production or the performances. The actresses gave it the old college try and sometimes that's enough. But I will say that it was strange to sit in an audience of mostly naked people watching a play performed by naked women talking about their vaginas when you could plainly see their vaginas. It gave the performers a vulnerability that comes from being naked onstage, and the audience seemed extremely appreciative of their efforts. But then one thing I've noticed about nudists is they are very appreciative of any activity that reinforces their choice to be a nudist. Now that I think of it, most people are like that.

...

I don't know if she was inspired by all the naked people around her or felt some kind of peer pressure, or perhaps she was just up for the challenge, but my research assistant began taking tentative steps toward having her own nonsexual social nude experience. Every evening, after dinner, we would bring our wine back to the room and sit naked on our private verandah, letting the night breeze whip around us, watching the stars, listening to the dull thud of the waves against the hull as the ship slowly plowed the Caribbean. From there she tried a simple stroll down the corridor outside our stateroom sans clothing as a test, and then, realizing that no one was really looking and, honestly, who were they to judge, she began to make quick sorties around the boat. A simple trip in the elevator. A hop down the stairs. A topless excursion to the espresso bar. Or we would sit naked on the promenade deck, which was shaded, reading and looking out at the ocean.

The more time you spend naked in the company of other naked people, the less awkward it becomes. It is not, in my experience, a normal thing to walk around a salad bar—or a casino or library—without clothes. But that's what was happening. Nude had become the norm.

Bare Necessities, the Austin, Texas–based company that chartered the cruise, says, "Our mission is to provide relaxing, entertaining and health-conscious vacation opportunities that offer non-threatening, natural environments where the appreciation, wonder and compatibility of nature and the unadorned human form can occur." Which, to its credit, is pretty much what was happening. We were nakationing with our fellow nakationers.

This was the fifty-fourth nude cruise that Bare Necessities had chartered since Tom and Nancy Tiemann founded the company in 1990. Bare Necessities offers several nude cruises a year, trips like the Big Nude Boat tours of the Caribbean; luxurious European cruises on clipper ships that churn the Mediterranean from Italy to Croatia to the Greek isles; and journeys to places like Fiji and Vanuatu in the South Pacific. On the company's website it claims that 70 percent of its passengers are repeat customers and I don't doubt it. Almost everyone we talked to had been on a Bare Necessities cruise before and was planning to go on another. It's one of the more compelling aspects of the experience, because Bare Necessities has managed to create a community, or at least a place that feels like a community, of loyal customers, many of whom plan their yearly vacations around these cruises. They're not kidding when they guarantee that "you'll vacation with some-one you know." People were hugging and reconnecting and picking up where they left off from the last cruise. Which is not to say that we felt like outsiders. Arrive as a single male and you might be met with indifference or outright hostility, but show up with a pretty blond research assistant on your arm and nudists could not be friendlier.

One night we shared a table in the dining room with two retired couples, whom I'll call Larry and Donna and Gary and Brenda, couples who'd initially met at a nudist camp in Colorado and had become close friends. They had been on about a half dozen cruises together, and for this voyage they'd splurged on private poolside cabanas for the week. We were invited to stop by and enjoy the splendor of the cabana anytime. As Donna said, "You can recognize Larry by his cock ring."

And she wasn't kidding. One afternoon I strolled past the poolside cabanas on my way to the espresso bar and Larry and Gary were splayed out on loungers, eating chocolate-dipped strawberries and sipping champagne, living the good life in their hand-knit cock rings. Apparently the crafting of a macramé cock ring requires some trial and error to get the correct fit; or as one of their female friends explained, "Frank started getting a hard-on when I put his on, so he had to take it off."

Being naked in the company of other naked people cre-ates a kind of camaraderie, a nonsexual intimacy, that you just don't see in typical social settings or on a textile vacation. It's an unusual experience.

I had arranged to meet Nancy Tiemann while on the cruise, but unfortunately it became like one of those missed connection ads you see in the back of an alternative weekly and we never were able to meet up. I believe her when she says that things get "hectic" behind the scenes. However, after the cruise, I managed to ask her a few questions.

Nancy is a fit and attractive sixty-year-old Texan, a woman who does yoga and is involved with the local farmers' market in Austin. Because what she does—run a company that provides nude cruises around the world—is unusual, I was curious how she got started. Was she always a nudist?

"The year was 1989. My husband and I were scheduled to take a scuba diving trip on a live-aboard dive boat in Belize. It was a long-awaited trip for me, an overworked and underpaid bank officer with high blood pressure. My husband was also stressed and we were both desperately in need of a getaway. When he got word from a county court judge that one of his clients was due to be deposed on the day we were scheduled to leave on our trip, he made a quick call to the boat operator and was told that we could still catch the boat in Belize the following week; however, it was chartered by a group of nudists."

This news didn't go over well.

"I was so angry that he would even suggest this sort of thing that I tossed the literature he handed me into the trash. Later that evening when I was cleaning up the dinner dishes, I saw the brochures in the trash can. I lifted the small brochure out of the trash. I was taken by the woman on the cover. No beachcombing Barbie here, but rather a fortysomething woman talking about social nudism, how it had changed her life. She spoke of body acceptance, of letting go of her preconceived notions on public nudity and our society's unrealistic ideal of beauty and perfection.

Intrigued, I flipped through the pages and saw more 'real' women in different stages of life . . . As I read their stories I found myself relaxing a bit."

I was curious if she'd ever tried skinny-dipping before she got this brochure.

"I first did it on a dare when I was thirteen years old. It was at Janie McFarland's sleepover party in her backyard pool. I remember how good it felt! And skinny-dipping was something I enjoyed from time to time . . . after dark . . . in the privacy of our backyard pool."

So she and her husband decided to roll the dice and booked the trip.

"'What the heck,' I thought. 'If the people are too weird, if all the nakedness is just unbearable, we'll scuba dive and then retreat to our cabin and read.'"

This accidental vacation led her to a life-changing epiphany.

"Our experience over the next seven days, of vacationing sans clothing, was so positive and the people so extraordinary that I felt that I would never be quite the same again. And the more we talked to others on board, the more it became apparent that trips like this were few and far between. Mainstream travel opportunities were simply not available to the nudist world."

An entrepreneurial nudist was born. The rest, as they say, is history.

"It didn't happen overnight and it took some planning and a lot of good luck, but the bottom line (pun intended) here is that I happily and openly quit my day job and started a tour production company designed to cater to nudists looking for mainstream travel opportunities. Bare Necessities Tour and

Travel, Inc., was born in September 1990 with the filing of corporate papers. Since that time I have been living my best life, doing what I love the most, traveling with like-minded people and building a community."

It's the community part of the Bare Necessities experience that surprised me. There's what I can only call a friendly vibe among the passengers, like you're part of a secret club. I asked Nancy how she felt about creating this kind of experience.

"You know, I feel a tremendous sense of satisfaction. Not that I did it alone by any stretch. It grew more organically than that. As extraordinary as my story may seem, it would not be so were it not for the people I have met along the way. Nudists, or those who choose to travel where clothing is not a priority or necessity, seem to be more laid-back, have a better sense of self, and are simply more friendly, compassionate, and easy to get to know. And having no clothes on is a real equalizer. It's difficult to recognize the soccer mom from the Fortune 500 CEO . . . and no one cares. And isn't that what a vacation is for? To get away, enjoy the company of others, and come home relaxed, stress-free, and happy."

By almost any measure, Bare Necessities has been a success. I have to admit I'm impressed by the sheer gumption of a young woman who not only decided she wanted to spend her time nude—which, if you think about it, would lead some people to have her committed—but who actually quit her job and made it happen. I asked Nancy if there was a secret to her success, just in case someday I find myself having a life-changing epiphany. Her answer revealed that blend of modesty and no-nonsense-ness that is typically Texan. "There is no secret, really. If you are in the hospitality/service industry, be hospitable and provide a service."

...

Bare Necessities isn't the only nude cruise provider on the high seas. There are other companies plying the waters, with names like Dream Pleasure Tours, Castaways Travel, and Travel Buff. In case a boat full of naked people just isn't exciting or unusual enough, some of these cruises are for swingers and boast of a "hotter" environment than you might find on a typical nude cruise. Although the swinging is, apparently, not without rules and conditions. Castaways posted a warning on its website that stated: "Public sex is NOT permitted nor condoned."

All this freedom and friendship and food doesn't come cheap. My stateroom, priced on the low end of a variety of options, came to over $3,000 for the seven-day trip, or roughly $500 a day. More if you calculate our alcohol consumption. But that's only a couple hundred dollars more than you'd pay for the same itinerary on a textile cruise.

There were other ports of call on the cruise: we took a ride down something called the Jamaican Bobsled and drank Red Stripe beer in Ocho Rios; toured the Cayman Islands Public Library—all the proof you need that I am a nerd—and drank Caybrew lager in George Town; strolled along a forest trail on a small island off the coast of Honduras and then quenched our thirst with a Salva Vida beer. Perhaps you see a pattern emerging. None of these activities involved nudity and, if I'm being honest, it was a relief to put on some clothes and venture out into the world. But for those travelers who wanted to stay anti-textile, there were nude excursions available at each port of call for anyone who wanted to pay for them. Although at the beach in Honduras, the nudists from the ship stripped and skinny-dipped and no one said anything, even though it was supposedly against the rules. I think for the locals, pragmatism trumped any moral misgivings they might've had, and having happy tourists eating and drinking on their beach was more profitable than turning them away just because they weren't wearing clothes.

I was especially proud of my research assistant. She managed to put her initial reluctance and discomfort at being naked in public aside. And ultimately I think she was surprised to discover that she actually enjoyed herself. Her tentative forays around the boat grew bolder and she started to get the hang of being a nudist, and by the end of the trip she was sporting a sarong and walking topless in a 5k cancer charity walk-a-thon around the decks with hundreds of other naked men and women.

Because she is so friendly, we suddenly had people asking us if we'd put a deposit on the Big Nude Boat cruise for next year, or if we were going on the one after that, the cruise called "le Carnaval del Caribe" that would celebrate Mardi Gras in Guadeloupe. Surprisingly, or at least it was surprising to me, most of the people we talked to had already put deposits down on these cruises. At the time I felt as if we'd been accepted into the nude cruiser community, but with hindsight I think it might have more to do with people enjoying my wife's company.

...

Late one evening, my research assistant turned and chinged her wineglass against mine. She looked at me and said, "This is nice."

We were sitting on the private balcony outside our stateroom drinking a bottle of wine and looking at the lights of the southern coast of Cuba twinkle in the dark as the ship plowed through the night. It was cool and breezy, but not cold, so we sat on our towels in the nude and felt the air whip around our bodies. It was an amazingly pleasant feeling, almost as nice as swimming in the water in the Bahamas. I'd gotten used to seeing naked people everywhere and I'd gotten somewhat more accustomed to being naked with all these naked people. I can't deny that the combination of a crisp Sancerre, balmy Caribbean breezes, a clear and starlit night, the Cuban coast, and my alluring and naked research assistant weren't situational factors influencing my thinking. But was I a nudist? Had I reached some kind of hedonistic tipping point?

Naked at Lunch

I was sitting under a tree by a small lake in the Austrian Alps. The lake was nestled in a valley not far from the little town of Mandling, the surrounding hills crisscrossed by trails used for cross-country skiing in the winter and hiking in the summer. A shallow stream gurgled down the mountain, feeding into the lake. The sun was shining, birds were chirping in the trees, dragonflies were zipping low over the water, and the shore was littered with naked people lying in the sun or swimming quietly in the lake. It was about as pastoral a scene as pastoral gets: naked humans communing with nature, surrounded by the bucolic vibe of the sylvan. This is what the French naturist Durville brothers were talking about, what the health food fanatic from Stuttgart, Richard Ungewitter, saw as the salvation of humanity from the machine age. This was the escape from the urban that New Yorker Kurt Barthel aspired to, the hedonistic individualism of anarchist Émile Armand, the simple pleasure that left-wing beachgoer Lee Baxandall fought for. It was a stress-free, groovy slice of arcadian paradise.

I opened my backpack and took out a cheese sandwich wrapped in wax paper and a couple of fresh apricots.

Richard Foley, free hiker extraordinaire and ringmaster of the Naked European Walking Tour, sat down next to me. Polly, Richard's dog, trotted up with a stick in her mouth and flopped to the ground at our feet. The three of us sat there quietly for a while.

I finally broke the silence by thanking Richard for organizing the hike and for letting me come along and share what had turned out to be a challenging and profoundly enjoyable experience.

Richard unwrapped a sandwich and fed a little meat to Polly, and then turned to me and said, "After this book is done do you think you'll be a naturist?"

It was a good question and one that I didn't have an answer for at the time. I shrugged and said, "I don't know."

When I look back at all the people I've met and the experiences I've had in the course of writing this book, I'm struck by the realization that, well, society just doesn't get it. The nudists and naturists I've met are not kinky freaks and weirdos, they're not exhibitionists or voyeurs or pedophiles; for the most part they are friendly people who just want to enjoy the sensual pleasures that life has to offer, just like foodies and wine snobs, people who go to spas or concerts or sporting events, and people who stop and smell the roses— basically anyone who does something for the pure pleasure of it. Nudists enjoy the sensation of sun and wind and water on their bodies. And I would argue that unless one has some sort of debilitating skin condition, everyone enjoys these sensations. Nudists are just brave enough or honest enough to go all the way. So it begs the question: Is society punishing and stigmatizing nudists because it's afraid of the pleasure they're having? Is it that rich vein of Puritanism running through our psyche that says pleasure is bad? If that's true, we, and I mean all of us, need to see a shrink.

It's like some weird disconnect. If you look at celebrity gossip websites or magazines at the supermarket, it's pretty obvious that American society has an obsession with scantily clad celebrities and their nipple slips and miniskirt upshots. We are entranced by the erotic transit of partially dressed celebrities walking the red carpet. And yet we can't let someone go skinny-dipping without being offended. Maybe it's some kind of self-shaming mechanism for the guilt we feel about ogling celebs. Are we that immature?

If so we need to grow the fuck up. Accept that humans are sexual animals, that we're born with bodies, that we all look basically the same. Even the hottest young buck strutting on Black's Beach has the same body as the seventy-five-year-old grandpa sunbathing on the Big Nude Boat; the only difference is time and, perhaps, the tolls taken by a sedentary lifestyle and a taste for fried food.

Society needs to come to terms with the fact that some of us like pleasurable pursuits. A person shouldn't feel guilt or shame for being naked any more than someone should feel guilt or shame for enjoying a ripe peach. So what if people want to go skinny-dipping at the beach? If it really bothers you, maybe you need to take a long look at yourself and figure out *why* it bothers you. Just because you're offended doesn't give you the right to keep someone from enjoying their own body and the environment. Two things we all share. Two things that are free of charge.

And if, after lengthy soul-searching and a few sessions of group therapy, we're still not able to wrap our heads around the idea of "nudity is okay in all contexts," then how about some official set-asides for the people who want to be naked? Beaches and lakes and hiking trails where clothing-optional recreation is permitted; places where naturists and nudists have equal protection under the law. In fact, places where nudists would be protected from photographers and Internet pornographers who post "amateur" photos of naked men and women. Is that too much to ask? I don't think so.

After writing this book am I a nudist?

No.

I'm not ready to join AANR and spend my days playing pickleball. Not yet, anyway. And I seriously can't imagine ever dancing to the oldies wearing nothing but a T-shirt, socks, and sandals.

I wasn't a nudist when I started this journey and, if I'm being truthful, I'm not a nudist or a naturist or an anti-textile now. Not that I think there's anything wrong with any of those labels. They're just not my scene.

I feel the same way about the libertines with their penis jewelry and their wife-swapping clubs at Cap d'Agde. I think it's awesome that they're into it, I can even see the carnal appeal of random sex with strangers in a disco filled with bubbles, but it's not for me, not these days, anyway. I'm not even sure I would go on a cruise ship again, textile or nudist, even though I had a good time on the Big Nude Boat.

And still I'm changed. I think before this I would've been slightly uncomfortable seeing naked people at the beach or hiking along a trail. I might've thought they were part of some freaky sex cult. At the very least it would've made me nervous. For sure I wouldn't have felt comfortable stripping down and joining them. But now, if they promised not to start a drum circle, who knows? Why not? It may not be de-alienating, but it is empowering to actually not give a fuck what people think about how you look. It means you're okay with yourself. You take ownership of who you are.

Would I go out of my way for a nude experience? Probably not.

But I do know that if I ever find myself on a secluded beach somewhere, or if I'm hiking through the mountains and there's no one around, or if my wife wants to sit outside at night and share a bottle of wine in the buff, then, if the weather's nice, fuck yeah, I'll be taking my clothes off. It feels good.

Acknowledgments

I am deeply indebted to the work of nudism historians Cec Cinder and Mark Storey, as well as Chad Ross, Daniel Freund, Brian Hoffman, Ross Velton, and Nina Jablonski for their excellent and informative books and articles.

I'd also like to thank the people who were kind enough to lend their voices to this book: San Francisco supervisor Scott Wiener, Dr. Dana Jo Grenier, Bob Tarr, Lisa Lutz, Richard Foley, Conxita Fornieles, Pascal Hausser, Roberto di Mattei, Vittorio Volpi, Mayor José Blanco, Pilar Guerra, Mara Amster, Stuart and Karla, Harry De Winde, Maarten van der Zwaard, Augustus Stephens, Erica Davies, Sharon Seymour, Felicity Jones, Juan Carlos Pérez-Duthie, Robert Proctor, Nancy Tiemann, and Bob Morton.

Big thanks to my editor Jamison Stoltz for his style, intelligence, and continued enthusiasm; to Morgan Entrekin, Judy Hottenson, Deb Seager, Justina Batchelor, Allison Malecha, Amy Vreeland, Charles Rue Woods, Gretchen Mergenthaler, and all the great people at Grove/Atlantic for their hard work and continued support; to Nancy Tan for making me look smart with a superb copyedit; to Tom Cherwin for an excellent proofread; and to Mary Evans, Julia Kardon, and Brian

Lipson for representing. Special thanks to Simona Supekar for early reads of the manuscript, Geoff Dyer for his friendship, Dog and Pony, Claire Howorth for the merkins, Hind Boutlejante and the Guérif family for getting me drunk in Paris, and Olivia Smith and Jules Smith for putting up with it all. I want to give a super-special shout-out to the best and bravest research assistant a writer could ever have, Diana Faust, who makes every day fun.

Selected Bibliography

Barcan, Ruth. *Nudity: A Cultural Anatomy.* Oxford and New York: Berg, 2004.

Brook, Daniel. *A History of Future Cities.* New York: W. W. Norton, 2013.

Carr-Gomm, Philip. *A Brief History of Nakedness.* London: Reaktion Books, 2010.

Cinder, Cec. *The Nudist Idea.* Riverside, CA: Ultraviolet Press, 1998.

Crane, Diana. *Fashion and Its Social Agendas: Class, Gender, and Identity in Clothing.* Chicago: University of Chicago Press, 2000.

Darter, Larry. *American Nudist Culture.* N.p.: s.p., 2011. Smashwords e-book.

Egger, Liz, and James Egger. *The Complete Guide to Nudism and Naturism.* 2d ed. Hereford, UK: Wicked, 2009.

Foley, Richard. *Active Nudists: Living Naked at Home and in Public.* Aschaffenburg, Germany: Ed. Reuss, 2009.

———. *The World Naked Bike Ride.* Addlestone, UK: RFI Technical Services, 2012.

Freund, Daniel. *American Sunshine: Diseases of Darkness and the Quest for Natural Light.* Chicago and London: University of Chicago Press, 2012.

Fussell, Paul. *Thank God for the Atom Bomb and Other Essays.* New York: Summit Books, 1988.

Gay, Jan. *On Going Naked.* Garden City, NY: Garden City Pub. Co., 1932.

Hanson, Dian. *Naked as a Jaybird.* Cologne and London: Taschen, 2003.

Hoffman, Brian. "Challenging the Look: Nudist Magazines, Sexual Representation, and the Second World War," in *Sexing the Look in Popular Visual Culture.* Ed. Kathy Justice Gentile. Newcastle upon Tyne, UK: Cambridge Scholars, 2010.

Ingebretsen, Ed. "Wigglesworth, Mather, Starr: Witch-Hunts and General Wickedness in Public," in *The Puritan Origins of American Sex: Religion, Sexuality, and National Identity in American Literature.* Ed. Tracy Fessenden, Nicholas F. Radel, and Magdalena J. Zabrowski. New York: Routledge, 2001.

Jablonski, Nina G. *Skin: A Natural History.* Berkeley: University of California Press, 2006.

Lange, Ed, and Stan Sohler. *Nudist Magazines of the 50s and 60s.* Los Angeles: Elysium Growth Press, 1992.

Lippman, Matthew. *Essential Criminal Law.* Los Angeles: Sage, 2013.

Robson, Ruthann. *Dressing Constitutionally: Hierarchy, Sexuality, and Democracy from Our Hairstyles to Our Shoes.* Cambridge, UK: Cambridge University Press, 2013.

Ross, Chad. *Naked Germany: Health, Race and the Nation.* Oxford: Berg, 2005.

Royer, Louis-Charles. *Au Pays des Hommes Nus.* Paris: Les Éditions de France, 1929.

Singer, Mark. *Somewhere in America: Under the Radar with Chicken Warriors, Left-Wing Patriots, Angry Nudists, and Others.* Boston: Houghton Mifflin, 2004.

Storey, Mark. *Cinema au Naturel: A History of Nudist Film.* Oshkosh, WI: Naturist Education Foundation, 2003.

Surén, Hans. *Die Mensch und die Sonne*; rev. ed. *Mensch und Sonne: Arisch-Olympischer Geist* [Humans and the Sun: Aryan Olympic Spirit]. Stuttgart, Germany: Dieck, 1924; Berlin: Scherl, 1936.

Swaddling, Judith. *The Ancient Olympic Games.* Austin: University of Texas Press, 1980.

van Driel, Mels. *Manhood: The Rise and Fall of the Penis.* London: Reaktion Books, 2008.

Velton, Ross. *The Naked Truth about Cap d'Agde.* Villa Park, IL: Scarlett, Oh!, 2003.

Webster, Nesta H. *The Socialist Network.* London: Boswell, 1926.

Notes

Interview with a Nudist

1. Cec Cinder, *The Nudist Idea* (Riverside, CA: Ultraviolet Press, 1998), from the preface.

2. The general definition of a "nudist."

3. hedonist-international.org

Skin in the Game

4. Nina G. Jablonski, *Skin: A Natural History* (Berkeley: University of California Press, 2006), p. 43.

5. A. Hamish Ion, *The Cross and the Rising Sun: The British Protestant Missionary Movement in Japan, Korea, and Taiwan, 1865–1945*, vol. 1 (Waterloo, ON, Canada: Wilfrid Laurier University Press, 1993).

6. Russell W. Chesney, "Theobald Palm and His Remarkable Observation: How the Sunshine Vitamin Came to Be Recognized," *Nutrients* 4, no. 1 (Jan. 2012): 42–51.

7. Daniel Freund, *American Sunshine: Diseases of Darkness and the Quest for Natural Light* (Chicago and London: University of Chicago Press, 2012), p. 99.

8. "RCPCH Launches Vitamin D Campaign," Royal College of Paediatrics and Child Health, Dec. 14, 2012, www.rcpch.ac.uk/news/rcpch-launches-vitamin-d-campaign.

9. "Too Much Sun Cream Results in Leicestershire Boy's Rickets," BBC News, May 14, 2013.

10. Jablonski, *Skin*, p. 59.

Gymnophobia

11. From Didion's essay "Some Dreamers of the Golden Dream" in the collection *Slouching Towards Bethlehem* (New York: Farrar, Straus and Giroux, 1968).

12. From Fussell's collection *Thank God for the Atom Bomb and Other Essays* (New York: Summit Books, 1988), p. 182.

A Very Brief History of Early Nonsexual Social Nudism

13. According to Grant Barrett's *Official Dictionary of Unofficial English: The Slang, Jargon, and Lingo That Are Revolutionizing the English Language* (Chicago: McGraw-Hill, 2006), "junk" burst onto the language scene in the late 1990s.

14. Daniel Brook, *A History of Future Cities* (New York: W. W. Norton, 2013), p. 96.

15. The Fabian Society was founded in 1884 and is still active today. According to its website, "the Society is at the forefront of developing political ideas and public policy on the left" (www.fabians.org.uk).

16. Crawford's letters to Carpenter are reprinted in *The Nudist Idea* by Cec Cinder.

17. Vishwas Kulkarni, "World's First Nudist Colony Was in Thane," *Mumbai Mirror*, Apr. 24, 2010.

18. From the 2003 London Royal Academy of Arts exhibition catalog *Kirchner: Expressionism and the City, Dresden and Berlin 1905–1918*, ed. Jill Lloyd and Magdalena M. Moeller, available at static.royalacademy. org.uk/files/kirchner-student-guide-13.pdf.

19. Richard Ungewitter, *Kultur und Nacktheit: Eine Forderung*, n.p: s.p., 1911.

20. And Ungewitter wasn't alone. Another early nudist philosopher, Heinrich Pudor, author of the 1906 pamphlet *Nackende Menschen: Jauchzen der Zukunft* (Naked Mankind: A Leap into the Future), was also concerned about German society's unhealthy habits.

21. Chad Ross, *Naked Germany: Health, Race and the Nation* (Oxford: Berg, 2005), p. 4.

22. Ibid., p. 20.

23. Ross, *Naked Germany*, p. 17.

24. Ibid., p. 151.

25. Jan Gay, *On Going Naked* (Garden City, NY: Garden City Pub. Co., 1932).

I Left My Cock Ring in San Francisco

26. From an interview Fishback gave to the local *My Naked Truth TV* public access cable TV show.

27. San Francisco City Council meeting as reported by Heather Knight, November 24, 2012, in the *San Francisco Gate* article "Supervisor Olague eager for low-key life."

28. Neal J. Riley, "S.F. Barely Passes Public-Nudity Ban," *San Francisco Chronicle*, Nov. 21, 2012.

29. Lisa Leff, "San Francisco Nudity Ban Upheld in Federal Court," *San Jose Mercury News,* Jan. 29, 2013.

30. Geoffrey A. Fowler and Vauhini Vara, "Proposed Ban on Public Nudity Offends Some in San Francisco," *Wall Street Journal,* Oct. 3, 2012.

The Rise of Nudist Clubs in America

31. Cinder, *The Nudist Idea*, p. 563.

32. From Allan Bérubé, *Coming Out under Fire: The History of Gay Men and Women in World War Two* (New York: Free Press, 1990).

33. From Hoffman's essay "Challenging the Look: Nudist Magazines, Sexual Representation, and the Second World War," published in *Sexing the Look in Popular Visual Culture*, ed. Kathy Justice Gentile (Newcastle upon Tyne, UK: Cambridge Scholars, 2010), p. 78.

34. Mike Lawler, "Treasures of the Valley," *Crescenta Valley Weekly* May 23, 2013.

35. "People v Hildabride," *Michigan Law Journal,* Feb. 2009.

36. Lee Gregory, "History of Pasco Nudism," Pasco Area Naturist Development Association (PANDA), Naturist Capital USA, www.naturistcapitalusa.org/history.htm (accessed June 7, 2014).

37. Mark Storey, *Cinema Au Naturel: A History of Nudist Film* (Oshkosh, WI: Naturist Education Foundation, 2003), p. 47.

38. Felicity Jones, "AANR East Taking Social Nudity into the Future," Young Naturists America, Apr. 29, 2013, youngnaturistsamerica.com/social-nudity-aanr-east-interview/.

Vera Playa

39. This figure is from the Ministerio de Vivienda (Spanish Housing Ministry).

40. As reported in Angeline Benoit and Harumi Ichikura, "Spain's Worst Year for Work Leaves Rajoy Counting Cost," *Bloomberg*, Jan. 20, 2014.

The Man in the Fishnet Diaper

41. I'll quote from the version translated from the French by Alejandro de Acosta, originally published in Sébastian Faure, ed., *Encyclopédie Anarchiste*, (Paris: Librairie Internationale, 1934), available via the Anarchist Library at theanarchistlibrary.org/library/emile-armand-revolutionary-nudism (accessed June 7, 2014).

42. Ross Velton, *The Naked Truth about Cap d'Agde* (Villa Park, IL: Scarlett, Oh!, 2003).

43. Matthew Campbell, "France's Nudist Mullahs 'At War with Swingers,'" *Sunday Times*, Nov. 23, 2008.

The Naked European Walking Tour

44. Whitman described his air baths in *Specimen Days*, first published in 1882 by Rees Welsh and Company, Philadelphia.

45. The full German title is *1, 2, Frei! Das NacktAktivBuch* (Berlin: MYm, 2005).

Sex and the Single Nudist

46. Diana Crane, *Fashion and Its Social Agendas: Class, Gender, and Identity in Clothing* (Chicago: University of Chicago Press, 2000), p. 2.

47. Translated from the Italian by Roger Friedman and published in *Zone 4: Fragments for a History of the Human Body*, ed. Michel Feher with Ramona Naddaff and Nadia Tazi (New York: Zone, 1989), p. 237.

48. Ruth Barcan, *Nudity: A Cultural Anatomy* (Oxford and New York: Berg, 2004), p. 172.

49. Susan Donaldson James, "Lawsuit Alleges Maryland Nudist Camp Promotes 'Swingers,'" ABC News, Aug. 29, 2013.

50. "Etiquette," Maryland Health Society, www.marylandhealthsociety.com/etiquette.html (accessed June 7, 2014).

51. James, "Lawsuit Alleges Maryland Nudist Camp Promotes 'Swingers.'"

52. Katie J. M. Baker, "Nudist Colony Just Can't Get Rid of This One Naked Lady," *Jezebel*, Aug. 26, 2013, jezebel.com/nudist-colony-just-cant-get-rid-of-this-one-naked-lady-1126752612.

53. "Statement on Sexuality," Gay Naturists International, gay naturists.org/about/# (accessed June 7, 2014).

54. Fuck for Forest, www.fuckforforest.com/en/about.html (accessed June 7, 2014).

55. Danny Wicentowski, "Sex Positive St. Louis Bowls in the Buff at Saratoga Lanes," *Riverfront Times*, Apr. 22, 2014, blogs.riverfronttimes.com/dailyrft/2014/04/photos_sex_positive_stl_bowls_in_the_buff_nsfw.php.

Trends in Genital Topiary

56. Ashley Fetters, "The New Full-Frontal: Has Pubic Hair in America Gone Extinct?," *Atlantic*, Dec. 13, 2011.

57. Debra Herbenick et al., "Pubic Hair Removal among Women in the United States: Prevalence, Methods, and Characteristics," *Journal of Sexual Medicine* 7, no. 10 (Oct. 2010): 3322–30.

58. Allan Edwards, Keith Gilbert, and James Skinner, *Some Like It Hot: The Beach as a Cultural Dimension* (Oxford: Meyer and Meyer Sport, 2003), p. 118.

59. "Smooth Naturists," Euro Naturist, www.euronaturist.com/smooth.htm (accessed June 7, 2014).

60. "About SCN" and "Frequently Asked Questions," SCN, www.smooth-naturists.co.uk (accessed June 7, 2014).

61. Vanessa R. Schick, Brandi N. Rima, and Sarah K. Calabrese, "Evulvalution: The Portrayal of Women's External Genitalia and Physique across Time and the Current Barbie Doll Ideals," *Journal of Sex Research* 48, no. 1 (Jan. 2011): 74–81.

62. Amanda Hess, "On Beauty: For Women, a New Look Down Under," *New York Times Magazine*, Dec. 1, 2013.

Free Beaches

63. Baxandall coedited *Marx and Engels on Literature and Art* with the Polish philosopher Stefan Morawski (St. Louis, MO: Telos Press,

1973). See also *Radical Perspectives in the Arts* (Harmondsworth, UK: Penguin Books, 1972).

64. Lee Baxandall, "New York Meets Oshkosh," in *History and the New Left: Madison, Wisconsin, 1950–1970*, ed. Paul Buhle (Philadelphia: Temple University Press, 1990).

65. Cinder, *The Nudist Idea*, p. 624.

66. Cinder, *The Nudist Idea*, p. 593.

67. Quoted from the court opinion written by Justice Stanley Mosk, *In re Smith*, 7 Cal. 3d 362, available at scocal.stanford.edu/opinion/re-smith-22890 (accessed June 7, 2014).

68. Davis, Edward M. "Letters to The Times: Chief Davis Cancels His Subscription," *Los Angeles Times,* Aug. 20, 1975.

69. Hanauer, Gary. "Nude Beaches 2012," *San Francisco Bay Guardian,* July, 7, 2012.

70. Housed in the American Nudist Research Library and mentioned in Jerome Pohlen, *Oddball Florida: A Guide to Some Really Strange Places* (Chicago: Chicago Review Press, 2004).

71. From the short film *Celebrate the Freedom*, directed by Michael Cooney, 2000.

The Fall of Nudist Clubs

72. Douglas Belkin, "Wearing Only a Smile, Nudists Seek Out the Young and the Naked," *Wall Street Journal*, May 2, 2011.

73. Patrick Barkham, "A Stitch in Time," *The Guardian,* May 31, 2007.

74. "About Young Naturists America YNA," Young Naturists America, youngnaturistsamerica.com/about/ (accessed June 7, 2014).

75. Bill Briggs, "Naked Truth: Aging nudists seek new skin in game as ranks dwindle," NBC News, Aug. 3, 2013.

World Naked Whatever Day

76. "About," World Naked Bike Ride, wiki.worldnakedbikeride.org/index.php?title=About (accessed June 7, 2014).

77. From the introduction to naked gardening on the World Naked Gardening Day website (wngd.org).

78. Quoted in Laura T. Coffey, "Not Dirty to Play in Dirt on World Naked Gardening Day," NBC News, May 13, 2011.

79. From Breasts Not Bomb's mission statement on www.sherry glaser.net/bnb.html.

80. From Carr-Gomm's excellent book *A Brief History of Nakedness* (London: Reaktion Books, 2010), p. 95.

81. Page Six, *New York Post,* Jan. 27, 2009.

82. Wells Tower, in his essay "The Old Man at Burning Man" in *GQ,* Feb. 2013, wrote about the nonstop nudity of the festival and his own feelings about it as he attended a "Human Carcass Wash" in hopes of getting a shower. "Until now, if given the choice, I'd have preferred to have a hole of large diameter drilled in my foot rather than be naked among strangers. But I am trying here, friends, so there is nothing to be done but to remove one's clothes. I disrobe brusquely, a little angrily."

83. See coedtoplesspulpfiction.wordpress.com.

Funwreckers

84. According to some postings on the "ThongBoard" forum, an online community devoted to "thonging" (wearing those tiny string bikini bottoms), the park rangers used to sneak up on nudists and "were very nasty for several years."

85. *United States v. Biocic,* 928 F.2d 112 (4th Cir. 1991).

86. That would be a violation of Penal Law 245.01 (exposure of a person). A person is guilty of exposure if he appears in a public place in such a manner that the private or intimate parts of his body are unclothed or exposed. *People v. Santorelli,* 600 N.E. 2d 232 (N.Y. 1992).

87. Ruthann Robson, *Dressing Constitutionally: Hierarchy, Sexuality, and Democracy from Our Hairstyles to Our Shoes* (Cambridge, UK: Cambridge University Press, 2013), p. 58.

88. Ibid.

89. *Weideman v. State,* 890 N.E. 2d 28, 31 (Ind. Ct. App. 2008).

90. Joel Feinberg, *The Moral Limits of the Criminal Law,* vol. 2, *Offense to Others* (New York and Oxford: Oxford University Press, 1988).

91. "About GotQuestions.org," Got Questions Ministries, www .gotquestions.org/about.html (accessed June 7, 2014).

92. Sahih International translation.

93. The mission statement of Got Questions Ministries is "Got Questions Ministries seeks to glorify the Lord Jesus Christ by providing biblical, applicable, and timely answers to spiritually related questions through an internet presence."

94. John Hall, "'And They Were Naked—and Not Ashamed': Church Allows Nude Worship," *Daily Mail*, Feb. 11 2014.

95. Pope John Paul II, *Love and Responsibility*, trans. H. T. Willetts (New York: Farrar, Straus and Giroux, 1981).

96. Mark Storey, "The Offense of Public Nudity," *Nude & Natural*, Winter 2002.

Brave Nude World

97. Nick Alimonos, "Nudity Is the Future," *Writers' Disease*, blog, Apr. 23, 2013, writersdisease.blogspot.com/2013/04/nudity-is-future.html.